THE NEW YORK COPS

THE NEW YORK COPS

COPS

An Informal History

BY GERALD ASTOR

Charles Scribner's Sons • New York

For Sonia, my kind of cop

CONTENTS

ACKNOWLEDGMENTS

Acknowledgments are due to Harcourt, Brace and Jovanovich for permission to reprint sections of *The Autobiography of Lincoln Steffens,* copyright 1931. Permission to reprint sections from *Mr. Dooley Remembers* by Phillip Dunne, copyright 1963, has been granted by William Morris Agency. The New York Civil Liberties Union has granted permission to reprint sections of its report on the Yippie Demonstration at Grand Central Terminal (1969).

I would also like to thank the office of the Commissioner of the New York City Police Department for its help and for the time granted to me by numerous members of the Department.

THE PRINCIPAL CASE FILE

Crime created the New York City Police Department as it did the police in other American cities (in Europe on the other hand, the origins of the police lay mainly in the need for protecting the sovereign and suppressing insurrection). Some social scientists, speculating over disorders in the ghetto and the university in the 1960s, have begun to question whether the police themselves are not an essential part of a system that spawns crime. It has been suggested that crime rates would drop if police, particularly white ones, were withdrawn from the ghetto and if policemen did not invade campuses that are in the thrall of student rebels.

Undeniably the use of force, even legally, may provoke violent reaction and escalate crime. The role of the system in creating the conditions that spawn crime is well documented. But an existential reality must also be recognized; the city is a savage place.

Every day, the chief officers of the New York City Police Department receive a copy of a report summarizing the most important cases in a twenty-four-hour period. It is an anatomy of crime, violence, race hatred, civil dissent and disturbance, the fractures of law and order that confront the police constantly. Reading the "principal case file" discourages notions of cities without police. Here, for example, are some of the contents of the file from 9:30 A.M. October 1, 1968, to midnight October 3. (The names of individuals have been left out.)

10/1   9:30 A.M. One patrolman injured at a barricade set up around Intermediate School 55 in Brooklyn during the teachers' strike. A FN (female Negro) struck the officer on the head and arm with a lead pipe.

10/1   10:15 A.M. At I.S. 55 a rock hit Patrolman _____.

10/1   10:45 A.M. Man in Queens while "in residence" was shot by "unknown MN (Male Negro) three times." The "Perpetrator" fled.

10/1   10:30 A.M. Queens, "_____MN, 36, shot by _____ during an altercation. The perpetrator was arrested."

10/2   12:30 A.M. Brooklyn, "_____MW shot in the left leg during an altercation with an unknown MW. Perpetrator fled on foot."

10/2   3:30 A.M. "_____, a police trainee, was arrested with two other young men for 'malicious mischief of autos.' "

10/2   3:35 A.M. At 132nd Street and Seventh Avenue "_____MN sustained gunshot wound right leg by _____MN. Aided to hospital, not serious. No arrest at time."

10/2   4:48 A.M. "_____MW, found DOA by friends, gunshot of head, rifle at feet."

10/3   12:45 P.M. Brooklyn, _____MW shot by _____MW. Victim DOA. _____ arrested.

10/3   1:35 P.M. "On stakeout duty at _____ Motel, Patrolmen _____ & _____ observed two unknown MW break a vent window in 1968 Buick and rifle the contents. When the perpetrators attempted to start the auto, the patrolmen, in civilian clothes, approached the auto and the perpetrators ran to another auto and started to drive off. As the auto was leaving the curb, Patrolman _____ jumped in front of the auto, showing his shield and the driver of the auto attempted to run down Patrolman _____. He fired two shots from his service revolver at the auto. The perpetrators escaped, no injuries, no property damage."

10/3   2:30 P.M. "_____MN, during an altercation with _____FN same address was stabbed to death. Aided, pronounced DOA at Coney Island Hospital. Arrest made."

10/3   8:20 P.M. "Radio car responded to a Bronx call of 'disorderly youths, may have guns.' Between 2805 and 2185 _____ Avenue, an unidentified man fired one shot at patrolmen. The two patrolmen returned four shots at perpetrator who fled. No injuries, no property damage."

10/3   11:10 P.M. "_____ held up by one unknown MW and

FW. Knocked subject to the ground, took $1,000 and fled on foot. Aided treated at Staten Island Hospital for laceration of eye and mouth and released."

10/3   11:55 P.M. Bronx, "_____MN, 40, in rear yard of residence was shot in the left side of chest by one of three unknown MN during an altercation. Perpetrators fled scene. Aided DOA."

This was not an unusual period of police activity. In the following week there were four trucks hijacked, one subway train accident with ten injured, one bank holdup, one prisoner escape and one escapee recaptured. A girl was shot and two other females pistol-whipped; two burglars fleeing the police fell off a roof and one died from his injuries. A vehicular homicide by a hit and run driver occurred in Manhattan and fifty members of the Students for a Democratic Society seized two buildings at New York University. Both buildings were subsequently evacuated with no arrests.

The principal case file does not cover every serious crime that blights New York City. There are a few offenses that get special reports. A good many go entirely unreported or are graded as routine. The victim of a mugging considers his misfortune serious, but this offense has become too commonplace to be worthy of the principal case file. And in many instances people who have been mugged or stuck up, or beaten in a family quarrel fail to notify the cops. On other occasions, the officer summoned to the scene determines that the paper work involved will be too much trouble and unless pushed fails to submit an account of the crime.

Beyond the principal cases reported, and those that ought to be but are not part of the daily record, the New York City police must cope with an average of two bodies a week fished out of the water. The Emergency Service Division revives a couple of asphyxiation cases per week, and another pair perhaps do not survive. Each week roughly 1,500 cars are reported stolen and nearly 3,500 burglary complaints require police attention. Assaults number 400 a week, and in the same time span between 50 and 60 charges of arson must be investigated. All these are felonies, which totalled 434,000 in 1969.

Misdemeanors involve, per week, almost 3,000 petit larcenies, 300 "dangerous drug offenses," 150 prostitution charges, 1,500 deeds labelled "criminal mischief," a hundred assaults less serious than those rated felonious, and about fifteen arrests for "jostling and fraudulent accosting." Misdemeanors, with 147,000 motor law offenses included, totalled 535,507 in 1969. But as with felonies a substantial number of such crimes go unreported.

The job of the New York City police does not begin or end with crime. All ambulance requests, and there were 577,167 in 1969, must go through police communications. The 30,000 hack drivers of the city fall under police supervision for licensing and testing of cabs. The statistics for 1969 show 14,024 persons reported missing and the police located 13,183, a clearance rate of 93 percent. The police laboratory assisted in 37,416 criminal investigations for 1969 and the photographic division snapped 110,693 prisoners, of whom 46,812 entered the rogues' gallery for the first time. That year fingerprints figured in the arrests of 116,066 criminals. The Department's motor vehicle fleet contains more than 1800 cars, including fifty "unmarked traffic pursuit cars" and seven "unmarked sedans." In many instances officers use their own autos to avoid recognition by the underworld. To cope with this amount of crime and to man its bureaus and equipment, the Department has better than 32,000 members who are supplemented by several hundred civilian employees. This works out to one cop per 230 citizens.

But numbers are only part of the Department's problem. There are also the factors of population density, attitude toward law and order by both police and public, the duties demanded of an officer, and a sadly ignored factor, the history of the city and its police force. History's effect cannot be underestimated, for past performance and tradition influence much of the quality of police work today.

CHAPTER I

THE MEANING OF
A POLICE HISTORY

"When I go to bed at night," said Mayor Robert F. Wagner, "I say a special prayer for the safety of the city. Then I say a special prayer of thanks that nothing bad happened in the police department."

Wagner's prayers were well spoken, although perhaps he should have reversed the order. For the life of New York City, as well as other American cities, has been inextricably intertwined with the vicissitudes of the police force.

One means for measuring the quality of life in a civilization is by studying the limits of action for the individual. In one sense, the border between the lawful and the criminal defines a society. More particularly, the attitude toward these limits by those who live with them is a trustworthy guide to the morality or the real ethic of a society.

In primitive groups, tribal pressures can control deviant or antisocial behavior. But in industrial, urban civilization, limitations upon individuals can no longer be enforced by public pressure. Just as citizens who can no longer handle their political decisions through town meetings have elected delegates to make decisions, they have chosen representatives—the cops—to handle deviant or antisocial behavior.

One of the luxuries of such a system is that the citizen is divorced from responsibility for control of the criminal. The police are interposed between the "outs" and the "ins," and they suffer the painful consequences of anyone who gets between warring parties. The fact that the police are in the hire of the "ins" does not mean they are wholly at peace with the law-abiding. For the latter regularly change the rules or often accept them only when they do not restrict their own behavior, thus occasionally lining up with the outsiders.

The life and times of the New York City police is a history not only of the struggles of the criminals, the law enforcers and the law abiding but also a chronicle of the shifting mores and morality on which the battle has been fought.

Gambling and prostitution offer the most obvious examples of ambivalent attitudes and shifting mores. Without exception, police commissioners have agreed that they can never entirely suppress gaming. Policemen, a century ago, groused that the courts threw out gambling arrests on legal technicalities. In that period, the hack politicians who sat on the magisterial bench often gave freedom to the gamblers for their contributions to political clubs rather than for the sake of the Constitution. In the twentieth century, especially in the last decade, it has been concern for civil liberties that has often turned illegal gamblers out of court. Whatever the reason, the policeman's reaction has been that no one really wants him to stifle gambling. He also observes that the state endorses parimutuel betting at the race track (and shares in the revenue), and also runs a statewide lottery. And that an attempt to curb games of chance at a street bazaar brings the wrath of the church down on his head. The policeman can be pardoned for a lack of zeal when faced with the policy game, the poor man's effort to get rich quick, or with the bookmaker accepting $2 to $10 bets from people who aren't able to take a day off from work and go out to the track.

Prostitution, largely as a result of changes in morality, no longer finds the market it once had. At the turn of the century, restless men who had left behind their families, wives, and sweethearts roamed the city. Respectable girls treasured their chastity; demand created a supply of vice. Today women outnumber men in New York City. Fornication and adultery, although crimes according to statute, do not antagonize either public opinion or the District Attorney. The oldest profession, once a heavy industry, now operates more as a cottage trade. Call girls with their own places of business plus street walkers serve out-of-towners and those, who, in an era of easy sexuality, can't or won't find other partners. A procurer may be involved but white slavers and Syndicate influences appear to have been eliminated. Police suppression of prostitution becomes difficult, reflecting the lack of interest by the citizens.

As the central figure of a history, the New York City policeman is an easy target. His imperfections are clearly visible for he is the most scrutable of all those concerned with the limits upon freedom. The criminal takes pains to keep his actions hidden; the "law abiding" have divorced themselves as much as possible from dealing with outlaw behavior. The policeman is also vulnerable because by the peculiar twist of modern social criticism there is a fascination with the criminal as a "good man" gone wrong.

On a less philosophical level, a cop's best work, his prevention of crime, cannot be measured, cannot even make interesting reading. Quite possibly a community that found itself without criminal acts would ascribe its perfection to its home life, recreation facilities, and churches. The community might even decide that it was so virtuous that it needed fewer cops.

New York City has never been faced with such a situation, however. By 1860, something like one resident in ten had a criminal record. Some newcomers from the Old World had been given the choice of emigrating or passing long years in prison. The city was a violent place almost from the beginning. It was once a frontier; it had been fought over by the colonizing nations and by Indians. Firearms and other weapons were part of its tradition from birth. The explosive growth of the New York population, without any control placed over the number of residents or their utilization of natural resources, kept the city a frontier well into the twentieth century. (And it can be argued that for the nonwhite population still pouring in from the South or Puerto Rico the city is still frontier territory.) Pacification depended entirely upon the establishment of order by the police. The political forces of New York's infant democracy immediately saw in the police a valuable adjunct. The cops supervised the elections, put the pressure on sources of money and votes while attempting to control crime and vice, and "civilized" the new settlers.

The cop expresses the ambivalence of many Americans toward the abstract values that are supposed to underlie American institutions. While private citizens can prattle about freedom of speech, condemn or applaud draft card burners, support civil rights, or warn what will happen "if niggers move into the building," the cop is out in the street facing people who have gone past the stage of mere talk. And nothing in a policeman's training can totally expunge his own background. Cerebration may be part of every cop's work but his bag also includes the use of brute strength, his blackjack, night stick, and pistol.

Nonviolence has never been an accepted American philosophy. The New York cop no more grew up worshiping a turn-the-other-cheek viewpoint than did any other American nurtured on tales of the frontier, the violent Revolution, the Civil War, the body-contact sports hero and his commercial equivalent, the "hard-nosed" businessman. The hoariest cliche of the Department says, "There's more law in the end of a night stick than in a library of Supreme Court decisions."

We speak traditionally of the war on crime, and the policeman becomes the civil equivalent of the soldier patrolling the frontier. There is, however, a significant difference. Wars begin when the high command orders its forces to invade or create an incident that provokes a war response. The discretion of the front line soldier is limited. Even if he commits an act of aggression the commanders can repudiate him. The individual soldier is also restrained by the knowledge that his enemy too bears arms and an act of war means retaliation. Contrast that with the policeman. He has tremendous discretion in the use of force. He operates with the assumption that the enemy is not legally entitled to respond with force. He can start a war (or riot) and has.

The policeman cannot be measured by his successes. We cannot count the crimes that didn't occur because he patrolled his beat and didn't coop. We cannot enumerate the graft he refused. So we must turn to his failures. In New York City there have been innumerable investigations, police scandals, and breakdowns in what is called law and order. The cop is a convenient scapegoat. But it is the society that placed him in charge of its morality that is un-masked by an investigation of the police. It is that society that is smeared by any scandal involving its guardians and it is that soci-ety that is ripped when riot occurs.

CHAPTER II

FOREIGN ANTECEDENTS

History takes no note of the appearance of man's first cop. But when Hammurabi, around 2000 B.C., created his Babylonian Codes of Law it is a reasonable assumption that he also employed a facsimile of a police corps to enforce his rules. More than likely throughout antiquity, police power resided in the hands of the military or the palace guards.

From the sixth century A.D. on, small numbers of Parisians were enrolled into night watches. In the fourteenth century, Charles V, of France, probably created the first seemingly civilian police system. The ranking official, however, became a military officer. This French police became one more arm of despotism and concerned itself with maintaining royal control. The French did not put a truly civil police on the streets until 1829.

Across the Channel, Oliver Cromwell provided a form of police through a constabulary of mounted cavalry. They battered English freemen with merciless savagery until the restored King Charles II assumed the throne in 1663 and replaced them with a night watch and day constable system. The night watch, called Old Charlies in deference to their creator, offered little protection. Most were elderly men, barely able to wield cudgels and no match for outlaws.

In the New World, a Schout Fiscal (Sheriff Attorney) enforced the rules in New Amsterdam for the Dutch West India Company. The Schout Fiscal maintained order and carried out sentences of the governing body, including hangings. After dark a watch armed with rattles guarded the city. But the Schout Fiscal and the Rattle Watch disappeared in 1664 when the British assumed command. Under the British garrisoned troops enforced decrees.

When the British troops finally evacuated New York City in 1783, the town fathers sired an infant police force. It was not an impressive specimen. For a population of over 25,000 in 1786, the watch numbered one captain and 28 men. Still using the English pound sterling, the city allowed £1724 a year for the watch which was strictly a nighttime force. The captain received eight shillings a night; the common watchmen were paid three shillings.

Within a few years a fee system lifted the watch's incentive and income. A constable serving a warrant got one shilling, sixpence, plus another sixpence for each mile of travel. Collection of a 20-shilling fine earned the officer one shilling; taking a defendant into custody earned a shilling and conveying a prisoner to jail a similar fee.

The first waves of immigrants soon washed over the city shores, and as landlords began to cut up buildings to house the newcomers slums were spawned. Crime and vice boomed. The watch added 20 men in 1789; by 1801 two captains, assisted by two deputies and 72 men, required a budget of $21,162. Four jails now housed the watch's human take. Prices for services remained fairly stable although the police switched to the decimal money system. For 19 cents a constable delivered a summons. For 12½ cents he took a man into custody and on every $2.50 fine, 12½ cents went to the arresting officer.

In spite of the fee-splitting, the watch offered little protection to the city. Constables were paid too little to make the job a full-time occupation. Teamsters, stevedores, and mechanics worked at their trades during the day and then dozed at the watch by night. During 1802, records show 120 watchmen caught sleeping on post and fined. The following year 140 paid penalties for this offense. Rowdies delighted in tipping over huts with snoring watchmen inside. From the top of City Hall and Bridewell Prison a pair of watchmen did their best to keep the city awake by bellowing the traditional "All's well" cry on the hour.

As crime thrived, the Watch Committee of the city strove to keep up with the pace by recommending bonuses for "good arrests." On July 8, 1805, $23 was awarded to a group of marshals and watchmen for capturing "The Portuguese Francisco," an alleged murderer. Five dollars went to one Richard Nixon, $2 went to each of the others, and Francisco went to the gibbet. The responsibility of the watch was extended to guarding Potter's Field because student doctors were stealing corpses from the graves. Along with that duty the watch was also expected to look out for fires, suppress crime and disorder in the streets, and light the street lamps.

The rewards and fees failed to improve significantly the performance of the watch. A committee petitioned the New York legislature for still bigger financial incentives to the officers: "In perfecting . . . a police, the activity of the inferior officers and agents of the police magistrates is every way important and competent. Rewards are consequently necessary to stimulate such activity."

Watch members ordinarily wore their regular working clothes and the motley of fashion did little to build esprit. A styled hat was proposed in 1820 but the stevedores, mechanics, and laborers preferred to remain in mufti. Citizens complained of the difficulty in determining who belonged to the watch and for a time a painted plate was attached to the watchman's own hat. In the late 1820s the watch adopted the traditional leather hat of firemen. Varnished twice a year, it became "as hard as iron," according to a contemporary historian. To the public, the watch became known as Leatherheads or Old Charlies, in memory of English forebears. Every Leatherhead carried a 33-inch club to help him keep the peace.

The watch was New York's major police force but its responsibility extended only to the hours after dark. Whatever crime occurred during the day belonged to a pair of city-appointed constables in each ward and some marshals assigned to the courts. The day police force limited itself to keeping peace on the waterfront with "staves of office," and protecting people from the "extortionate demands" of the hackmen. The watch did little more than look out for fires and raise an alarm over riots.

It would not be misleading to observe that the function of the police was basically to keep thieves, rioters, and purveyors of vice from disturbing the respectable elements of the city. What happened to the poor in their warrens concerned the police very little. The policy was basic in police thinking for the nineteenth century and a good part of the twentieth. Indeed, there may be some cause to believe that the police still consider their basic function the protection of the middle class and its neighborhoods from the invasions of the poor and criminal elements.

The pattern appears in any society based upon democratic capitalism. Whoever owned property could expect police protection, generally from the have-nots. Outside of democratic capitalism the police served only as an arm of the ruling aristocracy and its favored friends. A major conflict facing modern cities arises from the demand that police protection extend beyond the preservation of the propertied and their chattels to the lives of the poor whose net worth is near invisible.

At the turn of the nineteenth century, daytime law enforcement owed its survival mainly to one man, High Constable Jacob Hays, "a police force all himself," according to Augustine Costello in *Our Police Protectors,* the first history of the N.Y. police published in 1885. Born in Bedford, N.Y., in 1772, Hays received an appointment as a marshal in 1798, became High Constable by grace of Mayor Levington four years later. For a time Hays doubled his duties by captaining the watch. He was relieved of this obligation in 1804. However, successive mayors for nearly fifty years renewed Hays's appointment as High Constable.

The one-man police force patrolled some eighteen hours a day. Among his skills was a technique for breaking up street arguments before they turned into riots. When a belligerent crowd gathered, Hays circled the perimeter knocking off hats with his wooden staff. As the victims stooped to retrieve their headgear, Hays would shove them with his foot or hand. The tactic piled up bodies in a sort of barricade and contained the combatants until Hays could draw off ringleaders or delay action until other law enforcement officials arrived. Unlike a dismal series of successors, Old Jacob avoided major violence when dealing with a mob. He left neither broken heads, bruised bodies, nor appetites for revenge in his wake.

Although the early nineteenth century saw almost weekly riot-

ing or large scale brawling in the streets of New York, Hays never
called out the state militia. "If you send for the military," said
Hays, "they will kill someone, and that will bring trouble; then
there will be the trouble of burying them; and that will be the
greatest trouble of all." Hays's success with mobs did indeed stem
from his realization that violence begets more violence. In fact, the
British civil police force, created under Sir Robert Peel, owed its
early acceptance to its firm but restrained handling of mobs. Previously, British troops savagely slaughtered Englishmen threatening
civil disorder.

Along with quelling street disturbances, Hays built himself
something of a reputation as a detective, although even at that
early date there is evidence that the informer rather than shrewd
deduction or even hard work usually provided the answer to the
question of who did it. In the fashion of modern police, Hays kept
an amazingly large file on known criminals and their habits of
work. Only Hays kept his catalogue in his head. So respected was
his knowledge of rogues east of the Mississippi that police officers
in Europe corresponded with him seeking information on safecrackers and forgers who might have left the United States to seek
fortune in Europe.

The intrepid Hays was no more fazed by the robber barons
than he was by common thieves. While he was High Constable the
fight for control of Hudson River shipping between Commodore
Cornelius Vanderbilt and the Livingstone family kept the waterfront a snarl of legal and physical skirmishes. At one point the Liv-
ingstones secured an injunction to restrain the Commodore and it
fell to Hays to serve Vanderbilt. In a letter the Commodore recalled, "I was mad enough to defy the whole Livingstone tribe, old
Hays included, but when I caught a glimpse of his calm and smiling face and a twinkle in his eye which singularly enough said, as
plainly as words could express it 'if you don't obey the order of the
court and that damn soon I'll make you do it by God!' I concluded
to surrender. I didn't want to back down, however too hurriedly
and I said that if they wanted to arrest me, they should carry me off
the boat, and don't you know, old Hays took me at my word and

landed me on the dock with a suddenness that took away my breath."

Despite the singlehanded success of Hays, when an 1843 Alderman's Committee studied police performance, it recommended unification of the firemen, watch, and constabulary to protect New York's 350,000 people, a figure that included 50,000 transients with "the usual proportion thereof whom are wicked and debased." The aldermen reported that, aside from the watch, 100 marshals, 31 constables, and 16 day police comprised the city's defense against crime. All, including the watch, owed their jobs to politics.

In fact, the 350,000 residents struggled to survive with the barest municipal services. Almost from the beginning citizens had recognized the threat of fire to their tinder box buildings. As early as 1731 the city fathers bought two engines from London for pumping water and six years later the first volunteer fire companies organized. Wildly spreading blazes continued to threaten the entire city. One conflagration in 1835 nearly leveled the town from Wall Street to the Battery. By the time it died out, six hundred buildings had gone up in smoke and firemen from New Jersey, Philadelphia, and Baltimore had been summoned. Most of these never got to New York but bogged down at Perth Amboy, New Jersey, waiting for transportation. Firemen on the scene were hampered by a water shortage.

The 1835 fire and the cholera epidemic of 1832 convinced New Yorkers that they needed cleaner and more available water. Engineers selected the Croton River, forty miles upstate in Westchester County as the source for it and built a dam, flooding many local farms. The piped water flowed to a large reservoir on the site of what is now the Public Library at 42nd Street and Fifth Avenue. By 1842, New Yorkers were drinking Croton water and it remains the principal source of potable water today.

The Croton supply ended any shortage of water to pour on fires but the city continued until 1865 to rely upon volunteer fire companies. These were really social and political clubs (much like some vamp units in suburbia today) and they controlled their own membership. The city supplied the equipment but the men bought their own flashy uniforms and fought fires in highly individual

manners. Rival groups, who sometimes arrived at fires simultaneously, waged pitched battles with cobblestones, clubs, and knives
for the right to put out the fire which blazed on while they skir-
mished in the streets. William Marcy "Boss" Tweed started up the
ladder of political power as a member of the "Big Six" Fire Company.

In 1865, the same year metropolitan fire districts were established, the city finally set up sanitary services to deal with filth in
the streets. The police department was allotted money to contract
for street cleaning but their administration of it was so corrupt the
responsibility was taken away from them in the 1880s.

The gestation period for city services was obviously too long
and the infant municipal departments could not seriously cope
with the problems they were facing. As New York moved toward
the middle of the nineteenth century it was already well on its way
toward becoming a jungle of slums and corruption.

No one could doubt that within the cesspool of the tenements
vice, crime, and corruption flourished and that the police even if
willing to enforce laws faced an insurmountable problem. For
example, the Five Points (a section named for the intersection of a
number of lower Manhattan streets near the present day Foley
Square) was off limits to the law. Costello remarked, "Certainly as
no spot of ground on this continent had the reputation of having
been the witness of more crime, so no spot had such repulsive features or where want and woe were more apparent. Every house was
a brothel, the resort of persons of every age, sex and color. Every
store a dram shop, where from morning till morning the thieves
and abandoned characters of the town whetted their depraved
tastes and concocted future crimes and villainies." The police
stayed out of sections such as the Five Points and hoped that the
residents of these areas would confine their activities to the neighborhood.

In the area Roman Catholics and Protestants engaged in
small but bloody crusades against one another. Gangs of toughs
ravaged the streets, the Bowery Bhoys, a motley of young adults,
setting the pace with a distinctive uniform of chimney tops or plug

hats, fireman's red flannel shirts, tight calfskin boots, high heels, and a deserved reputation for street brawls.

The Five Points region contained picturesque alleys known as Murderer's Alley and Cow's Bay along with an acre of open ground called Paradise Square. Whatever the names, the streets all lay sodden with filth. Ten feet below ground level, windowless cellars housed lodgers, rats, and vermin.

A contemporary survey of a Five Points tenement said, "In this one room the cooking, eating and sleeping of the whole family and their visitors is performed. Yes—and their visitors: for it is no unusual thing for a mother and her two or three daughters, all of course prostitutes, to receive their men at the same time and in the same room, passing in and out and going through all transactions of their hellish intercourse with a sang froid at which devils would stand aghast."

Secondhand stores and pawnbrokers covered the Five Points, the chief business being resale of stolen goods. The saloons sold liquor to anyone with the price, and children were among their customers.

The Dead Rabbits, an Irish-oriented offshoot of the native American Bowery Bhoys, swarmed through the Five Points. Their insignia consisted of a pole with a dead hare. The ruler of the enclave was "Captain" Isaiah Rynders, a New Orleans gambler and knife fighter, who thought slavery was God-inspired. Prostitutes, vice dens, gambling halls, fences—all had Rynders as a partner, whose chief contribution was to keep the police from interfering with their operations. Rynders supplied immunity to criminals through the newly formed Tammany Political Club.

Respectable citizens, alarmed by the lawlessness, took quasi-legal action to control it. George W. Matsell, a bookseller, became a police magistrate in 1840. Like his English counterparts with their Bow Street Runners, Magistrate Matsell organized his own vigilantes to patrol the city. They prowled the wards of New York, "breaking up many places of evil resort through physical exertions," says Costello. Years later, Matsell was accused of accepting bribes from the city's leading abortionist.

CHAPTER III

THE BIRTH OF
THE DEPARTMENT

The tide of immigrants from the Old World rose to the flood stage by the 1840s. With no operating laws governing building codes, sanitation, health, or the number of people to be crammed into an apartment, the landlords packed immigrants into lower Manhattan in a density never before seen in the world. New York held 290,000 people to the square mile in 1855, London only 175,816.

Tenements mushroomed on whatever space was available, without regard for ventilation or sunlight. Some shacks became islands surrounded by taller structures with threadlike alleys as the only access. At least one child died of suffocation because of the absence of air within a tenement.

Fetid paths, inadequate sewage, polluted water, disease-spawning marshes, and barriers to the sun made the city a fever and plague resort. Hundreds died during periodic epidemics that festered during the first half of the nineteenth century. Small boys hawked coffins at $4 apiece on street corners during outbursts of yellow fever or cholera.

In the early part of the century, the better-off citizens hired laborers to haul away garbage and offal for dumping into the neighboring rivers. The poor depended upon sporadic collections of waste, which much of the time lay heaped in alleys and gutters. Swine roamed the streets scavenging. Their chief competition was small children searching for edible treasures. Not until 1867 did an ordinance forbid owners to let pigs run free in built up areas.

As late as 1890, Jacob Riis saw a family with boarders who

fed their hogs in a cellar that held eight tons of manure. He noted one 12 × 12 room containing five families totaling twenty people of all ages. An old brewery building put up in 1792 had been turned into a tenement that housed nearly 1,000. Its population was well-integrated, with Negroes and Irish sharing the premises and not a few interracial marriages.

The city began to take notice of its slum problem in 1857. In 1869 the Board of Health ordered windows cut in 46,000 buildings. But it was already too late. The profiteers of the tenement played a large role in the city's political machines. The mass of money involved controlled enormous civic muscle. The exploitation of land and tenants, the pressure for maximum returns on the investment in real estate became a prime factor in New York politics and police conduct. By 1890, landlords expected to net 40 percent return on tenement investments and profits ran as high as 100 percent.

The actual birth of the New York City Police Department was now at hand. The Municipal Police Act of 1844 abolished the night watch and empowered the mayor to select two hundred men to police the city twenty-four hours a day. In recognition of Matsell's devotion to a purer New York, he was named superintendent. His salary was set at $1,250 a year, the patrolmen's at $500. The Act designated an official uniform; singlebreasted blue frock coat, buttoned to the neck with the initials M.P. on the collar. But the 1844 attempt to establish a professional force foundered as aldermen blocked appropriations. A year later the demand could not be denied and a full time police department was established.

The 1845 reorganization of the police called for 800 men to replace the 1846 members of the night watch, dock masters, inspectors of stages, carts, and hydrants. The guardians of the law wore no uniforms but a star badge of copper adorned their left breast, making them either "coppers" or in honor of the incumbent mayor, Harper's men. (Partridge's *Dictionary of Slang* attributes the origin of the designation "copper" not to the badge but to a theatrical term for captures or arrests.) George Templeton Strong, a diarist who minutely recorded the events of the era, thought so little of the founding of the department that he failed to record the event in his papers.

New York's 1844 municipal police act had called for a uniformed body of men but the Americans, like the British, harbored deep animosity to the military connotation. The police themselves preferred to work in mufti. The uniforms had provoked assaults and were abandoned with the 1845 law. To enable the men to perform more efficiently, the city created station houses. Citizens now had a place to go when in search of a cop. In addition, indigents were lodged in station houses.

In their first six years of operation, the New York City police busied themselves with 144,364 arrests. Of these, 13,896 were for assault and battery, 20,252 for disorderly conduct, 36,675 for intoxication, 29,190 intoxication *and* disorderly conduct, 14,454 for picking pockets. Among the more exotic arrests were 187 for bastardy and 171 for something called "constructive larceny." There were 1,484 booked for insanity, 64 for murder, 68 for rape, 138 for insulting females in the street, and 11,347 for vagrancy. A force of 1,000 achieved this record of arrests. Conspicuous in its absence is any significant figure for arrests for crimes against property.

The newly established department was expected to deal with riots. The bourgeois and the new industrialists realized that nothing could be more destructive of their new prosperity than to have the swelling urban populace go amok and smash shops and factories.

British experience had taught Americans that the employment of the military to quell riots spilled blood that stained memories for decades. The newborn New York City police had five years to plant themselves before they faced the first hurricane of a populace gone berserk. The occasion for riot in 1849 was a theatrical performance at the Astor Place Theatre. While touring England, the American thespian Edwin Forrest felt that his British counterpart, James Macready, slighted him. When the latter scheduled a series of appearances in New York, Forrest and his friends pumped the bellows on smoldering anti-British sentiment. The American actor allegedly declared that Macready ought never be allowed to appear on a New York stage. Posters appeared on the city streets, just before Macready's opening: "Workingmen: Shall Americans or English Rule in This City? The crew of the English steamer [then anchored in the harbor] has threatened all Americans who shall dare to express their opinion this night at the English Aristocratic Opera House. We advocate no violence but a free expression of opinion onto all public men! Working men! Freemen! Stand by your lawful rights."

Some citizens of the period saw the hand of Isaiah Rynders behind the agitation but credit for whipping up the anti-British sentiment generally belongs to E. Z. C. Judson, whose pen name, Ned Buntline, graced a number of best-selling adventure tales of the day.

Quick to resent the invasion of Macready were Rynders' Bowery Bhoys. On the night of May 7 they filtered into the theater and disrupted the proceedings by tossing things onto the stage even though Macready wasn't even on the bill. The players gave up in the third act. Three nights later, Macready took the stage for his version of *Macbeth*. Police Chief Matsell, sensing the temper of the city, wanted the show to be canceled. But the promotors had sold out the house, and they insisted it was up to the mayor to provide adequate protection.

Macready took his stance on stage; behind him a sign affixed to the proscenium announced, "The friends of order will be quiet." The actor recalled, "Looking at the wretched creatures in the parquet who shook their fists violently at me, and called to me in savage fury, I laughed at them, pointing them out with my truncheon to the police." Matsell's men, stationed inside the theater, hauled away a number of troublemakers; one was stripped near naked as the patrolmen dragged him through the aisles.

A steady clatter of paving stones reverberated against the building as a mob pelted the theater. From a theater window, a hooligan leaned out and shouted that he and his fellows inside were being arrested. The crowd turned even more rowdy. Its disposition failed to improve when a cop seized a hose and sprayed it with water on what was a chilly evening.

On stage, Macready continued over the rumbling belligerents in the audience. "While deeds of real crime and outrage were roaring at intervals in our ears, and rising to madness all around us," the play was finished with Macready expiring in the death of Macbeth. Musket fire sounded outside. The actor sneaked out of the theater in disguise, sought refuge in a house for three hours, slipped out of the city to New Rochelle where he took a train to Boston. There he caught the first boat back to England.

Outside the theater, 320 police, marshaled by Matsell, faced thousands of pushing, shoving, rock-throwing drama critics. Troops were called out to reinforce the Matsell brigade but the fury of the throngs only increased. Paving stones flew through the air, bloodying the militia men who told city officials that they could not hold the line unless they turned their guns on the rioters.

Mayor Woodhull hurried to the scene and the militia commander General Hall, bleeding freely from a stone-inflicted wound on his face, requested permission to open fire. But Mayor Woodhull feared the political consequences of drastic action. Unable to accept his responsibility, Woodhull ducked out to a hotel, leaving the General to bear the consequences of any action taken.

Hall's officers gave an order for the crowd to disperse but in the confusion of jeers and skirmishes the command was unintelligible. It is questionable that words could have brought order at this point. The soldiers discharged their muskets over the heads of the mob in a last gesture of forebearance. The reaction was a chorus of shouts that the soldiers had only blanks. A second volley went into the crowd but only two citizens fell wounded. The remainder, either unable to detect the slight diminution of their ranks or else misinterpreting the reluctance of the soldiers, resumed the attack. Musket muzzles flashed again, and this time the toll was heavy.

Patrolman William McKinney supplied a semicoherent account: "I was knocked down myself, I endeavoured to arrest one of the men who was killed but he was taken away from me, and I was dragged across the street to the curbstone. This man, after he was killed was taken inside into the opera house. He was shot. I saw him inside. He was throwing a stone when I arrested him." Aside from McKinney's victim, twenty-one other persons died in the Astor Place riots in what must be history's greatest bloodbath based upon an acting performance. More significantly, the young police force had failed in its first joust with civil disorder.

For well over one hundred years after the Astor Place riot, the police in New York, as in other cities, struggled unsuccessfully to cope with large-scale civil disorder. Few departments bothered to develop tactics that could disperse an outraged mob. Worse, police discipline, as at Astor Place, tended to break down. Isolated acts of police savagery or indiscriminate use of force only inflamed rioters more. At Astor Place the force could at least claim ignorance, inexperience, and a lack of cohesion that hampered concerted action. Within a few years, however, the authorities recognized these crippling deficiencies and began to take steps to correct them.

CHAPTER IV

METROPOLITANS VS. MUNICIPALS

Requirements for joining the force in 1853 were simple. A prospective cop had to be a citizen, be able to read and write, and know the "first four rules of arithmetic." A doctor's certificate attested to physical fitness and twenty-five character references were required from citizens. A committee consisting of the mayor, recorder, and city judge appointed whomever they favored among the eligibles. The men continued to work in civilian clothes; their only concession to uniformity was the badge of office.

Pressure to put the police into uniforms began to grow. Citizens claimed that a badge could not be readily seen and the generally lackadaisical performance of the police was ascribed to the absence of the proper dress. James W. Gerard, a private citizen, made a study of the London Police, bought a British police uniform and wore it to a New York fancy dress ball. When Gerard was well received, police leaders were encouraged enough to send a squad of uniformed men to the Crystal Palace Fair as a uniformed drill team. Although the demonstration received favorable comment, both rank and file rebelled at the suggestion they don uniforms. The coppers held an indignation meeting in front of Chief Matsell's office. When ordered to buy uniforms they refused, denouncing the garb because it gave them the look of "footmen." Inspector Thorne argued that a uniform is a "badge of servitude."

However, someone convinced Thorne to wear a uniform to the next meeting of the police at Military Hall. A number of patrolmen complimented Thorne on his new suit, none recognizing it as the hated uniform. While Thorne, in the uniform, sat listening, a series of speakers denounced the prescribed uniform in "strong language," said Costello. Thorne then rose and said if they did not accept the uniform they would eventually be dropped from the department. He added that only the coat was actually required.

Those at the session supposedly agreed, said Costello, "Well, if that be what they call the uniform, it is a first class thing."

Later, Matsell encouraged his subordinates to wear brass buttons supplied by the city. He promised to attend the Department's annual target practice excursion, giving it greater cachet, if the men would adopt the brass buttons.

The first uniform consisted of a blue coat with velvet collar and nine black buttons, later supplanted by brass ones. Although Inspector Thorne insisted only the coat was necessary the men were also supposed to wear gray trousers with a one-inch black stripe running down the sides. Cloth caps completed the ensemble and in the event of a fire or riot hard leather firemen's caps were used. The uniforms had an immediate effect; 25,000 arrests were made in the first six months of 1854, 2800 more than the previous half year. The record was attributed to the greater pride in work policemen took as a result of the new uniforms.

The dress was the first major step in establishing discipline. For the first time the cop was separated from his peers in New York. The pattern of isolation and submission to authority that exists today dates from the acceptance of the uniform. The police department was not simply a rabble of peace keepers; it was an organization with visible symbols. The policeman now possessed an identity and in the violent flux that has been traditional in the U.S. an identity has never been a mean prize. In fact police experts today insist that the uniform that confers position and power upon an individual remains a strong attraction to recruits.

Quite aside from the inability to handle eruptions in the streets, the municipal police, even in uniform, failed to impress respectable citizens. Democratic Mayor Fernando Wood flourished at City Hall in 1857 while his Tammany Club, then enjoying the first of its many reigns, rumbled with internecine strife. A Tammany thug, Bill "the Butcher" Poole (he owned a slaughterhouse) fell before bullets from thugs in the service of an Irish immigrant, John Morrisey. As Poole's life ebbed he mumbled, "I die a true American." A public funeral filled the city streets with marching bands, civic organizations and the inevitable fire brigades. With Bill Poole noisily laid to rest at the cemetery the trip back to town turned into a brawl between the anti-Catholic Know Nothings and the men of Ireland. Poole followers and Morrisey men shot it out on Broadway pausing only to loot stores. Under Mayor Wood, an intimate of the leaders of commerce and society as well as a friend of thugs, the municipal police made little effort to stem such carnage in the streets. Upstate, however, the Republican legislators decided, as so often since then, to save New York from itself.

Amendments to the New York City Charter by legislators in Albany abolished the municipal department and replaced it with the Metropolitan Police Force which was subject to commissioners appointed by the governor. Mayor Wood refused to be deprived of what he considered his private police force and denounced the state's action as unconstitutional. Some of the Municipals joined the new force, others stayed with the city police.

One of those who signed on with the state-created lawmen was George Walling. Like Matsell, Walling swung a heavy club. Costello described an encounter between a burglar and Walling. "A scientific twirl of his locust [night stick] and he laid the ruffian prostrate in the gutter." (Dead, actually.) Walling in his memoirs tells of receiving the dubious assignment of arresting Mayor Wood in City Hall. When Walling arrived, the Mayor's fifty guards permitted him to enter because most of them had served earlier alongside him. Inside Wood's office, Walling announced the purpose of his visit. "I shall have to take you out forcibly if you resist." The palace retinue gently eased Walling out of the building.

Then Daniel D. Conover, appointed by the state as Street Commissioner, marched on City Hall and also attempted to oust Fernando Wood. Conover was roughly handled and bounced out of the building. The Street Commissioner, armed with a warrant for Wood that accused him of inciting to riot and violence, organized a band of Metropolitan cops to assault the Wood fortress. Passersby were treated to the sight of two rival police forces going at one another with clubs by the seat of city government. The out-numbered Metropolitans fell back from the onslaughts of Fer-nando Wood's platoons.

Once again Walling was assigned the task of arresting the res-olute Wood. Accompanied by the sheriff and one other man, he made his way to the mayoral redoubt. Wood angrily banged his staff of office on the floor, "I will never submit." To confirm Wood's resistance his man, Matsell, poked his head in upon the conference to advise Wood on the state of the battle outside: "We've beat them off." He neglected to add that the skirmishing had spread to side streets with opportunists beginning to sack sur-rounding stores.

An unlucky coincidence proved to be the Mayor's downfall. While the police pummeled one another in the streets, the Seventh Regiment happened to be marching down Broadway en route to a boat for Boston. The foes of Tammany and Wood sought out the commander of the troops and begged for his help. The Seventh Regiment detoured to City Hall and halted the brawling in the streets. Inside, Matsell said, "Well, our game is up."

Fernando Wood accepted service of legal papers from the state. The Mayor was not prepared to yield without a struggle in the courts, however. The question of which police force held juris-diction went to the judges while the two blue-coated armies strolled the streets, more interested in punishing one another than in en-forcing any laws. Injured Metropolitans sued Wood for their in-juries and won. He was strong enough politically to get the city to pay the $250 damages to the litigants.

While waiting for some binding legal decision, members of the old force were threatened by Wood with immediate dismissal if they heeded the orders of the state-appointed commissioners. Both police forces patrolled the streets nightly in an irregular manner. The miscreants arrested by the Metropolitan Police were frequently rescued from custody by the Municipals and set free. And those who were brought to jail or court won their release through the in-tercession of aldermen or by magistrates who owed their position to Mayor Wood's political machine.

Wood finally surrendered to a court order on the police issue but the Metropolitans remained under strength for many weeks. Some of the more boisterous sections of the city suffered no restraint for a long period of time. Encouraged by the weakness of the lawmen, the two leading gangs of toughs, the Bowery Bhoys and the Dead Rabbits, moved to meet in mortal combat. Residents of the city in 1857 foresaw the coming struggle as, on the night of the Independence Day holiday, swarms of toughs roistered in the streets looking for trouble. July 4th traditionally brought turbulence to the slums. The respectable folk appealed to sixty former Municipals to serve until after the holiday without pay. They agreed but the State Commissioners haughtily rejected volunteers from the ranks of their erstwhile competition. As evening fell, hoodlums began shoving people from the sidewalks into the refuse-strewn gutters. The few Metropolitans in the Five Points district offered no resistance.

Early in the morning, a band of Dead Rabbits, reinforced by allies from the Plug Uglies, assaulted a policeman. He fled, taking refuge in a saloon that happened to be headquarters for the Bowery Bhoys. The Dead Rabbits made their declaration of war with a shower of paving stones, shattering every pane of glass in the groggery. The Bowery Bhoys rallied and charged with clubs and stones, driving the enemy off. Both sides then salved their wounds with drinking and boasting in the favorite resorts.

While the Bowery Bhoys boozily plotted strategy for the future, the Dead Rabbits launched an attack on another hangout of their enemies. They smashed the furniture and glassware, drank the liquor, and retreated to their Five Points stronghold. Their women, however, considered the failure actually to confront the Bowery Bhoys an act of cowardice. Stung by the tirades of the ladies the Rabbits grabbed a lone policeman, tore off his clothes, and beat him bloody. He staggered back to headquarters, and a squad of twenty-five policemen hurried to skirmish the Dead Rabbits. The patrolmen ran into a barrage of rocks, bricks, and glass from the rooftops and streets and retreated.

The Bowery Bhoys could not be so easily discouraged. They attacked. Artillery of stones, bricks and bottles, the ammunition supplied by women and children, enabled the Dead Rabbits to fend off the assault. The Bowery Bhoys backed off a short distance, threw up a barricade of wagons and began pelting the enemy with missiles. The Dead Rabbits also put up ramparts and the riot turned into a pitched battle along military lines. There were clubbing charges and pistols began to pick off combatants. Men fell in the streets to be stomped by the boots of the contending armies. Bodies of dead and wounded lay scattered over the area.

A large party of police marched to the scene but with 1,000 rioters embroiled the police could only lay hands on an occasional straggler. Looters took advantage of the concentration of police and the disorder spread into neighboring streets. Isaiah Rynders, who owed much of his success to the backing of both gangs, was persuaded by the city leaders to appeal for peace. He appeared between the barricades and called for a truce. The Bowery Bhoys replied with oaths and brickbats, and there is no indication the Dead Rabbits appreciated his efforts. Rynders bolted. Bruised by his reception, he advised Police Commissioner Tallmadge to call out the troops. For a day, a nervous quiet broken by sporadic skirmishes fell on the city. The Bowery Bhoys bruited rumors that the Dead Rabbits intended to pillage the stores of the Bowery, while the Five Pointers gossiped that the Bowery Bhoys and their allies among the Know Nothings planned to sack St. Patrick's Cathedral.

As dark fell, hundreds of partisans rose to the battle and the streets again became a bloody field. The battle raged just three blocks from a police station but no patrolmen appeared in the streets. The Seventh Regiment was recalled from Boston and, with the moonlight playing upon their bayonets, marched on the fighters and broke the back of the riot. Six people died, a hundred were hurt.

As New York moved toward the '60s, little over 1,000 Metropolitans provided protection for a population of 820,000. The city thus had only 150 more cops on duty than it had when the number of New Yorkers was only 350,000. The ratio of one officer to 804 citizens compared unfavorably with London's one to 226. Nor were the Metropolitans evenly distributed throughout the city. Some officers patrolled a desolate two-mile beat, barely covering the territory once during a tour. Precincts with 40,000 people in them had only eight men on duty during a day. The vital statistics of the late 1850s showed 7,779 retail liquor shops, 496 known brothels, 84 houses of assignation, and according to historian Costello, "185 low groggeries where thieves and fallen women daily and nightly resorted." Police headquarters in lower Manhattan near Mulberry Street lay in the center of the criminal area with hangouts like the House of Lords and the Bunch of Grapes. Patrolmen on the way to headquarters stopped off a block away to gamble.

Shootings and knifings went on regularly within the shadow of the station house. Dan Lucey killed a bartender; Reddy the Blacksmith killed Jimmy Haggerty; Peter Mitchell made $300,000 accommodating skilled thieves and fencing for them before he hung himself from a whiskey tap. Saloonkeeper Bunker fought off four assailants who chopped off four of his fingers, then stabbed him six times in the stomach. He carried his fingers to the hospital, but he died from his abdominal wounds. Big Pickles, a renowned strongman and thief, carried off a 500-pound safe on his back.

In this scabrous section of town, five-year-old Lucie Zucheri-chi was carried from Mulberry Street to Presbyterian Hospital dying of cirrhosis of the liver, from hard drinking. Her abdomen was bloated from her diet and in the hospital she lisped, "Give me whiskey, little drop of whiskey and I'll give you a kiss." The police also picked up Romelt Vikonski as a "drunkard, tobacco fiend and hardened criminal." Romelt was eight.

All this tumult and savagery continued unabated near police headquarters, the nerve center for control of crime. Said one thief, "The nearer the Church, the closer to God."

The police department was now a fully functioning municipal service but it continued to lag behind the needs of the city and its residents. The force was ill prepared for pressures developing from the Industrial Revolution, now picking up a full head of steam. There was money, big money, in building New York and in governing it. The police department was an obvious tool for controlling the city and plunder. To add to the stresses on the police department, the Civil War with all of its internecine confrontations lay just ahead.

CHAPTER V

GROWING PAINS
AND THE CIVIL WAR

As the North and South squared off for the wrack of Civil War, the New York City police were forced to busy themselves with matters closer to home. (An 1860 ordinance burdened the undermanned department with the responsibility for scouring the filthy streets. Later, the responsibility would turn into an asset as shrewder officers recognized that street cleaning could be one more source of loot.) Meanwhile the pursuit of criminals continued to flag. Some 71,000 crimes were recorded in 1860; 11,294 were against property and 59,836 against people. Two years later it would be discovered that one-tenth of all New Yorkers had police records, no mean figure considering the haphazard record keeping of the era.

The Civil War in its first years had sat very poorly with New York. The city was largely Democratic and did not support Lincoln for the Presidency. A long tradition of anti-Negro behavior marked New York and merchants had a considerable stake in business as usual with the South. New Yorkers and particularly Tammany, with political allies in the South, sympathized with the Confederate cause enough to make officials take special precautions when President Lincoln visited the city in 1861. The police department, however, cooperated most heartily with the War Department in Washington. During the war, the police picked up soldiers who overstayed their leave and carried them off to Fort Hamilton in Brooklyn which was outside of the Metropolitan Police's jurisdiction.

The decision to compel able-bodied men to serve in the

Union Army brought on the greatest disorder ever to imperil New York City. The draft offices opened in July, an unhappy time of the year for civil tensions throughout the city's history. Then, as now, simmering temperatures in streets and tenements lowered the kindling point.

In the words of Augustine Costello, the "methods adopted by the national government for the enforcement of the draft were not the most judicious possible." Captain Joel B. Erhardt, Provost Marshal of New York, happened to observe some able-bodied men erecting a building on the street. He ordered them to be registered for the draft. Not only did they refuse, they attacked Erhardt with crowbars and forced him to flee. By mid-July, says Costello, "the thirst for violence had grown furious, along with the craving for plunder, gratification of instincts of rapine and destruction."

Drafting began peaceably enough at the Provost Marshal's office, but a fire of undetermined origin leveled another draft office as soon as a police guard left. When fire companies arrived a mob began to stone them. Chief Engineer Decker of the fire department begged the rabble to permit his men to halt the spread of the blaze. The rioters agreed they had no quarrel with the owners of other property in the vicinity, and left the scene.

Near the Provost Marshal's office a band of patrolmen left their posts after a series of skirmishes with roving anti-draft crowds. Police Superintendent Kennedy came in mufti to survey the scene. The crowd recognized him and set up the cry "There's Kennedy, there's Kennedy." They pursued him. He was pummeled and hurled down a six-foot embankment and into a manhole.

The Superintendent crawled out and spied a familiar face. "John Egan, come here and save my life," the desperate Kennedy called. Egan helped bundle the battered Superintendent into a passing feed wagon that outran the fury of the mob and delivered him, nearly dead, to headquarters.

Police officials now began to realize the seriousness of the situation. A mob captured Sgt. Ellison, beat him unmercifully. They broke Patrolman Van Buren's leg, stripped Officer Bennett and clubbed him into unconsciousness for three days. A woman stabbed Officer Phillips. Officer Gabriel "received enough body blows to make a jelly of him, none that proved serious." Colleague Travis had his jaw and hand broken, teeth knocked out, and was left naked, while Patrolman Didway's eye was "bashed from its socket." Near City Hall, savage hand-to-hand combat only temporarily halted the progress of the rioters. With dead and wounded scattered in the streets the policemen made their escape only by using dazed rioters as human shields. In one of the more brutal episodes a Negro orphan home was burned moments after the children were led to safety.

Because Horace Greeley and his *Tribune* stood high in the forces of abolition, a mob marched on the paper's offices with a banner, "We'll hang old Greeley on a sour apple tree." Sgt. Robinson led a detachment to save the *Tribune* and "gave them a shower of locust" (the wooden billys). The newspaper survived.

Plainclothes operators tried to mingle with the rioters to discover where the next outburst of violence would occur. The police were recognized and were lucky to escape with only bruised and bloodied bodies.

With Kennedy *hors de combat,* Police Commissioners John Bergen and Thomas Acton took charge. The torrential force of the mobs could no longer be dammed by small squads and the authorities began mobilizing larger units of two hundred and three hundred men to be rushed to trouble sites. The most obvious of these lay at several factories used for the manufacture or storage of weapons.

The police succeeded in barricading themselves within one such arsenal just before the marauders arrived. The first of these to force his way in fell dead with a police bullet in his head. Eventually the police were forced to yield this stronghold; they had better luck in the battle for another storehouse of weapons. Rioters and police arrived more or less simultaneously at this carbine warehouse. A vicious fight for survival left scores dead and the carbines still in the possession of the police. "Brute courage yielded to determined bravery," said a contemporary report.

George Walling performed heroically in the draft riots. While leading his men against the rabble, Walling yelled, "Kill every man who has a club." He himself saw a fellow battering the door of a hardware store where guns were kept. One swing of Walling's "locust" killed the man.

Guarding a barricade, Walling was approached by Governor Seymour. Acutely aware of the political dangers from repression by police, Seymour complained to Walling of the number of dead lying in the street. "I can't help that," replied Walling. "They were there behind their barricades and we had orders to clear the street. ... If they come back I shall attack them again. ..."

Walling adroitly asked the Governor if he wished to give any orders. Seymour, recognizing the snare, backed off and advised Walling to get his instructions from his official superiors. (Later in the year, Seymour entertained charges of malfeasance against the police commissioners.)

The situation obviously was beyond the efforts of the police and although the Union armies could ill afford such diversions, troops were transported to the city to restore order. Included were some walking wounded, invalided home from combat. Many of these were too weak to be effective and they suffered heavy casualties. In one of the earliest confrontations of soldiers and citizens, the military commander, Colonel O'Brien, ordered his men to turn their howitzers on the enemy. The mob broke and ran, leaving dead and wounded lying where they fell. O'Brien made the error of returning to the scene of the battle by himself. He was captured, beaten and tortured, finally dying at the cruel hands of women during the night. Historian Herbert Asbury reported, "female auxiliaries inflicted the most fiendish tortures upon Negroes, soldiers and policemen captured by the mob, slicing flesh with butcher knives, ripping out eyes and tongues and applying the torch after victims had been sprayed with oil and hanged to trees."

The troops, freely employing rifles and artillery, gave the police the reinforcements they needed. The most successful tactic put the soldiers in the fore whenever a massing of the foe could be found. After bullets broke the ranks of the mob the police charged, swinging their clubs.

Through the alleys of the city Negroes were chased and slaughtered by the insurgents. A thug tossed an infant Negro from the top of a tenement to its death. A white woman, married to a

Negro, tried to save the life of her daughter and was murdered. A black male was knocked to the cobblestones and his head crushed with blows from a 20-pound boulder.

Commissioner Acton organized the large force of police to crush the insurrection finally. Augustine Costello interviewed Seth Hawley, chief clerk of the police, for his recollections of the final moments. "The Commissioner said to me, 'Now that this force of policemen must go out and face that mob, who shall lead them?' "

" 'Carpenter is the Senior Inspector and it is his place to take command,' " answered Hawley.

" 'Will he do it?' " Acton asked.

"He must do it, he will not refuse," remembered Hawley. "He's a gallant man. Never will I forget the words and action of Carpenter when I conveyed to him the message.

'I'll go, and I won't come back unless I come back victorious.' "

The rebels collapsed before the phalanxes of soldiers followed by the club-wielding police who showed no compassion for the slow of foot, to say nothing of those who offered token resistance. The draft riots were over.

Seth Hawley supplied Costello with an interesting footnote. "One lesson learned by the police is that in close contact with a mob there is not any weapon as effective as the club. [Hawley conveniently ignored the fact that without the rifles of the soldiers the police could never have been able to attain close contact.] The clerk added: "It was also found out that nothing could stand the strain for this kind of work like locust. In the early stages of the riot the men carried their rosewood sticks, and these splintered and broke as fast as the heads they were used on. Rosewood is heavy and seems solid but it lacks toughness and elasticity. Now, locust, besides being light, possesses these qualities. It does not split, is sonorous and gives out a sound like a bell. It is very rarely that I have seen a locust club broken. Since then locust has entirely come into use in the department."

In any event when the musical chimes of locusts on skulls no longer resounded through New York the costs in human suffering and money turned out to be enormous. Asbury listed 50 soldiers, 3 policemen, and 18 Negroes as known dead. Another 70 Negroes were missing; 300 soldiers received wounds. The rioters suffered 2,000 dead and 8,000 injured or maimed for life. Whole blocks of stores were gutted by fire or stripped by thieves. With troops as escorts the police scoured the nearby dives and recovered paintings, ornaments, mahogany chairs, carpets, and barrels of sugar. Of the hundreds arrested, only nineteen men were tried and convicted for their roles in the riots.

The jurisdiction of the metropolitan police began to spread after the Civil War. With the added responsibilities came new rules and the Department's organization became a ramshackle structure, amenable to corruption and inefficient for fighting crime. It was a mirror of the city's growth.

During the Civil War period, metropolitan police responsibilities were extended to include Jamaica, Brooklyn, Westchester, Flushing, and Staten Island. But when one spoke of New York he meant the island of Manhattan. The Bronx, Brooklyn, Queens, and Staten Island were outlying rural independent duchies. Final consolidation into what is now New York did not take place until 1898. Meanwhile, police in sailor garb patrolled the harbor while on land the bluecoats supervised pawnbrokers, junk boatmen, second-hand dealers, auctions, slaughterhouses, tenements, and hotels.

A new rule prohibited any member of the force from accepting gifts or rewards except for "extraordinary service rendered." Within a few years it became apparent that thousands of police were indeed rendering extraordinary service and for substantial rewards but hardly within the meaning of the regulation.

Crime in the rural suburbs particularly disturbed the public at this time. Police historian Costello remarks, "It was felt to be worthy of consideration especially to the population of rural districts how far police of the city protect against criminal classes. It became common that life and property were more safe in the city than in the rural districts."

Spirit sales thrived. 9,250 liquor stores satisfied the thirsty in 1866 but only 754 held proper licenses. The police also performed inspections of some 3,500 steam boilers and gave certificates to 444 persons operating hydrostatic boilers. Indigents continued to be housed at least overnight in the station houses and about 97,000 people received a lodging annually. The police returned to the bosoms of parents more than 8,000 missing children each year.

The statistics did not impress many New Yorkers. Respectable citizens had begun to take note of the desperate doings within their city. Diarist George Templeton Strong noted on February 12, 1869, "Crimes of violence—burglaries, highway robberies and murders—have been of late many and audacious beyond example. There has been much common talk, not more than half serious (but not much less than half) about a Vigilance Committee as the only remedy left us while the Judiciary continues elective, worthless and corrupt. I have thought this talk premature, although well aware that we shall probably be driven to that dangerous remedy before many years. But tonight's *Post* speaks of "secret meetings of respectable citizens" and of Vigilance Committees already organized and ready for action in *this* ward and in another. We want a *Vehmgericht* badly, but even in the best hands it would be a fearful experiment; and then it might so easily fall into the worst. . . ."

If the *Post* was correct that such Vigilance Committees had been organized, their sponsors must have given up very quickly, for there is no indication that any ad hoc groups were effectively at work at the time. A year later Strong reported, "At half past ten last evening, Delano [a friend] wending his way home from a dinner at John Astor's was set upon and robbed by three men on the corner of Fifth Avenue and Eleventh Street. Of course there was no arrest. Crime was never so bold, so frequent, and so safe as it is this winter. We breathe an atmosphere of highway robbery, burglary and murder. Few criminals are caught, fewer punished. Municipal law is a failure in New York and we must soon fall back on the law of self preservation. Among the most prominent candidates for informal execution are sundry ministers of justice—or rather of injustice—the most notorious scoundrels out of jail and far more nefarious than most who are in it. . . ."

The sentiments expressed by George Templeton Strong echoed through New York nearly a hundred years later. The themes of crime in the streets, a corrupt and inefficient system of law enforcement, and vigilante justice were composed at least a century ago. But the city in 1870 was going to have to get worse before reform could be mobilized.

CHAPTER VI

DISORDER AND DISILLUSION

As the 1870s dawned, two persistent ailments plagued the city. The first of these was deep-seated ethnic hostilities and the second was the involvement of almost the entire police force in the systematic looting of the city and its residents.

The national and religious hatreds within New York flamed up in 1871. The avowed cause was the strife of Protestant North Ireland against the Catholic South. Of the New York Orangemen, Costello remarked, "Both their religion and their politics were of a very pronounced type. They were, although a handful compared with the Catholic population, strong in their protection of their government and their fanaticism and bigotry kept ablaze in the North of Ireland the fires of religious intolerance and political persecution." (Costello was a native of Southern Ireland.) Scheduled for July 12 was a celebration of the anniversary of the victory of William of Nassau, Prince of Orange, over King James II.

A less than temperate George Templeton Strong noted the animosity in his diary. "Prospect of a faction fight on a large scale next Wednesday. The Orangemen turn out in force on that day to celebrate the Battle of Boyne . . . The Fenians, Ribbonmen, Greens and miscellaneous Irish scum of the popish persuasion propose a grand target excursion and picnic for the same day and avow their design to break up the procession and to bait the skein of the ugly bones of the processionals . . . The police and military are said to be ready for action. I hope they are. The lawlessness, insolence, arrogance and intolerance of these homicidal, ruffianly, popish Celts must be suppressed somehow. If all the braves of both factions could be brought together, well-armed within the enclosures of the Union Racecourse and kept there to fight it out . . . until both parties were exterminated, criminal justice in New York would be administered at a greatly reduced expense."

The parade sponsors, the local Orange societies, requested protection by both soldiers and police. Mayor Oakey Hall, the elegantly tailored puppet of the political boss, William Marcy Tweed, hardly sympathized with the Protestant Irish since his party drew much of its strength from the far more numerous Roman Catholic sons of Erin. Mayor Hall and Police Superintendent Kelso agreed to ban the parade. The marchers appealed to Governor Hoffman, and, true to the upstate code, he seized the opportunity to embarrass the New Yorkers. The parade was reinstated with orders for adequate police and military supervision. A total of five hundred cops took up positions along the line of march.

Costello, an eyewitness, said, "Hotblooded men and women, [for as usual on such occasions the weaker sex was well represented] poured maledictions on the heads of the Orange crowds." However, the procession moved along smoothly until forced to halt momentarily while the police broke up a small disorder blocking the way. From a nearby window a single shot was fired and troops of the Eighty-Fourth Regiment retaliated with a volley, although no officer gave them any order to discharge their weapons. Their bullets in turn triggered action from the Sixth and Ninth Regiments and the streets became a bloody battleground.

Strong observed the disorder from the fringe of action. He saw three or four bloody rioters being escorted to station houses, also twenty or thirty omnibuses packed with perspiring policemen roaring up Broadway.

Despite his vision from afar Strong managed to draw conclusions, all to the detriment of the Irish. "Talked with many people who had seen the collision but I could not ascertain its particulars. It would seem that Celts began firing down from roofs upon Orangemen and militia and charged the procession; that the militia returned the fire and killed some ten, some say twenty, some say sixty rioters. . . ."

He embellished his theme. "Yesterday there was a beastly riot uptown. A procession of Orangemen held a picnic . . . with their wives and children. They were set upon by a swarm of base and brutal Celts, such as those who burned orphan asylums and got up a Negro massacre in July 1863. The police intervened with good effect. Many Celts were knocked on the head; but many men, women and children of the assaulted party were killed or cruelly mauled and maimed. Pity there was no grapeshot for the assailants. Execrable Celtic canaille! The gorilla is their superior in muscle and hardly their inferior in moral sense."

The final total for the 1871 fiasco was officially set at 11 dead, 67 wounded civilians, 2 dead police. Short, but bloody enough, the Orange riots demonstrated the fierce enmities within the city population and their explosive potential. The police had again failed to handle a civil disorder. During the late '60s and early '70s, Boss Tweed and his booty-hungry tribe ate high on the municipal hog. The subsequent collapse of the Tweed Ring failed to shake up the police force. Reformers were so busy searching out corruption among aldermen, councilmen, and civil officials that they paid little attention to the police. But it was the men in blue who supervised the elections that kept returning the Boss and his confederates to office. And while Tammany looted the city treasury, the cop on the beat supplemented his income with tribute from illegal enterprises and outlaws. A few years after Tweed's destruction Costello, at the time a friendly chronicler of police history, noted that there "was a good deal of complaining . . . that too much deference was being paid by them [the police] to the comfort and interest of the criminal as a class and too little peace of mind to taxpayers and citizens."

A Select Committee of the State Assembly in 1875 looked into the city's rising crime rate and summarized their findings: "Again and again houses of prostitution that were disorderly have been 'pulled' [a police term for raided or arrested] and the inmates taken before the magistrates and again and again magistrates have dismissed such cases either from an honest opinion that the testimony was insufficient for a conviction, which was assuredly in most cases erroneous or from some other less credible motive." The committee reported that a number of those who were arrested obtained bail for the Court of General Sessions but never stood trial. Many of them continued their criminal careers. The complaint that the judges as well as the police were responsible for continued crime was to be a recurrent theme in the frequent investigations into New York's evils. But nothing significant came of the Assembly report.

The 1875 committee also suggested that patrolmen generally were appointed through political influences. Absenteeism averaged 408 daily out of a total of 1,946 men supposedly available for duty. The requirements for becoming a member of the force in 1877 were simple enough. The candidate had to be able to read and write English, be a citizen, a resident of the state for a year, and without a criminal record. He had to be under thirty, at least 5'-7½" and 138 pounds, in good health, and of good moral character.

The candidate now needed only ten petitioners to recommend appointment. On his application he was advised that no favoritism or influence was permitted. A "man with a grog-blossomed nose or one who is uncouth," said Costello, "rarely passed muster."

After having been asked if he had ever suffered "the rheumatism or piles" he was asked whether he had paid, or promised to pay, any money toward influencing his appointment. (The purchase of admission to the force and promotion became a scandal within a few years.) About forty of each hundred applicants failed to make the grade.

The powers permitted the police went far beyond the most liberal interpretation of the Constitution's limits. The superintendent or a captain within a precinct could, in writing, empower any patrolman or detective to search the books or shop of a pawnbroker, vendor, junk dealer, auctioneer, or second-hand dealer if the officer sought property which he suspected had been illegally obtained. On a complaint of any two or more householders, the superintendent could permit police to conduct a raid for gambling, or for lewd or obscene activities. It was a far cry from the restrictions decreed by the Supreme Court eighty years later.

The police of each precinct had the names of doctors in their area who were willing to make emergency calls. If the patient could pay the doctor collected from him. Otherwise the city awarded $3 a call.

Augustine Costello closed his 1885 history with some observations upon police behavior and attitudes of the public. "The most vulgar conception [of a policeman] is a bloated drunken ugly brutal fellow, who depends on craft and political influence to retain his sinecure situation and who perfunctorily does his '60' minutes to the hour from pay day to pay day and from one blackmailed rum hole to another. These prejudices are fostered by newspapers which will call a 'police outrage' an act of self defense by an officer."

Costello averred that there was "the same exultant shout over a backsliding policeman as over a fallen minister or good citizen." He turned to a comparison with Europe. "In Europe it is not rare to see a police officer call on help from bystanders and get it. In the U.S. the request is greeted with a guffaw; an escaping prisoner gets more aid from the crowd than his pursuer." Concluded Costello, "Our free institutions tend to make men who enforce the law and deprive others of their liberty, objects of contempt." It was a lament that has been revived many times right to the present.

Costello admitted, "It is safe to say that nearly every appointment is made through personal or political influence." But far from decrying such procedures, he argued, "Those who cavil should remember that this means men who have lived long in the city and know it." He failed to include the Tammany-required qualification: to vote for the party's choice, regularly if not often.

George Walling in the final years of his life pronounced the failings of the police department an unhappy consequence of democracy. Municipal affairs are based on universal suffrage, reasoned Walling, and campaigns for office are organized not on what the cities need but the needs of the politicians. Walling refused to dignify the existing factions in his state as "political" parties. He called such a label a misnomer since the only reason for their existence in New York was "power and plunder . . . Judas Iscariot could be elected through the pull of a party," sneered Walling.

"All the sneaks, hypocrites and higher grade of criminals when questioned upon the subject, almost invariably lay claim to be adherents of the Republican Party . . . criminals of the lower order, those who rob by violence and brute force, lay claim in no uncertain terms to being practical and energetic exponents of true Democratic principles." Walling softened his condemnation: "Not to say every Republican is a sanctimonious sneak or forger, nor every Democrat a pimp, burglar or rough."

Walling offered two reforms. First, he said, "I would place the 'strange' woman under police surveillance"; second, he wanted election control removed from the police, a step that undoubtedly would have eliminated some of the problems of keeping the force honest.

Costello's history had the sanction of the police department and in fact he shared his profits with the police pension fund. Some fifteen years later Costello would sing a different tune, but at the time he wrote his book he blamed New York's crime and graft upon the public, not the cops. George Walling saw every defect in the organization that he had devoted himself to as a reflection on democracy where the vote and the dollar kept a cop from honest performance of his duty. What was clear to responsible citizens was that law enforcement in New York had created a massive opportunity for police blackmail, abuse, and graft. In the minds of most respectable leaders of the day the problem was not the system but a group of evil men who took advantage of it.

CHAPTER VII

DR. PARKHURST DECLARES, "DOWN WITH THE POLICE"

The Society for the Prevention of Crime was organized in 1878, the same year that William Marcy Tweed died a penniless jailbird. The first twelve years of the SPC made no mark upon the city and offered no threat to the felonius pursuits of criminals or the police. But in 1890, the Rev. Charles Parkhurst took charge. Instead of lofty appeals to the better nature of the city's rulers, Parkhurst wisely decided to aim lower and cease "cutting off the tops and apply ourselves to plucking up the roots." In *My Forty Years in New York,* a pastiche of autobiography, sermons, and speculations, Parkhurst said, "Our motto was 'Down With the Police.' "

A slight, respectably bearded man, Dr. Parkhurst may have fooled some of his foes by his mild mien but once he ascended to the pulpit he poured out hellfire.

The first salvo from Parkhurst was an 1892 sermon, "Ye Are the Salt of the Earth." "This then, is a corrupt world; and Christianity is the antiseptic that is to be rubbed into it. . . . In its municipal life our city is thoroughly rotten . . . a damnable pack of Administrative bloodhounds that are fattening themselves on the ethical flesh and blood of our citizenship . . . polluted harpies . . . under pretense of governing the city are feeding day and night on its quivering vitals. They are a lying, perjured, rumsoaked and libidinous lot."

Referring to the organization pledged to maintain the law, Parkhurst thundered, it "shows no genius in ferreting out crime, prosecuting only when it has to and has a mind so keenly judicial that almost no amount of evidence ... is accepted as sufficient to warrant indictment."

Parkhurst did not ignore the chief executive: "Every effort to make men respectable, honest, temperate and sexually clean is a direct blow between the eyes of the mayor and his whole gang of drunken and lecherous subordinates."

The District Attorney refused to heed Parkhurst's calls for an investigation until the minister apologized for his assertions about the DA's derelictions. When a grand jury did convene to look into Parkhurst's charges, the reformer could offer no evidence and found both judge and jury "distinctly uncongenial." After the judge complimented the veniremen for what Parkhurst considered a whitewash, the clergyman commented, "I retired cheerful but worsted."

The *New York Sun* denounced Parkhurst and urged that he spend his time in "prolonged prayer and penitence." Other papers also attacked him for failure to prove his case. Meanwhile, the Society for the Prevention of Crime harassed police and courts by hauling sinners into court and preferring charges against them for practicing vice. Some of the raids of the Society began to annoy the police, who counterattacked. They marched on a disorderly house and drove the forty girls inside out into the snow. The women were then tramped over to Parkhurst's house to protest that his efforts were destroying their livelihood, leaving them without a roof over their heads. Parkhurst invited them all in, served refreshments and, according to him, taught them who the real enemy was.

Dr. Parkhurst decided to collect his own irrefutable evidence. Through the Society's Superintendent, the minister made contact with a private detective, Charles Gardner. The latter agreed to give him a tour of the vice traps for six dollars a day plus expenses.

Two years after the excursion, Gardner, enmeshed in a plot to discredit him, wrote a book, *The Devil and the Doctor,* that detailed the high points of the minister's quest for proof of vice. Gardner began his book with a short tribute to his employer, comparing him to Dante: "... laughter dies on children's lips as he passes ... [he] seems to roll in a wave of darkness and silence, a faint yellow glow on his face. Awe-struck strangers ask who is it that passed? Hush, that is the man who went down into hell."

Gardner outfitted his client for the journey. "I told the doctor that he must put on a suitable suit of clothes and change his appearance as he would not be allowed even in a fairly respectable 'joint' for clergyman was written all over his face."

To disguise him, Gardner gave Parkhurst a pair of checked, black-and-white trousers, "seedy but loud enough in pattern to make noises in the next block." Because the private detective stood well over six feet, the waist band came up near Parkhurst's shoulders. Gardner completed the outfit with a doublebreasted reefer jacket and a red flannel sleeve rag tied about the clergyman's neck.

A third member of the expedition was a somewhat effete parishioner of Parkhurst's, John Langdon Erving. Ultimately he suffered a mental breakdown, traceable in part to the pressures resulting from his voyage into sin and the commotion that followed disclosure of his role.

At the saloon of Tom Summers on Cherry Street, the trio had an opportunity to buy stolen watches and other pawnable rewards of thievery. While the bazaar went on about them, small children toddled into the saloon with old whiskey bottles, pans, jugs, and tin cans for potables.

Through streets choked with bums, whores, hoodlums, and police, Gardner guided his companions to their first experience in a house of ill-fame. At the door, inmates were "soliciting people to enter the resort with the same air that a Grand Central hackman asks you to have a cab." "A big, fat, greasy woman" tried to foist her charms upon Erving, and Gardner himself became the object of the affections of a lady "old enough to have been the mother of Columbus."

The spectacle of this bordello was apparently so repulsive that the Rev. Parkhurst called it a night immediately after escaping from the place. His second evening on the town began in a hotel bar where, long after legal hours, whiskey continued to flow and a pair of policemen in uniform were among those enjoying the illegal libations. In one establishment a nineteen-year-old blonde began with Erving a "dance in which vice and shame, brazen faced, tried to thrust itself upon innocence."

As the disguised reformers left this place, volunteers from the Salvation Army requested contributions to save the denizens within. The detective was about to buy some tracts when Parkhurst stopped him. "I do not believe in the methods of the Salvation Army . . . I do not propose to aid their exchequer by buying their foolish paper. A Grand Jury indictment is the only paper that hole needs to convert it."

Gardner's descriptions of the prostitutes hardly makes sin attractive. "Dirty: I never saw such dirt. It was caked and crusted on hands and faces. Hair tangled and matted around rum flushed faces. Clothing scant, soiled, ragged and ill-smelling, half covering gaunt bodies . . . besotted and lust for liquor in their eyes." The whiskey in one den sold for five cents a glass and Gardner pronounced it sickening. Entertaining on the Society's money he bought drinks on the house for sixteen people and spent just 80 cents. In an even lower hell hole, the whiskey cost two cents a shot and the detective said it made the five cent brand taste like nectar.

Another sight that second night was a slum lodging house where a man got what passed for a place to sleep for a nickel to 15 cents. The chief product of such flophouses, aside from the breeding of vermin and disease, were hordes of voters to insure Tammany wins at election time. Policemen certified that these abodes were the permanent residences of the voters.

In the streets, Gardner bumped into a pair of city detectives who immediately recognized him. Dr. Parkhurst and Erving averted their faces while their guide chatted with his acquaintances. He explained his presence: "I've got a slumming party along." The police told him that he should have checked in at the station house because "Parkhurst has been raising hell."

One of the features of the third evening was a "tight house," where all of the inmates wore tights. Another special service was supplying girls of German background or French. Like restaurants, the bordellos attempted to appeal to ethnic tastes. Inside a Chinese opium palace, the party observed stupefied customers and seemed most appalled at a white woman who had chosen to live with a Chi-

nese. Some houses of ill fame offered shows. A girl smoked a ciga-
rette while standing on her head. She suggested to Parkhurst that
she would perform other and more interesting acrobatic feats for a
$3 fee but he declined.

At one saloon they were entreated to visit a nearby house for
special entertainment. "A boarding house for the most respectable
policemen in the city," laughed the lady who issued the invitation.

Somewhere along the line the police had learned of Dr.
Parkhurst's explorations. A clean-cut young man called on the
minister between trips and offered to show him some spectacularly
depraved spots. Gardner, with little difficulty, ascertained that the
visitor was actually a city detective. Gardner also became aware of
two men studying him while he awaited the arrival of his clients at
a disorderly house. He slipped away and managed to warn Dr.
Parkhurst to meet him elsewhere. The private detective was convinced that the police hoped to trap the crusader in a vice den and
thoroughly discredit him.

On the fourth and final evening the initial target was the
Golden Rule Pleasure Club. When the elaborately painted ladies
turned out to be men the shocked Dr. Parkhurst made a quick exit.
"I wouldn't stay in that house for all the money in the world,"
gasped the reformer.

At the House of Marie Andrea, the group witnessed an act
that became known later as Dr. Parkhurst's Circus. The girls,
dressed in Mother Hubbards, did erotic dances, the specifics of
which Gardner could not bring himself to describe. The House of
Marie Andrea was so infamous that Gardner took the liberty of
hiring an assistant to guard the party. The cost for viewing the
show was $5 a man. Parkhurst later labeled the affair "a sort of
gymnastic performance." At a French house later in the evening,
Gardner succeeded in bargaining the cost for the show down to $4
a man and Dr. Parkhurst rated the exhibition "the most brutal,
most horrible . . . that I ever saw in my life." On that note Dr.
Parkhurst concluded his search for evidence of sin and corruption.
The Society did supplement Parkhurst's work by sending Gardner
and some associates to test the efficacy of the Sunday closing laws.
The platoon of secret agents came back with a sheaf of affidavits

attesting nonconformance with excise laws. The entire investigation cost the SPC about $500 with a little less than half going for the minister's four-night expedition.

With his eye-witness catalogue of horrors and the affidavits as his arsenal, Dr. Parkhurst mounted the pulpit for a fresh assault upon Tammany. "Tammany Hall is not a political party but purely a business enterprise as much so as Standard Oil or the Western Union Telegraph and superior in respect to the perfection of its organization." After listing the dens of evil he had seen, the clergyman flung his gauntlet: "To say that the police do not know what is going on where it is going on, with all the brilliant symptoms of the character of the place distinctly in view is rot. I do not ask anyone to excuse or apologize for my language." He spoke of "an expensive temple of vile fascination where the unholy worship of Venus is rendered. I spent an hour in such a place yesterday and when we came down the steps I almost tumbled over a policeman doing picket duty on a curbstone. The bluecoated guardians of civic virtue will not molest a man if he enters." Flourishing affidavits of illegal liquor sales, he challenged his parishioners and the authorities with a Parkhurst paraphrase of Boss Tweed's snarl at reformers "Now, what are you going to do with them?" The affidavits were enough to convince another grand jury which examined the documents and listened to Parkhurst. But although the grand jury summoned police officials and patrolmen, it still could produce no evidence that would stand up in court. However, the presentment concluded that the police "are incompetent to do what is frequently done by private individuals with imperfect facilities for such work or else illegal and corrupt. The general efficiency of the Department is so great that it is our belief that the latter suggestion is the explanation of the peculiar inactivity."

Parkhurst had set in motion a mighty engine of reform. The spawn of the Society's efforts was the Lexow investigations that led to the first real reforms of the police. In a forward to Parkhurst's *My Forty Years in New York*, Judge John Goff wrote, "Particularly is the change made manifest in the attitude of the policeman to the citizen. No longer does he twirl and use his locust on the unoffending citizen as if it were his legitimate function . . . To Dr. Parkhurst beyond all other men must be accorded the credit for this great change."

The initial stone thrown by the Parkhurst Grand Jury back in 1894 had created a few ripples. First to drown was Superintendent William Murray, the Police Department's chief officer who resigned his post at the request of his civilian superiors. Murray joined the force in 1866 after having been wounded at one of the Bull Run battles. He rose in the ranks to captain. Augustine Costello records a number of Murray triumphs, ranging from the recovery of one million in bonds, to the capture of some abortionists and the tracking down of a group of masked burglars. Costello insisted that Superintendent Murray issued instructions with a view to "suppression of gambling and parading of the streets by women of immoral character." From what the Reverend Parkhurst saw the instructions apparently were not understood by the force.

Costello labelled Murray the cop who "has unmasked more crime and fastened the guilt on the perpetrators thereof than any man on the force with the exception of Inspector Thomas Byrnes." To succeed Murray, Byrnes was a natural choice.

Whatever reputation Murray held, Inspector Byrnes enjoyed an even better one. Graced with a white droopy moustache, and favoring the derby-style hat, Byrnes held the title of the world's greatest detective. He owed this renown to both his skill at solving crimes and his reorganization of the detective bureau which effectively reduced crime in the financial and jewelry areas of New York.

In 1882 the state legislature had created a forty-man squad with Byrnes as its head. The impetus for forming the new detective division came from the city's financial and jewelry areas which had been robbed heavily for years. Byrnes rented a Wall Street office and stationed ten men there from 9:30 in the morning to 4 P.M. Brayton Ives, the head of the New York Stock Exchange, asked Byrnes why he felt it necessary to spend money renting an office.

Byrnes, after pointing out that between one and two million dollars had been stolen within recent years, allegedly continued, "I said, if anything occurs in your office, you would have to send to police headquarters over two miles. In establishing this Bureau I intend to connect it, with telephone, to every bank and banking house in every part of New York, and you ought to have an officer from the time you ask for him by telephone ... in any of those banks or banking houses in ... one to five minutes."

The Stock Exchange promptly gave Byrnes a room in its own building and saw that it was connected by telephone to every financial institution in lower Manhattan. Byrnes bragged that from March 1882, when he set up his Wall Street office not a postage stamp was lost to a professional thief. The success stemmed in large measure from Byrnes' preventive measures. He drew "the Dead Line." No professional thief was to be found south of that line which was roughly Fulton Street. Byrnes' detectives would pick up any known criminal who crossed over the Dead Line and drag him off for interrogation, possibly tie him to a crime. At the very least, the professional faced a degrading shakedown and the era's casual habeas corpus procedures meant a stay in the Tombs Prison for several days. Professional detectives under Byrnes could enforce the Dead Line because they spent a great amount of time studying the rogues gallery or viewing lineups where as many as three hundred suspected thieves paraded before police daily.

Byrnes kept records of burglars, safecrackers, and the other specialists, which gave him a lead as to who might have committed a particular job. But beyond his vague suspicions of who might or might not have committed the crime, Byrnes was guided by the maxim: "a thief has three weaknesses, women, gambling, and drink." Thieves could always be found simply by searching the dens of vices. This theory for the detection and control of crime remained prevalent for many years. After a crime, it is still routine for police to comb certain bars, hotels, and hangouts in search of information and fugitives. Indeed, for many years shadowy resorts have been allowed to flourish, inspite of violations of the law, because police find that the information to be squeezed out of such places far surpasses their nuisance.

Byrnes, according to Costello, liked to believe that a soft word brought talk from the guilty. "Words of kindness are the only way to unlock the criminal tongue. Threats do no good with hardened criminals. I never met a thief in my life, provided he could benefit by peaching on his confederates from whom I could not find out anything I was desirous to know. There's no such thing as honor among thieves," stated Byrnes. However, he was also known as a skilled practitioner of the third degree.

Experienced, skilled in detective work, an innovator and theorist of police practices, this was the man who now confronted Parkhurst's charges.

CHAPTER VIII

THE GREAT
INVESTIGATION

The Reverend Parkhurst had at last tasted victory in his battle with the maggot armies of corruption. Upstate politicians and Republicans, hopeful of wounding the Tammany legions, called for a state study of the city's police. The muckraking reporter, Lincoln Steffens, who went to Albany when the clamor for an investigation became a roar found both parties eager to oblige the demands for an inquiry. The Democrats hoped, wrote Steffens, "a controlled commission might whitewash Tammany and shut up Dr. Parkhurst,"—"the Republicans because there was a chance to win the city away from the Democrats." Both parties had cause to be nervous when the Democrats advised their opponents that if the truth were to be exposed, then corruption would be revealed as a bipartisan affair.

The Committee, chaired by Republican Senator Clarence Lexow, nearly aborted at the start. The GOP-dominated state legislature authorized $25,000 for the Committee's work, hardly an excessive sum. Democratic Governor Roswell P. Flower vetoed the appropriation and appended a message of sorrow and rebuke. "No city has a lower ratio of crime." He bestrewed his veto message with references to a "junketing committee," the "avaricious appetites of counsel," and "bribery of witnesses." The Governor saw the proposal as an attempt to embarrass the Democrats.

The New York State Chamber of Commerce led by Charles Stewart and Gustav Schwab quickly guaranteed the Lexow Committee $17,500 and the Lexow hearings began March 9, 1894.

Later, state funds became available. As the hearings uncovered the extent of corruption, the Governor could not afford to veto appropriations.

Aside from legislators from both parties, the Committee included as chief inquisitors a trio of lawyers, John Goff, William Travers Jerome, and Frank Moss. Their weapons included information from Dr. Parkhurst and his Society for the Prevention of Crime, tidbits of gossip, and most important of all the power to subpoena witnesses and offer them immunity from prosecution.

Since politics motivated many of the committee, it is not surprising that the hearings started with the conduct of city elections, a responsibility of the police. A Republican poll watcher, F. H. Wolfertz, took the stand and told of having objected to an officer on duty at a polling place about a flagrantly illegal voter. The patrolman, said Wolfertz, removed the offender only after he voted. Outside, in the street, the cop released his prisoner. Wolfertz complained immediately. A pair of nearby loungers then pounced on the poll watcher and while the unconcerned officer looked on, they assaulted Wolfertz. Wolfertz filed a statement about the incident at headquarters only to be warned that if he continued to annoy the police he would be killed.

Another poll watcher reported that he attempted to supervise the counting of ballots. A number of unauthorized people crowded around. Somehow the poll watcher's hat kept being knocked down over his eyes whenever he attempted to oversee the tally. The policeman on duty sat quietly, taking no notice of the trespassers or the hat-tipping diversion. One witness testified that he saw detectives David Mallon and John Hock go from store to store ordering posters for an independent assembly candidate torn down. A pair of uniformed officers preceded Hock and Mallon to inform merchants whose campaign material was approved for display.

Large groups of men arrived at polling places to vote under assumed names, supplied from the registry lists. The patrolmen on duty ignored anyone who protested of irregularities. One applicant forgot his name as he was about to enter the booth and turned to ask his guide. The policeman remained undisturbed. A curious malady was the vague paralysis that seemed to seize so many New Yorkers on election days. Throngs of voters swore that physical disabilities required them to be aided inside the booth. Tammany men, showing great solicitude for these unfortunates, willingly accompanied them inside the closet to assist in the marking of ballots.

Witness Otto Rosalsky informed the Lexow Committee that, as an election official, he challenged a voter who answered to the name of Isaac Cohen. The Lexow Counsel asked, "Did you know Isaac Cohen? How could you draw the distinction between Isaac Cohen and the one who voted on his name?" Rosalsky averred he knew this was not Isaac Cohen although he had never met either gentleman.

"Do you mean there is such a marked distinction?"

Committeeman Sutherland interrupted, "He can tell the difference between an Irishman and a Hebrew."

Counsel persisted, "Is there anything peculiar about the physiognomy of the family of Cohen?" Rosalsky answered that the man who professed to be Cohen was "a big burly ruffian, with a red face, black moustache."

"Haven't you seen any Cohens with a red face, black hair, and big and burly?"

The police board lawyer now turned to more specific detail. "How was his nose, was it in a Hebrew cast of countenance?" That question of the Hebrew look was echoed by another poll watcher who remembered an illegal repeater because "he had a peculiar face and he voted a Hebrew name."

The Lexow Committee disclosed that the normal stream of naturalized citizens invariably turned into a torrent shortly before elections. Both political parties paid the naturalization fees for newcomers. A witness pointed out that Tammany regularly voted the inmates in the Tombs prison and Blackwell's Island, simply by listing prisoners as workers and guards.

After such testimony, the Lexow Committee denounced New York City elections. "During the years covered by the investigation, 'honest elections had no existence in New York. A huge conspiracy against the purity of the elective franchise was connived at and crime against the ballot was held high carnival.' "

From the voting circus the Lexow investigators moved on to gamier matters with a parade of madams, pimps, and brothel workers. One brothel keeper, Charles Priem, took the stand and caused a commotion by making a mere pretense of kissing the Bible. Senator Lexow sternly ordered him to open the book and kiss it after being sworn. Priem, an immigrant from Germany, kept a house for what he described as "fancy girls." He had operated for six years with only one raid. Captains Cassidy, Devery, Cross, McLaughlin, and Devine commanded the precinct in which he operated his business. Committee Counsel Goff asked, "Do you know anything about a wardman going around there and getting money from the houses of the neighborhood?"

"Oh God, yes," Priem answered, to the amusement of the spectators.

The wardmen, two plainclothesmen, reported directly to each captain. In practice the wardmen acted as collection agents for the police captains.

Priem claimed he paid $25 a month in the beginning, usually meeting the wardman on the street corner. Later his "rent" went to $50 a month. When Captain Cassidy moved to another precinct, Captain Adam Cross took charge and promptly raided Priem's establishment. A $500 lump sum squared the charge, then an additional $500 served as an initiation fee into Captain Cross's good graces; the $50 a month fee continued.

Goff asked, "Had you a new initiation fee to pay [whenever a new captain was assigned to the precinct]?"

Priem answered, "Why certainly, $300 to $500." Captain William Devery required $500 for his imprimatur upon the Priem business.

The brothel keeper recounted his conversations with Wardman Glennon on the stoop of the station house. "He said to me they meant business right away. I asked him what the price was and he said five. Said I, I ain't got it. Oh, he says. You can raise it, in half an hour if you want to." Glennon came to the whorehouse and Priem handed over $500. Then Glennon demanded the month's rent of $50 but the entrepreneur persuaded him to wait and collect $100 the following month.

Priem said he stopped paying toward the end of the Devery reign when the police advised that he would have to close up because of "the Parkhurst trouble." However, Priem informed the Lexow Committee that he fully expected to open up as soon as their investigation ended.

Aside from the regular collections, assorted wardmen and police would come around and say, "Now, Priem, Christmas is coming on, get ready." The holiday cost Priem another $100 a year.

Police Counsel Nicoll whose role in the investigation was to defend the Department began his cross-examination of Priem by asking why he failed to kiss the book when he was originally sworn.

"If it was a new one I would not hesitate for a moment, but I suppose there were so many kisses on that it wasn't necessary."

"You are so particular about whom you kiss or what you kiss?"

"Yes sir, in that line," answered Priem.

Rhoda Sanford, a widow, followed Priem to the witness chair. She turned out to be a less cooperative witness. She admitted having served one year as a housekeeper in a disorderly house before branching out on her own for two years as a madam. Mrs. Sanford, on orders from the Committee, produced her account book. One entry read, "C $500." Goff asked whether the initial signified "city officials." Mrs. Sanford thought it might. Goff pressed on, "Doesn't it stand for captain?"

"No sir, it did not stand for captains at all. I never seen the captains and don't know none of the captains."

Another entry listed a payment to "W. M." Mrs. Sanford in spite of the initials insisted that stood for William Ward and not "ward man." Somewhat disconcerted by Mrs. Sanford's resistance Goff asserted, "Mrs. Sanford, you said you only wanted an opportunity to tell what robbers the police were." The madam denied ever having made such a statement.

Like Mrs. Sanford, the next witness, a Mrs. Emma Jones, also claimed to know nothing about payments to the police. A pattern of newly bribed or recently terrorized witnesses unfolded as the hearings dragged on. Many promising candidates for the Lexow committee disappeared from town. Chicago became a nesting ground for specialists in vice and Europe supplied an investigation-free haven for police and high officials.

Augusta Thurow, a forty-three-year-old woman, cooperated fully with the investigators, however. She began her career as the owner of a rooming house which became a house of ill fame in 1890. "I could not get tenants to occupy the rooms and I took in women that said they lived with men that were their husbands," said Mrs. Thurow. "They would bring men in at night. One of the officers told me about it and said there would be trouble. How can I stop it, I said, when I am asleep?"

A policeman informed her, "There are women in the house there, and they are doing it, and you have to attend to it."

"I said, how will I attend to it?"

He replied, "I will send Bissert [the wardman]."

Bissert attended Mrs. Thurow and announced, "Where this house stands you can never put a church, and you can go on in business. I will see you in a month." She paid him $10 and Bissert set the toll at $5 a month for every girl in the house.

When Captain Docherty assumed command of the precinct, his wardman trotted around. Mrs. Thurow denied she was engaged in prostitution because she said she feared a steep initiation fee. Within a few days a raid shut down her place.

Mrs. Thurow pleaded guilty to operating a house of prostitution and paid a fine. On her way out of court, Detective Barney Meehan accosted her and advised a chat with Captain Docherty. The police commander spoke with her in the stationhouse and told her the wardman would visit her. Barney Meehan dropped in on Mrs. Thurow at her place to say that after elections she could open up for $25 a month.

Wardman John Hock confirmed to Mrs. Thurow that business would continue but he warned that Captain Docherty "would not stand for the notoriety of that joint for the price I was paying."

"I said I couldn't pay as much," continued Mrs. Thurow before the Lexow listeners. She told Hock, "Nobody gets robbed in my house, a quiet business." Part of Mrs. Thurow's quiet business consisted of girls soliciting from the front stoop. In spite of her pleas Detective Hock said $75 a month was a good rate for "a ranch like that." Unwilling to pay more than $25 Mrs. Thurow called on State Senator Roesch. The legislator and local political

leader offered to arrange things for his constituent on receipt of
$100 to $150. Thus advised and contracted for, Mrs. Thurow resumed her business. Unfortunately, Captain Docherty went to Europe and the captain acting in his place pulled the house.

The acting captain kept arresting the Thurow girls, and both
the proprietress and the inmates became restive. Each girl paid $1
a week to Augusta Thurow and contributed $10 toward the
monthly police tariff. Mrs. Thurow now complained to the precinct
commander, "This is a nice thing I am after paying Hock money
and I am pulled." The captain claimed her place had become too
well known and said she would have to move. He suggested she run
under the ensign of a cigar store or a cafe. And all he wanted was
$1000 for himself, $250 for Hock. Mrs. Thurow offered $500 down,
the rest on the installment plan. She commenced operations and
then Hock came around. "Business is on the bumerina," he announced. "Parkhurst is on the road, and you have got to lay low for
thirty days." But in view of her investment, Mrs. Thurow could not
afford a temporary shutdown. The police raided the establishment
and her lawyer said she would have to "do a little city time." The
aroused madam went to Parkhurst and "told him my tale of woe."

She traced her troubles to the greed of the police. They
wanted "to raid the ranch" because she couldn't raise her monthly
allotment to $70.

After Madam Thurow came Madam Katie Schubert who had
passed out business cards for her establishment. Mrs. Schubert had
retained a Dr. DeFalk as house physician who issued health certificates for the girls. Mrs. Schubert suffered no inconveniences at
the hands of either Captain Devery or Captain Cross. Each accepted a $500 initial gift and $50 a month. The only setback to Mrs.
Schubert came when Dr. Parkhurst himself, having visited her business on one of his four nights on the town, brought charges. The
judge fined her $250, which hardly slowed her operation. Each
prostitute charged $2 a customer and split the fee with the madam.

Madam Lena Cohen advised the Lexow Committee that her
girls received fifty cents a customer but she paid $40 a month rent
and her initiation fee to the police was $500. That sum she raised
on a loan which, with the usurious interest, cost her a total of

$1,000. Mrs. Cohen kept borrowing to stay in business and owed $1,500 when creditors forced her out of business.

Lucy Harriot, a Negro girl, testified that she worked on the streets. But she gave money to various madams who passed it on to the police, thereby winning her permit to streetwalk. Proprietresses introduced mobile forces like Lucy to the wardmen as their "cruisers." Sometimes Lucy worked with an accomplice in a "panel house." The customer would hang his trousers over the only chair in the room. While he consumed himself with passion, the accomplice in an adjoining room pushed open a wooden board in the wall and removed his purse.

Sometimes the victim discovered his loss after getting dressed or later, out on the street. He received no satisfaction from the police, who invariably told him that he had no business dealing with prostitutes. If the man persisted in his complaint the police pretended to search for the girl and then declared she had escaped. They also advised that further efforts to locate the thieves would result in unfortunate publicity.

The victim shuffled away, thoroughly discouraged, poorer and probably a little wiser. The police hastened to share the spoils with the panel gang. On one occasion Lucy Harriot and her assistant plucked $180 from a citizen, the wardman got $90, the madam $45, and Miss Harriot the remainder.

Lucy Harriot admitted that she had been arrested 107 times in two years, paid lawyers to barter her freedom thirty to forty times. Once the police hit her five times in a week. If she went to trial the sentences generally ran ten days or $10. Sometimes Miss Harriot felt it necessary to offer men on the beat a dollar "for cigars or a drink." She protested that she never made dates with policemen. "There is no money in it. I am looking for money and so are they."

When Madam Matilda Hermann went on the witness stand, Goff began: "I am very glad to meet you." She answered, "I am very sorry to meet you, Mr. Goff." He continued with small talk: "Now that you are back on your native heath ... I trust you will not have occasion to leave New York again?"

Mrs. Hermann was the first important witness to return from a refuge to go before the committee. She reluctantly admitted that she had come back of her own free will for rumors had circulated that friends of the committee had kidnaped her.

At the peak of her operations, Matilda Hermann had five bawdy houses going while maintaining a hidden respectability.

Matilda's schedule of payments added up to a comfortable income for the police. She paid Wardman Reynolds $100 to cover two of her houses. She agreed to pay an additional $30 a month toward the $300 initiation fee. Beat patrolmen drained some profits by standing in front of her places several times a week discouraging customers. For $2 the cops would move off.

She suffered several raids and it cost her $1,000 to open up again. Toward the end of her career she was arrested and bailed for $1,000. Her lawyer advised her not to show up for trial and she forfeited the bond. However, the police called her again and stuck her in the Tombs prison for eleven days.

Known as the "French Madam" or the "Gold Mine" to the police, Mrs. Hermann estimated that she paid to the police and the courts a total of $25,000 during her career. She could almost afford the extortion because her houses brought in between $1000 and $1,500 a month.

Mrs. Hermann's dealings with the police and the courts revealed some dazzling collusion and conspiracy with the law. After one arrest her lawyer advised Mrs. Hermann that a $500 payment would bring her simply a $100 fine on the charge of running a disorderly house. Meanwhile, the furniture from the establishment was removed to warehouse storage. In court, a policeman testified that the place was empty of furnishings and out of business. Mrs. Hermann paid the $100 fine on a Friday and opened for business on Saturday; the $80 storage charge was just one more cost of doing business.

Goff introduced testimony to show that the police encouraged Matilda Hermann to leave town to avoid testifying. Members of the police department collected a $1,700 traveling fund for Matilda Hermann after investigators began talking to her before the hearings. Mrs. Hermann met a dozen officers on a street corner one night and talked with them, shortly before the Lexow Committee convened. She confessed to a conspiracy for silence formed that night but Mrs. Hermann refused to name the twelve cops or to give the name of the officer who accompanied her out of town. She slipped away through Jersey City, went up to Montreal, and from there to Chicago where she joined a local colony of ex-madams. On her return to New York some attempts were made in Jersey City to keep her from appearing. When the train with Mrs. Hermann and a Lexow investigator arrived in Jersey City, a local detective accosted them and threatened to "break their faces." The commotion in the depot caused all participants to be brought before a magistrate. Matilda Hermann took up temporary residence in a Jersey City jail. A New York State Senator visited her there and begged her not to testify until after the coming elections. The Jersey City police chief, however corrupt his men were, cooperated fully with the investigation in New York and helped her to board a train and reach the city safely.

Goff used the Hermann case to offer an early conclusion: "In addition to paying the monthly tax and initiation fees raids were gotten up as an excuse to enable a policeman or a class of criminal lawyers to extort money." He asserted that madams were permitted to do business until fattened enough for shakedown. He also noted that the plunder of disorderly houses followed the business cycle. During financial depressions when the banks suffered reverses policemen were forced to raise money and they went to the easiest source, the prostitution enterprises and practitioners.

While the hearings proceeded the police quickly punished operators of houses of prostitution who cooperated with the Lexow Committee. Karl Werner, who testified that he had paid off Captain Adam Cross and managed a saloon, was arrested shortly after he appeared before the Committee and charged with having broken the Sunday liquor law. A businessman put up bail money for Werner but withdrew the bond under pressure from the police. While Werner contemplated the folly of being a friendly witness, another saloon, cheek to station house jowl in Cross's precinct, flourished seven days a week regardless of blue law restrictions.

Laughter attended many sessions of the Committee as madams, policemen, and politicians recounted their experiences doing business in the city. Indignation restricted itself to the newspapers and the reformers girding themselves for the coming elections. Graft and corruption had for so long been a commonplace for the city that there could be little shock to the citizens.

But the case of Caela Urchittel, revealed through an interpreter since she spoke no English, aroused horror. A widow with three children, Mrs. Urchittel opened a tiny cigar store to support her family. Two days after she went into business, Detective Borgelinae appeared at the store and demanded $50 to forestall arrest of Mrs. Urchittel as a prostitute. "You made $600," insisted Borgelinae, "and I want it." His partner, Detective Hussey, marched her through the streets from 11 P.M. to 3 A.M. He forced her to take down her stockings in the street to prove she was not hiding money.

Mrs. Urchittel finally gave the detective $25 that was her rent money; $12 went to the notorious red light commisar Max Hochstein, the rest to Hussey. The policemen insisted she turn over a similar sum the following day. Unable to raise the cash she sold her store. It was not enough for Hussey and Borgelinae. She was arrested as a prostitute and two boys perjured themselves in court, saying she sold them her favors for fifty cents. The court did not call her fifty character witnesses nor assign her a lawyer. Jailed three months, Mrs. Urchittel lost her three children who were dispersed to an orphanage.

A translator gave Mrs. Urchittel's plea to the hearing, "I lay my supplication before you, honorable sir, father of family, whose heart beats for your children, and feels what children are to a faithful mother. Help me to get my children. Let me be mother to them. Grant me my holy wish and I will always pray for your happiness."

Lexow counsel Moss told the Committee that Mrs. Urchittel haunted his offices begging for help to find her "shildren." With a heavy-handed melodramatic gesture the Committee restored the children to their mother during the hearing three weeks after she told her sad tale. For the first time in its history the Society for the Prevention of Cruelty to Children voluntarily surrendered children back to a parent from whom the youngsters had been rescued. Unfortunately the travail so debilitated Mrs. Urchittel that she died of heart disease a few years after.

At the time the Lexow Committee commenced its deliberations, the oldest profession could claim that New York served as a clearinghouse for much of the world. Both retailers and wholesalers set up shop in the city. The jobbers exported girls to entertain miners in South Africa, prospectors in Alaska, businessmen in San Francisco, as well as the bloods of such neighboring precincts as Newark, Philadelphia, Boston, and Chicago.

George Kibbee Turner in a 1909 issue of *McClures* cited an 1857 survey that listed 6000 women in New York as practitioners of the trade with almost one-third of them foreign born and of these a third Irish. By the 1890s a Methodist bishop took his own head count and sadly concluded that the 20,000 scarlet women in New York outnumbered the practicing Methodists.

Guy Kibbee Turner reported that the prostitution fief belonged to the Essex Market Gang or Max Hochstein Association. Trade meetings took place in saloons and coffee houses. The business association took on a social bond after the death of Sam Engel, brother of Martin Engel, a Tammany assemblyman in 1896 who represented the red-light district. On the trip back from the cemetery where Sam Engel was laid to rest, the mourners, a number of Jewish whoremasters, discussed the reluctance of their more respectable coreligionists to admit proprietors of prostitution into Hebrew burial societies. To accommodate their fraternity, the dealers at that point organized their own burial society, the Independent Benevolent Association.

Actually, although 1857 statistics listed Ireland as the chief producer of whores, Turner now found the ranks prevalent with Jewish, Polish, and Italian women. A redheaded Jewess brought premium prices in San Francisco. There were ethnic-centered houses that catered to fellow immigrants, many of whom left their wives and sweethearts behind when they came to the United States. Prostitution obviously thrived because of the shortage of women. Ignorant immigrant girls who were lured or tricked into their occupation supplied the basic demands. Some Italian peasant girls sailed to the United States with the promise of marriage but after their arrival their sponsors dumped them into the bordellos. In the Jewish community emphasis upon male offspring forced many females into vice even while their brothers began the long climb up to affluence. The foreign-born tended to staff the bigger pleasure palaces; the native-born worked alone or for a single manager.

Some of the recruits were enticed into the profession through "cadets," guileful youths who sought out the younger girls at the five cents admission dance academies or hiring halls for servants. The young men won the confidence and the favors of the innocent girls and usually promised marriage or else convinced them that unless they entered into prostitution the police would jail them or deport them. Cadets filled out their income by working as election repeaters and political errand boys. The cadet system spread from New York to other cities.

Writing after the turn of the century, Turner attributed the growth of prostitution to the decline in gambling revenues. Pressure from local businessmen who saw their reservoirs of purchasing power being drained by gambling hall operators had forced the police to curb the dens of chance. With that revenue cut off prostitution revenues came to finance political clubs and campaigns. Subsequently, the growth of municipal expenditures for goods, services, and capital improvements would eliminate vice as the financial support of political clubs and campaigns. Businessmen would become the stokers of political machines.

Experts like Superintendent Thomas Byrnes saw little hope for the suppression of commercial sin in 1894. Writing in the *North American Review,* while the Lexow Committee spent its summer recess searching for evidence against him and his men, Byrnes said, ". . . another great evil abounding in large cities . . . the social evil cannot be exterminated." The European tradition of "regulated quarters" said Byrnes would be a "plague spot," a "blot on the community." He theorized that the vice could and did hide in "respectable quarters" and "tampering with the social evil [the constantly reiterated label of the era] is a ticklish game." Byrnes concluded, "the more the public hears about it, the worse for the public." Byrnes thus joined those who believed that quiet vice that disturbs no one provides a necessary service.

Widespread prostitution and sexual exploitation of immigrant girls made abortion a profitable business in New York. In his book of memoirs, George Walling had devoted an entire chapter to abortion practitioners. The most famous of these was a Madam Restell. She achieved so much notoriety in her lifetime that youngsters pointed out her residence as the place built on the skulls of babies. Madam Restell had long been in her grave, a suicide, when the Lexow hearing convened.

What directed the Lexow Committee to the subject of abortion was a farcical melodrama of doctors, patients, police, judges, and lawyers that concluded with a surprise ending. But at the heart of the matter were unwanted babies and extortion.

Dr. Newton Whitehead went on the witness stand as the protagonist of the impromptu play. The physician's troubles began with an arrest for aborting a Miss Foos. Sgt. Frink, the officer who tagged Whitehead, suggested that an attorney, Emanuel Friend, could get Whitehead off. The helpful Frink advised Whitehead before the trial, "In all these cases, Doctor, we expect to have some money off them." The Lexow listeners could not have been surprised. They heard several times that policemen often gave such fuzzy accounts of their work in court that judges were forced to throw out the cases. Presumably, for $500 Frink would be a vulnerable witness against Doctor Whitehead.

The plaintiff, Miss Foos, claimed that she went to Whitehead for treatment of debility, had no idea she was pregnant, and that he placed her in a sanitarium. There, Midwife Stuvenohl, a notorious abortionist, delivered her of a six-months child and burned its body. Whitehead did demand of Frink why Midwife Stuvenohl was not arrested for the crime and the sergeant answered "she did not have any money and was not worth bothering with."

After depositing his bail, Whitehead said, he accompanied Frink and another detective to a hotel for lunch. Along with the advice about counsel and the price for a friendly arresting officer in court, Frink suggested, "If you ever want to run a young girl at this hotel nothing would be said."

The doctor met Frink and gave him $500 just before the trial. "You go around back the way you came," directed Frink, "and I will go the other way so we shan't be seen too much together and go into court." But in a three-hour delay while awaiting the judge, Counselor Friend managed to extract another $200 from Whitehead with the explanation, "I have to turn over 50 percent of it to the police." "That's how he [Friend] gets his cases," Whitehead volunteered to the Lexow Committee.

At Whitehead's abortion trial Frink said he knew the man who had gotten Miss Foos in trouble and that the father was married and had no money. The judge dismissed the case against the physician.

Three weeks later, Sgt. Frink arrested Dr. Whitehead on a similar complaint, this time involving a woman named Grace Fox. Once again Frink proposed lawyer Emanuel Friend, "He is our lawyer, the police lawyer," explained the sergeant. For convenience, Friend had a direct telephone wire into police headquarters. On this occasion, Friend took only $325 from his client. "Friend, not my friend but a friend of my pocketbook," remarked Whitehead to the Lexow Committee. Whitehead did not deny meeting Miss Fox and in fact he admitted that he suggested an abortion. However, he claimed the operation was never performed. When Whitehead was nonetheless indicted, Judge Koch denounced him and, seeking to discourage abortionists, set extraordinarily high bail. At the trial Grace Fox did not appear and the case was adjourned several times without ever coming up for a judgment.

For a third time, Sgt. Frink showed up on Dr. Whitehead's doorstep with a warrant for the physician's arrest. However, in return for $50 the policeman allowed the doctor to spend the night at home instead of the jail. Since the girl in this particular instance had no abortion nor had he even recommended one Dr. Whitehead began to suspect the motives of Sgt. Frink and his confederates. The physician went to see John Goff for some advice. Goff worked out a plan where a female go-between would try to trap the police in the abortion conspiracy.

Meanwhile Whitehead went back to the practice of medicine. A lady came to him with the standard complaint of being "in the family way." The physician, who obviously had included abortion in his repertory, told her that he no longer wished to handle that sort of case and indicated that both police and courts had been severe with him. The patient insisted "the gentleman who got me in the family way is a very influential man and he is a judge and can do a great deal for you, Doctor."

The doctor demurred, pointing out that he was held by a grand jury and nobody could help.

She asked, "Who is the judge?"

"Judge Koch."

"My God! He seduced me and got me in the family way five times and Judge Koch paid the bills."

On her advice Whitehead went to see Koch, who said, "Doctor, I am very sorry about this affair. I did not know that my girl had ever been to you." Still, Koch offered no help for the future.

Whitehead returned to Goff and it was agreed that undercover agent Annie Ruggles should follow Koch's inamorata in hopes of getting evidence that would trap the entire ring. But the pregnant woman tired of waiting for Whitehead to help her and used another and anonymous abortionist.

The practitioners of the day generally advertised as midwives and the estimate of the committee was that about two hundred of them plied their trade in the city. Corroborating Whitehead's testimony, a Dr. Hawker informed the hearing that over a period of six weeks he donated $2825 to Sgt. O'Toole, Sgt. Frink, and the favored attorneys.

The abortion testimony, like so much of the Lexow findings, did not go below the surface. No one expected, as in modern investigations, that legislation would prevent corruption. Instead the aim was merely to expose malfeasance and get the rascals replaced by more honest men. There was no suspicion that the code of laws and the ethics of the day encouraged corruption.

CHAPTER IX

THE POLICE RACKETS

Reading the testimony today, it is difficult to imagine how those at the Lexow hearings could have failed to recognize that the city's jerry-built laws provided a golden club for extortion, blackmail, and graft.

The New York City police left no opportunity for a dollar to slip by without a nibble from them. The cops plucked from $20 to $100 a year from fruit merchants for the right to pile produce on the sidewalk without fear of a summons. Illegal and legal signs both brought tribute to the police. Soda water sellers parked on the sidewalks with impunity after their association paid the police rent. Bootblack Frank Martine anted up $100 for the exclusive franchise to clean shoes at the station house at 67th and Third Avenue. It was not a very happy investment for Martine since his customers often refused to pay for the services rendered. Martine accosted Patrolman Gwinnen, "Why don't you pay what you owe me?"

"The next time you stop me on my way going across the street I will smash you on the jaw, you dirty Italian son-of-a-bitch," replied Gwinnen. The officer made his point even clearer by punching Martine's partner when that bootblack asked to be paid. A Gwinnen crony, Patrolman Looney, arrested the two shoeshine men and took them before the desk sergeant with the accusation that the bootblacks had been fighting. The desk man refused even to listen to Martine. In the back room Martine's partner underwent a severe beating with a belt. Martine went to Inspector Byrnes and charges were brought against both patrolmen. But the trial was delayed until the evidence—the welts and lacerations of the injured man—healed, and no disposition of the case ever was made.

Placido Galingo housed Spaniards and Cubans in his rooming house. One night three cops entered, battered Galingo and some friends, and collected $100 with the vague assertion that someone lost a lot of money playing dominoes at Galingo's. Galingo complained to Captain Haughery at the station house. The precinct commander responded with a punch to the face. As far as Galingo could learn a local madam had decided that the lodgings would be a profitable location and Captain Haughery felt that what would be good for the madam would be good for him. However, Bondsman Blumenthal instructed Galingo that the captain might be mollified if the roominghouse proprietor funded $50 a month to him. Blumenthal could not be subpoenaed; he had become part of the battalion of potential witnesses who roamed Europe during the investigations.

The police held the power to ban prize fights. The manager of Jim Corbett paid Captain Max Schmittberger $250 to allow Corbett to meet Mitchell in New York. But then the price went to 25 percent of the gate and Brady backed out, even though he lost $1,100 which he guaranteed to Mitchell. To recoup, Brady arranged for Corbett to fight three men in one evening. He billed the engagement as "Corbett to outpoint three men," and the suggestion was that there would be no lethal punches. Superintendent Murray, then head of the police, had publicly stated that he wouldn't permit any "brutal exhibition." With a $7,600 gate, however, Corbett gave the crowd more than their money's worth as he knocked his first two opponents senseless. Policemen hurriedly removed them from the ring. A slight delay ensued as the third foe, apparently a believer in the fight as advertised, refused to appear unless Corbett signed a document. The challenger demanded, "I want an agreement I am not to be knocked out."

In supervising elections the police board handled bids to print election ballots. When an outsider underbid the printer cronies of the board members they managed to void the low bidder's $43,000 contract. Their chum then lowered his bid through the simple expedient of not hewing to the original specifications.

The tangle of law wrapped around the sale of alcoholic beverages provided a prime opportunity for blackmail by the police. In the late 1880s, salesmen for a new wholesaler, Hollywood Whiskey, accompanied by policemen, began visiting saloon keepers. The wholesale liquor dealers' association reported that the retailers were advised of the "high favor with which it [Hollywood Whiskey] is regarded at headquarters." Rumors that Inspector Alexander Williams owned a share of the Hollywood firm circulated through the trade.

Prompted by the wholesale dealers' association, seven saloon proprietors went to Superintendent Murray and signed affidavits that they were not "coerced" by the police to buy Hollywood. The affidavits had been prepared by members of the police force. In 1890 the state legislature pushed through a bill that compelled all police to swear they were not interested in the sale or manufacture of any liquor, wine, or beer. Inspector Williams gave up his share of Hollywood Whiskey and salesmen no longer made their rounds accompanied by police. The action by the state legislature probably had less to do with a desire to correct police abuses than with appeasement of the liquor industry which was a powerful contributor to political funds. To further protect themselves from all forms of harassment, the liquor dealers concentrated on rigging grand juries with citizens whose property included liquor-selling establishments.

Along with the harassment of honest businessmen and conspiracy with dishonest ones, the cops were partners in the wide-open gambling of the day.

Games of chance and betting in all forms abounded in New York, and both were illegal. Policy or the numbers racket served as a major New York industry. An official report on policy described the phenomenon, "a species of petty gambling ... confined to itinerant venders of policy slips and to obscure places, chiefly in tenement houses, in the back rooms of liquor saloons, cigar stores and street corners ... it is well nigh impossible for persons not well known to policy writers to obtain slips.... Judging by the amount of money involved and the small sums one could bet, the policy writers must have had a very wide circle of acquaintances. One witness swore that to find a policy writer "just follow a nigger woman and you're sure to find one."

Each location or policy store was good for about $20 a month to the police. The city was carved into territories and the police helped the policy operators maintain their territory, driving out trespassers. With newspaper reporters constantly haranguing the public about the wide-open operation of policy, the police and the gamblers put on public shows to demonstrate that there was no substance to the complaint. Hangers-on impersonated policy writers at given times and the police duly arrested them for the official record, leaving the bona fide operators to continue their business without interruption by time in court or jail. Players were never arrested.

With so much money and so many players and operators involved the game had to be carefully controlled for fear of fraud, most particularly by counterfeiters. The winning figures came from Covington and Frankfort, Kentucky, painstakingly forwarded in a code decipherable by a mysterious figure, E. J. Conlon, in Jersey City. A sample telegram read, "To E. J. Conlon, Jersey City. Window Dear, Harvest, Lattice, Buggy, Signal, Emptiness, Welcome, Fortune, Legacy, Consent, Bank Post." Twice a day such signals came through to Conlon who telephoned the New York City number to the main backers or bankers. They forwarded the figures to the policy shops which made it official by printing up the numbers in their own print shops. Other major cities had their own E. J. Conlons.

Bets ran from one cent to $50. Children with schoolbooks sought out neighborhood policy writers while the cop on the beat benignly looked on. A good book carried $60 to $100 a day and an exceptional book handled $150. The best sources of income lay in the poorest districts of the city. The police themselves were considered "good players" (big bets) but, said one witness, "They are not always good payers." The policy writers, however, could not afford to cut off their credit.

As another diversion gamblers ran stores that conducted betting on the stock market. Seemingly furnished like a standard stock quotation room, the shops attracted from 100 to 150 players at a time. To make certain that the operators came out ahead fake quotations were posted when necessary. No stock certificates of course changed hands, and the odds against the players ran about 3 to 1.

One of the more instructive witnesses to appear before the Lexow Committee was George Appo who gave a short course in the green goods game, the popular con of the day. Green goods games swindled individuals who paid good money for counterfeit bills, worthless securities on scraps of paper.

As in all con games, the green goods caper depended upon the avarice of the victim. The steerer put together lists of people who had money and who might be susceptible to turning a quick and soiled dollar. Writers ground out circulars, the substance of which indicated that through some mischance the Treasury had printed an excess of currency which had fallen into the hands of a man willing to sell $3,000 worth for only $300.

Writers attached fictional addresses to their circulars and when victims replied by telegraph to the address listed, a member of the gang, employed by Western Union, held out the wires and delivered them personally to the green goods store. The technique protected the con men from traps, although testimony indicated that most of the police considered green goods operations a source of revenue for themselves.

Steerers arranged to meet willing correspondents in depots to prevent any interception by honest police or dishonest competitors. Once satisfied that the customer was bona fide, the steerer led him to the store where the turner embroidered his account of Treasury surplus. Prospective clients received samples of the excess, were even invited to go out and spend it. Convinced the stuff was genuine, and of course the samples were, the eager customer could often be talked into such absurdities as getting the entire state franchise for a few extra dollars. Then, while he signed a receipt or was distracted in some fashion, a substitution occurred. A duplicate satchel or box or trunk took the place of the original one. Such containers were always locked and the key handed to the client never fitted. The technique discouraged inspection of the goods until the victim was long gone from the premises, possibly on the way home by train, ferry, or carriage. The tailer observed the departure, ready to alert the gang in the event that the mark discovered his loss and hollered for the cops.

Detectives advised Appo and confederates of names to be

struck from the lists of prospects because the men in question had complained or could not be trusted. The police made no attempt to intercede or solve murders of green goods trespassers. "Stealing a guy" was considered by both the con men and the law to be a sin justifiably punishable by death and the execution was to be rendered by the trade.

While the city and surrounding small towns harbored an abundant supply of marks, the con game flourished. It perished in the 1920s, a victim of sophistication. But the Lexow hearings did squash police participation; at least the charge of officers cooperating was never raised again.

CHAPTER X

THE CLUBBERS

The tales of chicanery that unfolded before the Lexow Committee occasionally shocked the audiences but the cry of police brutality elicited the greatest indignation. After a committee hearing on the free and easy use of the lethal nightstick, the *New York Times* of October 3, 1894, described the accused: "... A hitherto unclassified body of men, to be known ever after as the 'clubbers of the New York police force' was gathered ... and exhibited ... as a collective example of the immunity from the law as to assault which is enjoyed by the ... police force." "The clubbers brigade" came together for the first time. "They were types who complained when Supt. Byrnes took away their night sticks that they were being left to the mercy of the criminal classes." According to the *Times,* some "looked the part," but many "mild-mannered policemen" also made up the brigade.

The Lexow investigation thus brought to a crescendo a theme that accompanied the birth of the police force, one which has seldom been muted in the history of police, excessive or indiscriminate use of police power against the civilian population. In time of riot, the club was the first line of defense for the city. Behind the baton stood the firepower of the military. Throughout the early history of the city the club had seldom proved sufficient to curb civil disorder. But in the years after the Civil War the club came to stand for all of the abuses perpetrated by the police. In 1887 William Browne privately printed a pamphlet, "Stop That Clubbing." Wrote Browne, "Every now and then the daily press furnishes reports of police outrages by violence and clubbing. Recently the number have become so great that the newspapers refer to them as epidemic."

"Shall we keep silence while these [innocents] are beaten by brutal policemen before our eyes, battered with murderous clubs, dragged through the streets as animals and flung bleeding on the cold stones of a felony cell without help, covering or food?"

Browne recommended: "Police commissioners should visit police courts to see the bandaged and battered." "Needless clubbing should be a five-year offense." Browne concluded with the opinion that the average sergeant, lacking in intelligence, "harsh, gruff, no grace of manners yet consigns people to cells." Browne's appeal obviously went unheard.

The Lexow hearings publicized a number of the assaults upon private citizens and brought out some interesting comparisons in the discipline wreaked upon patrolmen who broke bones and bloodied heads and those who committed simple derelictions of their duty.

At one point the proceedings of the Committee were interrupted by a citizen who burst into the inquiry fresh from an assault by a politician assisted by two policemen. The fugitive said that he knew nowhere he could be protected outside of the Lexow hearing.

Under the guidance of committee counsel the evidence of police brutality piled up. Patrolman Thomas Coleman had remained on active duty after sixteen charges against him, including four convictions by courts of brutal assault. Thomas Knox, a Columbia University student, spoke of a torchlight procession and bonfire by the sophomore class which ended at 11 P.M. when a squad of police barged in swinging night sticks. The students said they had a permit and Knox called the campus parade "extremely quiet," so much so that some boys termed it "quite a slow affair." The police appeared to be reacting to the decision taken a week earlier by the Columbia authorities to ban the city police from the college property.

A defense witness, Officer Richard Meany, who took part in the Columbia skirmish, disputed the student report saying the officers did not carry clubs. Meany himself had once been con-

victed of beating a man who fell behind in his installment payments on furniture.

Truckman and rigger Thomas Lucas appeared before the
Committee in disarray. "What is the matter with your face?" ingenuously asked the Lexow counsel.

"I was to the doctor twice, to the hospital."

"How does your face come in that condition?"

"Through a policeman's club."

"Are you a product of an artist with a club?"

"Well, it is a club done it," said the truckman. The police accused Lucas of attempting to free prisoners held for violating the
liquor law. In the Lucas version he had returned from a picnic and
fell asleep on a doorstep along with a friend. A policeman shook
him awake and Lucas discovered $4 was missing. He turned to the
cop and asked if the cop had any idea what happened to the
money. The officer laughed and ordered Lucas to leave the neighborhood.

That evening Lucas met the policeman and again mentioned
the $4. The patrolman answered with a blow from either a club or
his fist. "He beat me unmercifully in the gutter on the head and on
the face. I said for God's sake don't kill me altogether."

A bystander named McHugh tried to get the policeman to
stop. Another cop arrived and jumped McHugh. Both men were
arrested. At the station house a member of the force beat Lucas
until "the blood was running down by pailfuls out of my head."
Lucas needed twenty-seven stitches to close his wounds and Chairman Lexow commented, "Unless a man is a brute or a fiend in
human shape he ought not to use his club that way."

The episode involving Patrolman Henry Rohrig outraged the
Committee enough for them to make a point of it in their final summary of the testimony. Rohrig chased some boys playing ball in the
street, threw his nightstick at one and broke his jaw. Rohrig
claimed that the youth belonged to the Growler gang. Rohrig said
he feared a disturbance and was tapping his club on the pavement
to attract assistance when the stick bounced up and broke the boy's
jaw.

Police derelictions were sometimes punished, even if the punishment was unpredictable. Patrolman William McHugh, while on post, entered a bar, drank for two hours, and grabbed Mary Pot-chatko. He "made every effort to overcome her." "When remonstrated with by the husband . . . did strike him twice with club." The fine for McHugh was $49.31.

In contrast, Patrolman Henry Jacobi was assessed $98.62 for asking a druggist for a medicine not prescribed by the police surgeon in writing. And Isaac Weiner lost a day's pay for failure to report a dead cat during his afternoon tour.

The Lexow Committee put together statistics for a two-and-one-half year period of 1892–94 when 108 police were convicted of crimes, including 48 felonies. Only four men were expelled from the department and the others received fines of from two to thirty days' pay. In spite of some 56 assaults in the third degree, 45 in the second degree, one attempted rape, only one man was dismissed for clubbing a private citizen.

Through newspaper stories Lincoln Steffens and Jacob Riis sought to muster public outrage but Steffens at least discovered that clubbing could not simply be ascribed to the brutal nature of the men in uniform.

At the police station, Steffens wrote, "we saw two policemen half forcing, half carrying a poor broken bandaged East Side Jew into the office opposite that of the Superintendent of Police. There were officers and citizens all about us but Riis grasped my arm, and pointing to the prisoner as he stumbled in through the open door, he shouted—not, I think for me alone to hear: 'There you have a daily scene in Inspector Williams' office! That's a prisoner. Maybe he's done something wrong, that miserable Russian Jew; anyway, he's done something the police don't like. But they haven't only arrested him, as you see; they have beaten him up. And look—'

"The door opened and showed a row of bandaged Jews lined up against a wall in the inspector's office and while Clubber Williams sat at his desk, '. . . see the others, there's a strike on the East Side, and there are always clubbed strikers here in this office. I'll tell you what to do while you are learning our ways up here; you hang around this office every morning, watch the broken heads brought in . . .' "

Steffens stayed "to look at a specially wretched case; an old Jew, who plainly had been hit many times with the long night sticks: across the nose and eyes, on the side of the head, on his right hand, left arm or shoulder and his back. He was crying and shrank from the slightest touch. It was pitiful, and I must have uttered some sign of my disapproval for the old cop spoke.

" 'You're right,' he said. 'It's rotten work. Makes a man sick to see it.'

"I was relieved to find that there was someone that felt as I did, and a policeman, too; but he went on to say that what I was seeing was the bad work of a young policeman. 'They don't understand, they aren't taught as we were how to swing the stick. It's a formidable weapon, but there's a trick to it. One lick is always enough, if it is placed right.'

"So I gathered it was not an emotional but an esthetic criticism I was hearing, and I asked for more.

" '... You ought to know that a club, especially a night stick, is meant to knock a man unconscious. You can kill with it, you know, and you can batter a man all to pieces, like that striker just going in there. That's not necessary. All you got to do is to tap the extremities, head or feet, so as to send a current through the spine. If you land on the peak of the head your prisoner lays down; if you hit both feet exactly right ... it's the funniest sight in the world to see the effect of a proper lick with a stick on a man's two feet. You don't get the chance to try it often. In my day we old cops used to practice it very easy, on one another, and when you could do it you'd go out and find your bum. I remember the first time I got one just right. He was asleep on his back on a park bench, his two feet stuck out clear and even. Gosh, I was glad, and careful. I sneaked up on him from behind, knelt down, spit on my hand, and aimed. I was so nervous that I dropped my raised arm twice before I felt steady and ready. Then—say but then I let her go, I whacked level and straight, hitting the bottoms of both boots at the same instant, and well it happened, what they always said would happen. That bum rose, stiff like a stick; he didn't bend a knee or move an arm. I think he didn't wake up. He just rose up, running—I mean that he was running by the time he came erect, and with never a holler or a look behind, he was running hell-bent across that park ... It was beautiful; nothing like this.' "

Steffens, at the suggestion of the police, went to "a dirty East Side street corner to watch a shop where the sensible workers wished to return to work and the union pickets were to "try and keep them 'out.' I had no interest in the strike, in Labor and Capital, or any of that troublesome nonsense. I wanted to see why police clubbed people. And I saw."

While Steffens looked on three policemen stood on the corner by a "sweatshop." There was also a small group of spectators near the cops, "out to see the fun. For the rest ... Jewish men, women and children—all in their queer, black old clothes—going about their business. But one of the officers taught me to distinguish a procession of young men and women marching slowly at wide intervals along the street and turning around the corner. These were the pickets, the cop said, 'laying for scabs.'

" 'And there,' he added sharply, 'there comes a scab—with his father and mother to protect him.' He pointed and started toward a young man with an old Jewish couple a block away. . . . I saw the scared white face of the fellow and anxious looks he and his parents cast all about them. But I observed that everybody else recognized him, as the police did; the crowd stopped to look his way, and the pickets began to concentrate on the trio, the pickets and the police, slowly racing. Several pickets reached him first. Shouting and gesticulating, they grabbed him, and just as the three policemen and I ran up, one of the pickets yanked away the old people and another struck the scab, who dropped. My policeman's nightstick whizzed through the air, hit and knocked out the picket who had struck the blow, and the other pickets ran away. There were shrieks, calls, and a whistle. The parents of the scab were lying moaning and crying upon him; the police had to peel them off to lift him to his feet. He was bleeding from a cut on the cheek, and he was bawling as I had never heard a man bawl. With his father, mother and a policeman to escort him, he staggered to the shop, where he washed up and went to work. I stayed with my cop, who picked up the picket; his wound was a great bump on the back of the head and as he gathered his senses, he protested.

" 'What for did you——' "

" 'Ah shut up,' the policeman answered. 'Look a' here.' He seized the fellow's arm, held it up for him and me to see, a brass knuckle on his right fist. 'The emblem of the organization,' the policeman called it . . ."

"The prisoner was led away by my policeman, who, to my question, 'Police headquarters?' answered scornfully, 'Oh, no, we only take prisoners we club bad to the inspector; this one goes to court.' "

The chief effect of the Lexow testimony and the writings of Steffens and Riis was to lessen police attacks upon respectable citizens, including peaceful strikers. No one showed any horror toward police brutality against criminals. In fact, Riis distinctly approved of club work on young toughs. In the age of innocence it was still accepted that abuses of power when directed toward social outcasts or criminals, however petty, was not a subject for restraint.

CHAPTER XI

ROOSEVELT AND REFORM

The Lexow siege breached the police fortress, and, through the hole in the political structure, reform poured into the New York government. Out went some of the more obvious rascals and in came a new Police Board with two Republicans and two Democrats. Theodore Roosevelt, finishing a distinguished stint as Federal Civil Service Commissioner, was one of the 1895 appointees, all of whom were theoretically equal in power. But the tacit understanding was that Roosevelt ran the show. And in fact it was a show with T.R. entertaining newspapermen like Riis and Steffens by his noisy campaign for virtue among policemen.

Arthur Brisbane, writing features for the *New York World*, dashed off a prose ode to Police Commissioner Roosevelt: "Sing, heavenly muse, the sad dejection of our poor policemen. We have a real Police Commissioner. His teeth are big and white, his eyes are small and piercing, his voice is rasping. He makes our policemen feel as the little froggies did when the stork came to rule them. His heart is full of reform, and a policeman in full uniform, with helmet, revolver and nightclub is no more to him than a plain, every-day human being."

Writing to Anna Roosevelt, T.R. observed:

"I have the most important, and the most corrupt department in New York on my hands. I shall speedily assail some of the ablest, shrewdest men in this city, who will be fighting for their lives, and I know well how hard the task ahead of me is. Yet, in spite of the nervous strain and worry, I am glad I undertook it; for it is man's work."

Roosevelt and his colleagues dumped Superintendent Byrnes

and made Inspector Peter Conlin the acting chief. Conlin too failed to satisfy and an unsuccessful search for a man approved by all of the forces in government began. None of the reform commissioners, including T.R., could completely forget that control of the police brought political clout.

Operating as his own shoo-fly squad, Roosevelt sallied forth at night in a black cloak, a wide brim hat pulled down over his face. In the summers a black sash replaced his vest. Thus disguised, he lurked in the streets, hoping to catch somnolent, socializing, and dishonest cops. Those he caught suffered a tongue-lashing to be followed by discipline in the morning. Often T.R. dined in town, then made his rounds during the late night hours and wound up sleeping for an hour or two on a couch in his office.

In another message to Oyster Bay, Roosevelt recounted:

". . . After dinner I got my patrolman and spent three or four hours investigating the conduct of the police in a couple of precincts where I considered the captains to be shady. I make some rather startling discoveries at times. These midnight rambles are great fun."

The reformers quickly ran themselves aground on the tricky shoal of the liquor laws. To Parkhurst, Roosevelt wrote: "What I want is to see the law executed, and all the wrongdoers, no matter who, punished." Unfortunately for reform, the populace's Sunday thirst proved more powerful than any desire to see the law enforced. It did not take long for T.R. to realize that a law repugnant to the citizens was a tight handful of thorns. He wrote home, a few months after taking office, "I have now run up against an ugly snag, the Sunday Excise Law. It is altogether too strict; but I have no honorable alternative save to enforce it."

No prohibitionist, T.R. nevertheless tried to take the hard line on liquor law violations although the Lexow Committee had mounted a blizzard of evidence that the chief contribution of the excise regulations was to encourage blackmail and graft. Frenzied appeals by workingmen and saloon keepers for relief from intrusions of police failed to elicit a lenient approach from Roosevelt. "I do not deal with public sentiment. I deal with the law. I am going to see if we cannot break the license forthwith of any saloon keeper who sells on Sunday. This applies just as much to the biggest hotel as to the smallest grogshop."

The wets of the day began to snipe at T.R. At a Catholic Total Abstinence Silver Jubilee, State Senator Tim Sullivan shattered the dry good fellowship with an attack on T.R. Sullivan cited the case of a man who, because his favorite hangout was shut down on Sunday, stayed home and got drunk, thereby desecrating the Sabbath not only for himself but also for his wife and children.

Roosevelt's zeal for the letter of the law drew the fire of the newspapers also. The *Evening World* published a spurious tale of a mother unable to buy ice for her dying child because Roosevelt had ended Sunday sales of anything but food. The *Times* carried a heart-shattering account of a flower seller arrested for peddling five cents' worth of violets to an inviolate detective. The complaints about his appointee goaded even Mayor Strong. When an upstater approached the city's chief excecutive and asked for the loan of four top police officers to contend with a crime problem Strong answered, "All four are busy watching the girls who sold flowers and the poor devils who sold ice on Sundays."

Clutching at laws to dam the flow of booze on Sundays Roosevelt lobbied against an Albany bill that would have barred police from undercover work. Roosevelt pointed out that the only way to get magistrates to convict was to have a cop buy the illegal drink, gamble, or hire the prostitute.

Even within the administration he suffered opposition. City Comptroller Fitch refused to honor the vouchers of policemen who spent money paying for illegal drinks, gambling, or whoring. T.R. pleaded with Mayor Strong and submitted statements from two veteran officers that this was the traditional system for both catching the unlawful and refunding expenses involved. Roosevelt said he had added two limitations. "One was that no officer should perform any immoral act. The other was that when a disorderly house was raided, the men and women found therein should be treated alike, no discrimination being made because of sex." T.R. was possibly the first official to suggest that the "Johns" as well as the whores be called to account.

The Commissioner enjoyed some minor triumphs over the opposition. The London *Daily Mail* printed an item on the outrageous behavior of the New York police toward a visiting British couple, Mr. and Mrs. Ardenne Foster. According to the *Daily Mail,* Mrs. Foster was waiting for her husband outside a shop when a member of Roosevelt's force accosted her, roughed her up, then accused her of soliciting. Both Mrs. Foster and her husband spent the night in a New York jail before being released with apologies the following day. T.R. promptly looked into the *Daily Mail* story and discovered that Mrs. Foster was a well-known New York hooker and Mr. Foster held an equally long record as a pimp and minor criminal. The officer involved said that actually Mrs. Foster propositioned him. T.R. politely invited the *Daily Mail* to inform its readers of the true facts.

Critical to Roosevelt's purge of bad officers was the power to discharge men without legal proof of inefficiency or dishonesty. Whether the danger to the civil rights of police or, more likely, the threat to the future control of elections disturbed the state legislators cannot be determined. But they failed to pass the bill requested by Roosevelt, that would have given the Police Board the absolute right to hire and fire.

Frustrated in their efforts, Roosevelt and his fellow commissioners fell out over T.R.'s high-handed manner. With the Spanish-American War imminent, Teddy rushed off in 1897 to become Secretary of the Navy with a sense of relief. Shortly before his escape, Roosevelt confessed: "I have done nearly all I can do with the police under the present law; and now I should rather welcome being legislated out of office."

Roosevelt and reform gave the police a most needed dosage of honest administration at the top. While the city gagged on the astringents, the rank and file of police glimpsed the potential for advancement without political pull or payments and could feel some pride in their profession. At another level, T.R. hired the first female secretary for the department. He also turned aside the monied establishment's Protestant complaints against Irish Catholic policemen, saying that he found the latter as worthy and non-alcoholic as any segment of the population. He even recruited strong young Jews because he esteemed "the maccabee or fighting Jewish type."

Perhaps the most important innovation by T.R. was the imposition of strict discipline from above. His honest, firm hand forced every man in the Department to accept responsibility for his own actions. Every succeeding reform administration that has improved police performance has been characterized by a strong police leader. The more control he has exerted down through the ranks, the more efficient, the more honest, has been the Department.

CHAPTER XII

POST-REFORM BLUES

For the city, T.R.'s departure signaled another bacchanal. New York's first real flirtation with respectability ended with an angry divorce. Wrote Jacob Riis, "Honest government did not suit New York. It deliberately voted the dishonest crew back with vastly increased powers for mischief." Back came Tammany and with it, Bill Devery.

Red-faced, bullnecked, with a lush moustache, Devery had figured in much of the testimony taken by the Lexow Committee. Brothel owners and gamblers told of sharing their receipts with Devery and complaining witnesses recounted how, as a captain, Devery scorned their entreaties to enforce the law. He himself never appeared since he was traveling in Europe during part of the Committee's hearings and later was ill. Roosevelt's police board brought charges against him but Devery did not appear for the trial on the grounds of illness. Dismissed from the Department at this hearing, Devery won reinstatement in 1895 along with his favorite wardman, Glennon.

What distinguished Devery from most of his fellows was a roguish air that fascinated reporters and disarmed some of the less singleminded reformers. Lincoln Steffens wrote: "It was easy for Dr. Parkhurst and the other Christian ministers to hate Devery and reproach us for loving our enemy; they never met him. Not only I myself, every reporter I ever assigned to roast the man came back smiling and put the smile in his report."

The other side of Old Bill was described by the City Club report: "It was not until the appointment of William S. Devery as chief of police that the system of blackmail was centralized in such manner that 'protection' had to be bought from headquarters without any intermediaries and without the necessity of making a multiform division of the blackmail proceeds."

Devery had demonstrated his grasp of graft in a memorable address to the men under his command in 1893. "They tell me there's a lot of graftin' going on in this precinct. They tell me you fellows are the fiercest ever on graft. Now," pounding his fist on the desk, "That's goin' to stop! If there is any graftin' to be done, I'll do it. Leave it to me!"

Thomas Byrnes for all his faults attempted to wipe out crimes against property. Under Devery, even the records of crimes became fuzzy. The chief's robbery book showed only 2,784 crimes in eighteen months with stolen property amounting to $457,797. However, a tote of the robbery, felony, and complaint books by individual precincts recorded 14,168 cases with more than $1,200,000 worth stolen.

Devery's influence spread graft beyond Manhattan. Brooklyn, hitherto untainted, but now part of the city through the new charter of 1897, was assigned an inspector "to teach the Brooklynites how to graft." Closer to home, a friend of the chief, Bob Nelson, received the bail bond concession at the jail and cut five dollars out of every bond issued. The *New York Times* reported that gambling had been organized on an unprecedented scale. A Gambling Commission composed of city and state officials plus the head of the pool room syndicate met regularly to apportion licenses. "There are no leaks, no unauthorized places that can run for 24 hours without putting up or shutting up." The *Times* said gambling house keepers paid better than $3 million to stay open. The Chamber of Commerce denounced the police for widespread graft, protecting vice and crime and encouraging the lawless. Bishop Potter of the Episcopal Diocese protested to the Mayor. "Vice not only flaunts in the most open and ribald forms but hardworking fathers and mothers find it harder than ever today to defend their households from a rapacious licentiousness which stops at no outrage and spares no tenderest victim."

Reporters approached Devery for comment on the uproar and one asked about Bishop Potter's impassioned letter.

The Chief in his characteristic locution replied, "Touchin' on what?"

"About Bishop Potter's letter to the mayor."

"I won't say anythin' about that. I ain't got nothin' to say. When I have I'll send for you," answered Devery.

It did not take long for a state legislative committee to ape the Lexow hearings and take up the chase against Devery and the political boss, Richard Croker. Known as the Mazet Committee, the state group dipped into city affairs in 1899–1900. Sessions with Devery proved mainly that the chief had a very poor memory and was addicted to a prefatory "Touchin' on and appertainin' to" routine—"Touchin' on my personal affairs," "Touchin' on my administration," "I had some memorandums touchin' on the Broadway Gardens."

This last establishment turned out to be known locally as "Paresis Hall," and served as a meeting place for homosexuals.

An investigator before the Mazet Committee detailed the activities at Paresis Hall and its competitors, Manila Hall and the Palm. "These men [the homosexuals] conduct themselves there—well they act effeminately; most of them are powdered; they are called Princess This and Lady So and So and the Duchess of Marlboro, and they get up and sing as women, and dance and ape the female character, call each other sisters and take people out for immoral purposes." More to the police point, a witness identified Captain Chapman as having visited one of these establishments while it was engaged in its normal business, chatted with the proprietor and left.

Emma Hartig, a fifteen-year-old prostitute, told the Committee, "Within the last four months I was in four or five different houses." Emma had begun her career answering a German-language newspaper advertisement for the job of a waitress. The owners of these places used newspaper ads to entice girls into leaving home. Emma said of her first house, "They kept me quite nice there ... I did not like the place where I was but I would not return to home because the lady ... takes the place of a mother to me. I did not like to go back home because my father never treated me right."

The girl said that policemen in uniform visited houses in which she worked regularly. They never paid and as the youngest girl in the house Emma generally serviced the police trade. Mayor Van Wyck in his appearance before the Mazet Committee professed ignorance of open prostitution in his city. He was asked, "Do you know we now have male harlots thronging the streets, who have their peculiar places of resort which can be found as easily as any saloon can be?" Van Wyck professed ignorance and recalled that the British had suffered a scandal with Oscar Wilde.

But the main target of the Mazet Committee was Bill Devery. The chief offered no defense of his record on the extirpation of gambling stores. He could not recall a single arrest for gambling over the preceding three-month period. Nor did Devery show alarm when the Committee pointed out that his brother-in-law worked as a clerk for Al Adams, one of the most prominent members of the gambling profession in the city. On liquor law violations Devery cited forty excise arrests by his men, all of which the magistrates threw out of court.

When the Mazet Committee probed his personal finances Devery answered, "I refuse to answer on the advice of counsel." He did however blatantly claim, "I have never received a dishonest dollar or demanded one in my life."

Discipline under Devery naturally collapsed back to the pre-Roosevelt days. The departmental trials came under the direct supervision of the chief himself and if the results provided neither justice nor discipline for the force they did make excellent theater for those privileged to attend.

A patrolman who secured his appointment through the proper civil service channels filed a complaint against the supervisory roundsman; the latter returned the favor with charges of his own. The roundsman had nothing to support him while the patrolman brought three reputable citizens as witnesses to back his case. Devery fined the patrolman thirty days' pay: "If you're the kind of man we get from Civil Service, we don't want any more of them."

Another patrolman stood in the dock for being caught by a

sergeant kissing a girl in a dark hallway while he was supposed to be on post. Devery fined the offender, not for being off post, but for getting caught. Any man good enough to be a policeman would help a nice girl to a kiss, but the Chief added, "I would kiss a girl myself; there's lots of things I'd do and do do but I'll never get caught. And so I herewith fine you good and plenty for getting caught. Two days' pay." An officer went on departmental trial for recklessly firing his pistol in the street. Devery fined him thirty days' pay for "not hittin' nobody."

Devery's reign grew excessively grasping, even for the outlaws. The police-political combine that licensed all gambling took so much that the proprietors could not turn a profit from honest contests of chance. They began to cheat customers. Ladies who cruised the streets and entertained gentlemen in bagnios felt obliged to rob their customers in order to provide larger payoffs.

However disconcerting the greedy hand of Devery was upon the lawless, the effect was greater upon respectable people. A Committee of Fifteen organized itself and began compiling evidence that would oust police department incumbents. Investigators produced a file of sworn statements listing 290 separate apartments in 237 tenement houses where prostitutes violated the Tenement House Law. Police Commissioner Murphy, who thwarted an attempt by Albany legislators to rid the city of Devery, fulminated against the Committee of Fifteen and offered to "bet Mr. Baldwin [a member] anything up to $200 that there is not one such tenement house between the Battery and 14th Street." Murphy periodically delivered himself of vows to close up the gambling halls and pool selling parlors but raids by private civic groups uncovered pool sellers doing maximum business. The stubborn Commissioner continued to deny such places existed, even after the newspapers ran graphic accounts of such operations and gave names and addresses.

Only one poolroom was raided, apparently because it had been set up beyond the deadline established by Tammany between the courthouses and the ferries. Commissioner Murphy however remained a tower of indignation and ignorance. "I have every evidence from Inspector Clayton who has charge of the Queens

County District that such a condition does not exist." Murphy suggested that the vivid imaginations of reporters had painted a wrong impression of the places they visited. Another raid trapped seventy players including the President of the Board of Public Improvements who begged for anonymity saying he was only searching for a "wayward relative."

The gamblers' influence went to the very top of the politico-police pyramid. Patrolman McConnell, with mistaken zeal, interfered with a poolroom backed by State Senator Tim Sullivan. A complaint to the Commissioner followed and he in turn ordered Captain McCullagh to transfer McConnell to a less sensitive precinct. A mass meeting of women at Carnegie Hall scolded the police for their criminal connections. Newspapers continuously nagged at the poor performance and the knavery of members of the Department. The politicians decided to pitch Devery out in the forlorn hope that this act would satisfy the wolves of reform. The chief then plunged unsuccessfully into politics, running first for district leader and then for mayor. He then vanished for fifteen years. In his obituary in 1919, his former adversary, the *New York Times* noted that among his fondest possessions were thirty-six scrapbooks of clippings, most of them unfavorable.

CHAPTER XIII

THE BOSS

Chief Bill Devery, District Attorney Asa Bird Gardiner, and Mayor Robert Van Wyck held the public titles when the Tammany Tiger chewed up the reformers in the elections of 1898 but the ringmaster was Richard Croker. He began putting together his act shortly after Boss Tweed and company closed out their circus.

Throughout his career Croker insisted that he himself never touched "dishonest graft," a distinction that Tammany philosopher George Washington Plunkit used to cover money taken in blackmail and extortion from criminal activities including, of course, violations of the excise law. Lincoln Steffens in his initial streetside interview with Croker had learned that the roughhewn emperor of Tammany turned away accusations of political bossism with references to the hierarchy that ran Wall Street. "But they don't take graft in business," blurted out Steffens. "They don't take bribes from saloons, and they don't take away the earnings of the women of the street. How can you stand for that in politics?"

Croker remained silent while they walked along Broadway, then replied, "There is graft in Wall Street of course. . . . You mean that there isn't any dirty graft, like the police graft, don't you?" Steffens acquiesced.

"Police graft is dirty graft," Croker admitted. "We have to stand for it. If we get big graft, and the cops and small fry politicians know it, we can't decently kick at their petty stuff. Can we now? . . . This I tell you, boy, and don't you ever forget it: I have never touched a cent of the dirty police graft myself."

To the Mazet Committee that tried to chart the routes of the Tammany privateers, Boss Croker coolly declared, "I ain't no statesman. I am looking out for my own pocket first." Steffens in his peripatetic interview accused Croker of making money out of politics. "Like a business man in business," answered the candid Boss, "I work for my own pocket all the time."

Croker's appearance before the Mazet Committee could hardly be termed a success for the reformers. An attempt to lead off the questioning with a lengthy phillippic about Croker's power over Tammany caused the Boss to interrupt, "I am the leader of the party and I acknowledge it, and all of these people are my friends and I am going to stick to them all the time. I don't shy away from them." The gallery accorded Croker prolonged applause.

When the Committee tried to dig into Croker's financial status, the Boss invoked his right to silence. Frank Croker, his son, made a less impressive show as investigators dug into the young man's business career. Frank held a high post with the Roebling Company, the builders of the Brooklyn Bridge. A new subsidiary formed with Frank Croker as a principal stockholder specialized in fireproof construction, and the Mazet Committee found it odd that specifications for new schoolhouses called for techniques used only by the Roebling firm.

As political boss, Croker amassed enormous wealth. The business of the New York City government provided a number of Wall Street corporations with large profits. Railroads, utilities, steamship companies, construction—all of these depended upon the franchises and support of New York. Wall Street could not afford to have Dick Croker a loser when he invested in stocks and he was privy to inside information at a time when prices were easily manipulated and securities traded without regulation. He also interested himself in real estate, buying up tracts of land that became necessary for the expansion of the city or would be required by one of the subway or elevated railway lines.

Croker's organization began losing favor even with its traditional allies in the lower classes when the Mazet Committee in 1900 uncovered the ice trust. A favored corporation received priorities on the use of city docks to unload ice; the competitors were frozen out. Stock in the preferred ice dealer went to city officials and through the long sweltering summer the high price of ice brought complaints about Tammany from the poor.

The Boss lost his aplomb in another intra-Tammany squabble and the reformers seized upon the incident to flagellate all Democrats. Judge Joseph Daly, on the Bench twenty-five years, failed to issue a decision desired by Croker. The Tammany head openly attempted to discipline the jurist and snarled, "Judge Daly was elected by Tammany Hall after he was discovered by Tammany Hall and Tammany Hall had a right to expect proper consideration at his hands." The forthright equation of the political club's prerogatives with a magistrate's duties cost Croker the governorship for his party and ensured the election of Theodore Roosevelt.

To the Parkhursts of the day, Croker rated no higher than a common robber but to the Boss, his booty hardly seemed dishonest; he had been raised in the political spoils system and he knew enough of the business world, as he pointed out to Lincoln Steffens, to see that the lining of one's pocket was not determined by honesty. Business and government—and journalism, Croker said to Steffens—lay beyond considerations of honesty. William Allen White quoted the Boss, "I do not remember ever having done anything I ought not to have done, for I have done good all my life."

Croker never came close to being tried for crimes against the city government. When his health broke in 1890, he gave up his city post and never held public office again. No one could charge misfeasance or malfeasance against him. Possibly he had learned from the plight of Tweed. In 1901, Fusion, New York's perennial temporary marriage of disaffiliated Democrats, Republicans and independent reformers, swept the city and Croker fell from power. He exiled himself to an estate in Ireland. A Croker horse won the Epsom Derby and at 71 the Boss married an Indian girl some forty years younger than he.

Finley Peter Dunne, as recounted by his son Philip in *Mr. Dooley Remembers, the Informal Memoirs of Finley Peter Dunne,* mused about the Devery phenomenon and reform movements in a chapter on the Irish. "Bob Pinkerton [of the investigation agency] and I used to differ as to who was the best policeman in America. I don't mean the best detective ... it was policemen qua policemen, that is, officers of the peace. He thought Bill Devery of New York was the best, I thought Jack Shea of Chicago. . . . Both Bill and Jack looked with a good deal of contempt upon officers like the celebrated Inspector Byrnes whose fortune was made by scaring millionaires into the belief that there was about to be an uprising of anarchists and assembling an army of cops to surround a few hundred garment workers in Union Square who had gathered to hear a squeaky little tailor rant in Yiddish against the tyranny of Capital.

"Devery and Shea had the same antipathies. Both hated a thief as they hated a snake, and both grew savage when crimes of violence were committed in districts under their control. Prostitution and gambling they tolerated [an understatement in the case of Devery, certainly]. They looked with contempt on officers who took money from streetwalkers, as is the London practice. But, like the London police, they regarded gambling as a necessary evil—necessary to the principal officers of a well regulated police force who have families to bring up. It was not until Prohibition was put in force and crime became big business that the police in New York and Chicago began to grow rich by harboring and protecting murderers and kidnapers. You may be sure that under these two peace officers, the Als, the Dutches, the Rothsteins and the Luckys who have made fortunes by robbery and murder and kidnaping would not last twenty-four hours. 'Take the night stick to them, men,' were Devery's orders. 'These rats are only frightened by a beating. Give 'em the nightstick. They're not afraid of a revolver. Ninety-nine times out of a hundred an excited man will miss his mark with a gun. But you can't miss with a nightstick.' If Devery were chief in New York now, Mr. Lucky something-or-other, with a hue and cry out against him, wouldn't be drinking champagne in a New York hotel. He'd be lying on his stomach in some out-of-town hideaway with his lady-love applying poultices to his bruised rump.

"Jack Shea and Devery hated crimes of violence, and if you told them that organized bands of assassins existed in New York and Chicago without the purchased connivance of the police, possibly the district attorney, they would laugh in our faces . . . no money could buy them off from pursuit of these murdering thieves, blackmailers and kidnapers. But political killings were different.

And killings in the unending conflict between Ireland and the British government were acts of war." Dunne's appraisal of Devery hardly squares with the facts but Dunne's Mr. Dooley passed a shrewder eye over the failures of reform.

"As a people," he said, "we're the greatest crusaders that ever were—for a short distance. The trouble is the crusade doesn't last after the first sprint. The crusaders drop out of the procession to take a drink or put a little money on the ace and by the time the end of the line of march is reached, the boss crusader is alone in the job and his former followers are hurling bricks at him from the windows of policy shops. . . .

"It's this way: the lads elected to office and put on the police force are in need of a little loose change, and the only way they can get it is by negotiating with vice. Tammany can't raise any money on the churches; it won't do for them to raid a gent's furnishing store for keeping disorderly neckties in the window. They've got to get the money where it's coming to them and it's only coming to them where the law and vile human nature have a stranglehold on each other. A policeman goes after vice as an officer of the law and comes away as a philosopher.

"Well, the lads go on using the revised statutes as a sandbag and by and by the captain of the police station gets to a point where his steam yacht bumps into the canoe of the president of the Standard Oil Company and then there's the divvle to pay . . .

"It's been a dull summer anyhow and the people are looking for a change and a little diversion, and somebody who doesn't remember what happened to the last man who led a crusade against vice gets up and says he: 'This here city is a veritable Sodom and it must be cleaned out' . . . Lectures are delivered to small bodies of preachers on how to detect vice so that no one can palm off counterfeit vice on them and make them think it is good. The police become active and when the police are active, it is a good time for decent men to wear marriage certificates outside of their coats. Heinous monsters are nailed in the act of hoisting a . . . beer . . . husbands wait in the police station to be ready to bail out their wives when they're arrested for shopping after four o'clock; and

there's more joy over one sinner returned to the station than for
ninety and nine that have reformed.

". . . After a while people get tired of the pastime. They want
somewhere to go nights. Most people ain't vicious, Hennessey, and
it takes vice to hunt vice. . . .

". . . Men begin to say vice isn't so bad, that in fact it makes
life bearable and is good for business. The boss crusader gets
chased from town.

"Then the captain of police that's been spending his vacation
in the district where a man has to be a Rocky Mountain sheep to
be a policeman returns to his old place, puts his hat on the rack and
says, 'Garrity, if anybody calls, you can tell him to put it in an en-
velope and leave it in my box. And if you got a good man handy, I
wish you'd send him over and have him punch the Bishop's head.
His Grace is getting too gay.' "

Finley Peter Dunne and his alter ego had singled out the dev-
astating weakness in any movement led by the reformers of the
day. A certain amount of vice was necessary as an escape valve for
the lower classes who lived at bare subsistence level and even for
some of the middle class which found life at the turn of the century
intolerably dull. Boss Croker's analysis explained the source of political power: so long as government failed to provide welfare and
social service to the poor, a political organization filled a function.
In the United States it was not reform that finally began to curb
political machines; it was the dole started by Franklin D. Roosevelt
and the New Deal in the 1930s.

CHAPTER XIV

EARLY
MINORITY PROBLEMS

New York has a long tradition of unfriendliness to black people. In 1712, an outbreak of violence in the community left several whites dead. On the flimsiest evidence, nineteen Negroes were executed and a law was passed: "No Negro or Indian slave above fourteen years should appear in the streets south of Fresh Water Brook [now Pearl Street and Park Row] in the night after an hour succeeding sunset without a lantern by the light of which they may be plainly seen or else to be in company with a white person." Negroes could not fetch water on Sundays except from a pump or well next to their hovels and the punishment for doing so was forty lashes.

By 1741 Negroes accounted for 20 percent of the population of 10,000. In the spring of that year, anti-blacks fabricated a Negro plot to murder whites. Officials arrested 154 blacks, burned 14, and transported 71. Also executed were four whites, including a clergyman. A hundred years later, before the birth of the city police force, a theater audience took umbrage at remarks on American manners by a British actor. Unable to catch up to the critic, the spectators swept through the streets, venting their fury on passing Negroes, and climaxed the spree by an attack on the proprietors of an Abolitionist newspaper.

The barbarisms inflicted upon Negroes during the draft riots eloquently bespeak the prevailing attitudes of the majority of New York whites. Toward the end of the nineteenth century black people were systematically excluded from churches, schools, and other similar institutions. Other ethnic prejudices also gnawed at the city. George Templeton Strong spoke for a number of his contemporaries on the low esteem felt for the Irish. Riis wrote that the Fresh

Air Fund could not find places for children of Italians. In 1906, former Police Commissioner William McAdoo examined the crime problem in New York and dwelt extensively upon the animosities between the newcomer Italians and Jews. McAdoo also regretted the "Tenderloin type of Negro." He called this specimen a "disgrace to his race" who had a bad effect upon "decent colored people." McAdoo described the Tenderloin Negro as generally armed with a razor or pistol, flashily costumed with jewels and foppish tailoring. "Race prejudice and brutality by white ruffians was no excuse for the better Negroes who should disown and drive out the criminal kind of colored man," asserted the former police commissioner.

McAdoo foreshadowed mid-twentieth-century debates. He remarked that if arrested, "Negro ruffians" claimed race prejudice, and riots and outbreaks arose out of such alarms.

McAdoo, an influential leader of the day, concluded that some locality within the city should be made available so "decent colored could live away from the ruffians." Housing segregation already had begun to corral the Negro and McAdoo blazed his stiffest condemnation at social mingling of races. "Mixed race resorts, besides running counter to violent racial prejudices and traditions, is an unmitigated and disgusting evil and should be regularly under surveillance. A Negro beast, holding a white woman, even a depraved one—in captivity, arouses the fierce spirit of lynch law."

But it was not a white woman "in captivity" who touched off New York's first full-scale race riot. It was a black woman in the hands of a white cop. On August 12, 1900, in midtown Manhattan, Arthur Harris, a Negro, saw his wife in the grasp of a white man in civilian dress. Harris attempted to free his wife from her captor who announced that Mrs. Harris was under arrest for soliciting on the streets. The white detective, Robert J. Thorpe, clubbed Harris who retaliated with a penknife and stabbed him. Thorpe fell to the street where he died. Harris disappeared into the warrens of the slums.

Thorpe enjoyed a certain popularity with his colleagues and his funeral three days after the murder attracted a large number of police mourners and citizens. In the wake of the burial, the police began to talk of revenge. Negroes who dealt with cops daily over the split on numbers, gambling, and whorehouses, quietly closed up their businesses as word spread that the police intended to take their vengeance that evening.

The *New York Times,* on August 16, the morning after the riots began, gave a policeman's view of their genesis. The newspaper reported that two women strolled by the house where Thorpe's body lay. One woman said something about the poor dead policeman. Whereupon, Spencer Walters, "a drunken negro . . . came up behind the women and with an oath drew a revolver." A passerby disarmed Walters and a patrolman arrested him. Another Negro, said the *Times,* came on the scene wildly firing his pistol. Whites then set upon him and beat him unmercifully.

A *Times* reporter watched a well-dressed Negro woman flee an angry crowd. She saw a policeman and requested safe escort. "God bless you, Mr. Cop. Let me walk along with you as far as my house," she entreated. But the officer snarled, "Go to hell, damn you."

The mob started for her but their attention was distracted by a nearby Negro male. She escaped; he was not so lucky. When he turned to the same patrolman for help, the answer was a club smash on the head. Preliminary reports to the *Times* spoke of pistol fire by colored men and Captain Cooney supposedly suffered a fractured kneecap in a skirmish with the blacks. Most of the early *New York Times*'s information proved to be false. As reporters covered the street war, their accounts stressed more and more the actions of whites and police against Negroes.

Some units of uniformed men attempted to halt the outbreak of violence on the night of August 15. On one occasion, a cop saw a well-dressed white man haranguing a crowd of whites. The cop ordered him to move on but he refused, saying he was a policeman himself. Unconvinced, the uniformed man batted the orator unconscious. When searched, the victim turned out to possess both a badge and a police-type gun. Hauled to headquarters, he turned out to be a detective who only a few days earlier had brought shame upon the department for arresting a small girl on the charge of plucking a piece of ivy from a city-owned shrub. He was later suspended from the force after Chief Devery singed him with a sulphurous scolding.

After the first flush of arrests, Magistrate Cornell took note of the absence of whites. "Now if accounts are true, I don't see why you have no white men here," he told officers in his court. "Apparently they acted like beasts, jumping on cars and attacking colored prisoners indiscriminately." Cornell also thought it peculiar for Negroes to be charged with possession of weapons which were not produced in court.

As the disturbances moved into a second night, the lawmen found ready allies in gangs of young toughs who began hunting down Negroes and thrashing them. Officers stood idly by, benignly observing the punishment being meted out. They intervened once, when two Negroes sought sanctuary within a hotel. The police entered and drove the runaways back into the fists and feet of the mob.

Afterwards, a witness stated that he "saw a colored man enter a corner saloon, kept by a man named Gallagher.... I noticed three policemen in the saloon. A mob yelled bring him out. Several rioters entered the saloon, came out and formed in a semicircle, evidently waiting for something." The police hustled out of the bar clubbing the Negro "unmercifully." Then they threw him to the crowd. He escaped eventually, yelling, "For God's sake, don't kill me. I have a wife and two children."

Another Negro, Stephen Small, received a severe drubbing aboard a streetcar from two officers. They halted the attack only when several whites protested. A street gang then spotted Small and stopped the trolley. He hid beneath a seat but only the screams of terrified female passengers saved him from any further harm that evening. The following day when the city had quieted down, Small, heavily bandaged, met a policeman in the streets. "You look as if you had been in the scrap," said the patrolman. "They ought to have killed you," and he thumped Small on the back with his billy.

Some of the victims were saved by compassionate white women who barred their apartments to the search and pummel parties. "What kind of a woman are you, to be harboring niggers?" demanded a cop of one Samaritan. Dozens of black men were yanked into station houses where men in backrooms hammered them until the screams aroused complaints from nearby apartments. Residents swore they heard shouts, "Kill the black son-of-a-bitch," coming from the station houses.

One desperate Negro, William Elliot, borrowed a .22 caliber pistol to protect himself. Captured by patrolmen, he was escorted to the precinct headquarters. Captain Cooney accused him of carrying a concealed weapon. As Elliot was led to a cell a cop tripped him. "Another policeman struck me on the jaw with his fist; then another struck me on the back of the head with his club. And all of the policemen in the muster room jumped on me, yelling 'kill him, kill the nigger.' I still stood up and received many punches. I begged for mercy and did not weaken until an officer struck me in the temple with his billy." As they were kicking and beating Elliot, Captain Cooney rushed in, "Don't kill that man in here. The reporters are out here . . . lock him up." The peaceful arrest of Arthur Harris, the killer of Detective Thorpe, failed to halt the fury that lasted three days and nights.

The Police Board held an inquiry when the carnage ended. It conducted its own investigation of the events and did not permit counsel for injured Negroes to interrogate witnesses. All black witnesses were considered by the Board to be hostile. Officers stoutly contradicted any complaints about their behavior. It was such a transparent whitewash that 3,500 people attended a mass rally to protest police abuses of citizens. A speaker lashed out at conditions, "Brutality and insolence of policemen have increased greatly and the police commissioners seldom, if ever, convict officers for these offenses. Humble citizens of all races today are in more danger from policemen's clubs than they are from the assaults of criminals."

The 1900 riot distinguishes itself from all other New York City civil disorders in that the leading perpetrators also happened to be the men responsible for preventing such outbreaks. More than sixty years later a Presidential Commission warned of police actions that precipitated racial riots. The Commission referred to reservoirs of hostility built up by years of police abuse that overflowed into violence when policemen took action that ghetto people thought was unnecessarily harsh or discriminatory. Contemporary riots have resulted from the outpourings of black people venting their rage and frustration. The 1900 riot was a case of the police rioting. In the 1960s, the Chicago officers at the Democratic Convention and New York City cops confronted masses of dissenters before riots broke out. In 1900, the guardians of law and order simply went into the streets after individual blacks.

During Police Commissioner McAdoo's stewardship, crime was rampant. There was more horse-stealing in New York City in one year than in any state in the West. Thieves would spirit a horse and wagon off the streets and into a stable, clip the mane, dock the tail, bleach the hair, paint the wagon, and sell the rig within hours. According to McAdoo, crimes of the massive Jewish population were mainly crimes against property: swindles, robbery, pocketpicking.

McAdoo characterized the Jews as uninvolved in crimes of violence. However, only a few years later, Jewish gangsters conducted lethal war for control of gambling, killing without concern for race or religious preference. A generation later, Jewish descendants of New York's gangland arenas formed the spine of Murder, Inc.

But Commissioner McAdoo insisted that Jews limited themselves to thievery, particularly in the budding garment industry. He reported that agile thieves stole bolts of cloth and sold them to tailors; two days later the robbed merchant would find himself standing next to a lady dressed in his lost material.

The Black Hand began to get New York headlines in 1907 with the murder of Lt. Joseph Petrosino, the commander of a small squad of Italian policemen. Just how much of a reality the Black Hand was is a matter of conjecture. Arthur Warner, writing in 1909, criticized the police for attempts to use "English-speaking, English-thinking" methods against the Black Hand, which he called not an organization but a condition. Individuals, searching for an easy dollar, joined together to browbeat their ignorant, frightened countrymen out of money. The police, said Warner, spoke of conspiracy only to shift the responsibility to immigration authorities.

The Italian community of the city had long accepted the existence of the Black Hand and considered Petrosino their only defense. The Italian-born detective came to the U.S. at nine. He worked as a tailor, bank clerk, and sanitation man before joining the police. He began building his reputation with the immigrants in 1890.

Part of Petrosino's success was accounted for by his diligence. Of equal value was his ability to talk to his fellow immigrants in their tongue and in his soft-spoken manner get beyond the barrier of their fear in an alien land. He produced more convictions than did a total of any five other detectives in the department. So dangerous was his position that he courted a woman for many years before his prospective father-in-law relented and allowed his daughter to marry a man with so perilous a job.

In 1909, despite Petrosino's triumphs, only 50 of the 10,000-man New York Police Department were of Italian extraction. This tiny clutch of officers could not hope to work effectively with terrorism directed at an Italian population that ran between 500,000 and 750,000 people.

Petrosino was murdered in Naples, not New York, while on a police mission. His death spurred demands for links established with European secret police. Petrosino's murder set in motion a half-hearted effort to recruit cops who were able to cope with the myriad ethnic strains of the troubled city.

CHAPTER XV

THE BECKER CASE

One of the great reform commissioners was General Theodore A. Bingham who served from 1906 to 1909. When Bingham assumed his office he found he could trust few men to carry out orders. Like his predecessors, he sensed that the lack of tenure both on his part and on that of the mayor weakened authority. The political machine, on the other hand, displayed a hearty permanence that invited a cop's loyalty. Bingham noted that both high officers and the lower ranks belonged to Tammany cliques, "Sullivan Men and McCarren Men," he called them. Mayor McClellan, under whom Bingham served, transferred patrolmen and officers on advice of district leaders.

Bingham pushed through Albany a measure permitting the commissioner to reduce inspectors to captain without legal proceedings. The bill passed despite an $80,000 slush fund raised by policemen to defeat it. Bingham used his new power to remove four objectionable inspectors including Adam Cross and Billy McLaughlin, both of whom had come under fire during the Lexow hearings but had emerged unscathed.

Bingham won more than one skirmish in Albany but he nearly lost on two measures he felt detrimental for the continued effectiveness of police. One piece of legislation banned the use of clubs or "blackjacks." The bill passed both houses but the governor killed it with a veto. The other proposal, to bar photographs and the rogues' gallery, died in the legislature.

Breaking with the long-standing philosophy that criminal resorts should continue to exist because they provided convenient hunting grounds for wanted men, Bingham ordered two of his inspectors to root out the vice centers. When one proved slack Bingham ousted him. The proprietors of houses of prostitution streamed into court, defended by lawyers who were law partners of city aldermen, and the sheriff's counsel. The General exhibited little patience toward the legal niceties once his men made an arrest. He labeled defense lawyers "fixers and bellowers." The former, said Bingham, fake evidence; the latter bawl a few inches from the judge's nose "a diatribe concerning the rights of man and the oppression of the poor, stock cry of the professional criminal class and the politicians who defend them." Bingham also forced the corporation counsel to assign experienced lawyers to defend any policemen brought to bar for "oppression." He insisted criminals brought suits merely to bargain for an end to prosecution. When Bingham finished cleansing areas of Manhattan, he moved to Coney Island and elsewhere in Brooklyn.

A young man, picked up by the police due to a misunderstanding and then photographed for the rogues' gallery, gave Mayor McClellan the opportunity to bounce his nettlesome executive. Bingham, after being shoved out, scorned, "What Mayor McClellan will receive for doing this I do not know. Possibly he will be nominated Congressman from one of the districts below 14th Street or for governor next year."

Without Bingham to wield the scourge, conditions slipped back to normal. Some critics now referred to a Police Camorra, a secret society that functioned for the benefit of its members by preying on outsiders, just as the real Camorra or Black Hand did.

The membership of the Patrolman's Benevolent Association numbered 8,000 and lobbied for an eight-hour shift, but the bill failed to pass. Incensed at what they considered the failure of the captains and other high officers to support their demands, the uniformed force went on a one-day rampage. They turned New York into a "Sahara," shut down every saloon on Sunday, closed all bagnios, enforced every ordinance. The head of the PBA announced, "The word has been sent out that members must do strict police duty and enforce the laws. What the men are doing is due to the fact that they are incensed at the unfair methods of their superior officers." (In recent years, policemen denied salary demands have occasionally resorted to total enforcement of traffic laws as a means of pressuring the public.)

The PBA put together a "mortuary fund" of $150,000 that was used for burying reform bills in Albany rather than for funeral expenses for patrolmen. Of this money, $74,000 was later found in a safe deposit box and another $81,000 in a dirty shirt in the home of the PBA chief. District Attorney Jerome said the police had the "wealthiest and most powerful lobby" he knew about. The "black cavalry," as it was known in Albany, was reinforced by lobbies from the Detective's Benevolent Association and the Lieutenant's Benevolent Association.

The leading scandals in 1909 concerned not collaboration with vice but police brutality. Patrolman Martin Cahill, a member of the force for fifteen years, possessed the dubious record of fifty complaints by superiors for dereliction of duty, including two for assault. Cahill's reward for his meritorious service was election as Patrolman's Benevolent Association Delegate in 1905. From then on he received only the best assignments for duty.

Several cases where the police claimed they killed in self-defense provoked a thunder of protest. One officer entered a small grocery where he terrorized the storekeeper's family flourishing his pistol. He capped the show by shooting dead a twelve-year-old boy. At the station house, the killer ripped his coat and swore the child had attacked him. Brought to trial, the patrolman was convicted by a prosecutor skillful enough to demonstrate in court that the coat tear was self-inflicted.

Another bluecoat gunned down a Negro with the explanation to bystanders, "He was bad." Two other officers, however, discovered the only weapon on the dead man was a small penknife. The assassin attempted to arrange a conspiracy, "We'll say he slashed at me with a razor," but too many eyewitnesses came forward.

Dismal as the isolated cases of police behavior were, the actions of the District Attorney indicate that some limits were being set to the use of force by policemen.

On another front, the lawmen continued to serve as private soldiers for the moneyed. A millionaire's son went careening through the Tenderloin on a debauch. In one of his more euphoric moments, he bestowed a legal draft for $40,000 on a girl who had pleasured him greatly. When she attempted to cash it, a city cop who had been detailed to watch her snatched it away and tore the check into tiny pieces. He ordered her to disappear if she wished to stay out of jail.

Such indiscretions might have passed quietly but the city's crime had begun to burst out of the slum areas and bloody other streets. In August, 1903, a gang led by Edward Monk Eastman shot out the night against a couple of platoons of the Five Pointers whose titular boss was Paul Kelly. More than one hundred gangsters ducked behind pillars of the elevated trains and around corners while engaged in the shoot-out. The Gophers, a non-aligned army, took up positions and tried to pick off both Eastmans and Five Pointers: "a lot of guys was poppin' at each other," one said, "so why shouldn't we do a little poppin' ourselves."

A pair of police attempted to halt the battle early in the evening but retreated under a fusillade that put several holes in their uniforms. Finally a large squad of revolver-wielding officers blasted the two gangs out of their entrenchments and the night ended with three thugs dead, seven wounded.

The mortality rate was not terribly unusual but the duration of the fight and the damage to plate glass by stray bullets caused enough commotion to impel political leaders to demand that full-fledged confrontation end. The gangs agreed to a temporary truce but the skirmishes continued. Hardly a week passed that someone was not gunned down. Until the 1911 Sullivan Law made it illegal to carry a concealed weapon, most hoods went heavily armed. Those who had reason to suspect that the police were down upon them went to the extremes of having all pockets sewn shut so that in the event of a stop and frisk exercise, nothing could be planted by an enterprising detective.

The fights between the thugs centered upon control of the principal sources of illegal money, gambling, and prostitution. Although most gangs owed their allegiance to Tammany, the political organization could not enforce absolute discipline on the underworld duchies. It depended upon the Monk Eastmans to provide votes. But at the very least, politicians had to allow the gangsters to collect their tribute in return.

Eastman's was apparently the first of the modern criminal gangs. The Eastman group was not only a political apparatus in the service of Big Tim Sullivan, it was also a unit formed to steal and kill for profit. Its financial base and firepower gave the Eastman gang an independence not formerly enjoyed by the loose aggregations of hoodlums from earlier periods. It was no longer possible for a politician to control his underworld allies easily. In fact, the underworld was now beginning to buy the politicians and policemen, rather than serve as a subordinate or at best unwilling partner. The result was corruption for much higher stakes and much uglier crime.

Although Eastman held one of the more impressive reputations among racketeers, his name did not figure in the succulent scandal of 1912, the Becker case. The alliance of the underworld and the police had waxed fat at the trough of vice until 1912 when a peculiar combination of personalities and circumstances fused into a spectacular civic explosion.

After flagging for the first few years of the twentieth century and its reformers, gambling had made a prosperous comeback. Syndicates and individual pioneers did lively business throughout the city. There was relatively little attempt to disguise or limit such activities. There was little need to: the head of the Special Squad No. 1, the police strong-arm squad or "The Men," Lt. Charles Becker, a twenty-year veteran, was considered part of the combine that ran the show. At the very least, he and his fellow officers had a close association with the chief brigands and an easy tolerance toward the palaces of chance.

In 1912, one of the gambling-house operators was a pesky, unlucky fellow named Herman (Beansy) Rosenthal. Somehow Beansy's stores always seemed to encroach upon the territory allotted to larger and more influential men. When not being shut down by the police, Rosenthal's joints suffered the indignities of bomb throwers in the pay of rivals. After one raid in which Becker's strong-arm squad lived up to its name, smashing Beansy's expensive tables and in effect destroying his business, Rosenthal stalked the town bitterly complaining about his treatment at the hands of the police. He began to mutter that he intended to explode the entire nest of gambling corruption if he did not receive satisfaction. None was forthcoming and Rosenthal went to District Attorney Charles Whitman and poured out a tale of epic length. Whitman listened skeptically and offered no encouragement, indicating that the charges were too vague and lacked proof. Rosenthal tried to see the mayor, the police commissioner, and two city magistrates. They all turned him away.

Rosenthal then committed the unpardonable: he took his case to the newspapers. A band of reporters trooped to his home where he showed them his layout. He talked freely and named Lt. Becker as his partner, adding that the lieutenant boasted an income of between $7,500 and $10,000 a week from such dives.

The newspapers printed the information supplied by Rosenthal, with one major deletion. No one ever dared mention Becker's name for fear of libel. Rosenthal continued to protest publicly about the police investment in gambling, however, and Herbert Bayard Swope of the *New York Morning World* got Beansy to sign a notarized affidavit naming Becker. Armed with this document, Swope pestered a grumpy District Attorney Whitman, weekending on Long Island. DA Whitman agreed that Rosenthal ought to have an opportunity to chat with a grand jury. That was enough for the *World.* It printed Beansy's affidavit.

In the affidavit, Rosenthal swore, "The first time I met Charles Becker we had a good evening, drank very freely and became good friends.

"Our next meeting was by appointment on New Year's Eve 1912. . . . We drank a lot of champagne that night and later in the morning we were all pretty well under the weather. Lieutenant Becker put his arms around me and kissed me. He said, 'Anything in the world for you, Herman. I'll get up at three o'clock in the morning to do you a favor. You can have anything I've got.'

"And he called over his three men . . . and he introduced them to me, saying, 'This is my best pal and do anything he wants you to do.' "

According to Rosenthal the social relationship flourished at the Turkish baths, on auto rides, and on nights at the Elks Club. Becker kept telling Rosenthal that he expected to be a rich man within six months. Impressed, Rosenthal finally asked to borrow $1,500 and Becker answered, "You're on, on condition you'll give me 20 percent of your place when you are open." Rosenthal agreed. Then, according to the gambler, Becker insisted that Commissioner Rhinelander Waldo wanted him to raid Rosenthal. Beansy refused to accept even a token raid and Becker then lured him away from his establishment and broke up the place, arresting the two employees.

The District Attorney, true to his word to Swope, conferred with Rosenthal and arranged for him to appear before a grand jury the following day. The underworld could not ignore the challenge. The night before his scheduled performance Rosenthal supped at the Metropole, a midtown restaurant. A young man approached him and told him that somebody wanted to see him outside. The two walked out, the young man touched his hand to his head and four men stepped forward and began shooting. Rosenthal fell bleeding to death in the street.

The murder could easily be faulted on aesthetic grounds. No less than seven cops were in the vicinity and none of them gave chase to the getaway car. The number on the license plate was recorded slightly incorrectly but the slate-colored touring auto was quickly traced to another small-time gambler and rumored collector for Becker, Jack Rose. Known as Bald Jack, or Billiard Ball, Rose had contracted typhoid as a child and the disease denuded him of all of his hair including his eyebrows.

Whitman at first seemed reluctant to take quick action. It was the enterprising Swope who telephoned the DA in the small hours of the morning and told him of the loss of his star witness. Whitman seemed inclined to wait until morning to pursue the matter but Swope drove to his residence and Whitman greeted the reporter crankily in his pajamas. Swope managed to get the DA working, however.

Lt. Becker's original statement to the press regretted his lost opportunity to confront his accuser. "I would give anything in the world if this had not happened. It robs me of a chance to clear my-self. . . ."

When asked whether he knew Jack Rose, Becker answered, "Sure, I've raided him." From Jack Rose, however, Whitman learned the names of others in the conspiracy to silence Rosenthal, Bridgey Weber, Harry Vallon, Sam Shepps, and Charles Becker. Weber, Vallon, and Shepps all held positions similar to Rose. From Rose, Whitman also learned the identity of the actual men with the guns: Gyp the Blood (Harry Horowitz), Lefty Louis (Louis Rosenberg), Dago Frank (Frank Cirofici), and Whitey Lewis (Jacob Seidenshiner), all young musclemen from the Big Jack Zelig gang.

Whitman speedily indicted the four triggermen and Becker. He promised Rose, Weber, Vallon, Shepps, and Zelig immunity in return for their testimony. The fingering of Becker set off a volley of calls for the police department to be turned on the lathe of reform. An aldermanic committee under H. J. Curran opened up shop to hear from the disaffected. Police Commissioner Rhinelander Waldo, who had received a number of warnings about the activities of his strong-arm squad, still backed his men, "The city has never been more free of gambling."

Mayor James Gaynor also issued a *pro forma* statement. "I well know that you cannot wholly suppress gambling . . . especially among these degenerate foreigners."

The wheels of justice spun suspiciously fast in bringing Becker before the bar. Seldom does a murder case get to court within three months of the crime but this one did.

Becker and four of his colleagues were found guilty and sentenced to the electric chair. The killers went swiftly to their death; they had nothing to trade for clemency and there seemed little doubt as to their guilt. Becker's role could not be categorically proven without a confession by him. The most damaging evidence against him came from men whose character could hardly be classified as exemplary. The fact that four participants got away scot free in return for cooperating to send the other five to the electric chair also caused misgivings over Becker's consignment to the executioner. But Charles Whitman rode the conviction to the governor's mansion in Albany and when Becker's plea for commutation came to him as governor he rejected it. Rumors that Becker would tell all if given his life did not sway Whitman. The forty-three-year-old officer, a shrunken spectre of his 190 pounds, went to the death chamber in 1915, still protesting his innocence. His wife, a school teacher, carried on a decades-long campaign to clear her husband's name. She inscribed his tombstone, "Charles Becker, Murdered July 30, 1915, by Governor Whitman." A city official removed the epitaph on the grounds of libel.

Jack Rose bought a wig and became an evangelist against gambling, lecturing in churches and army camps. He died in 1947. The other principals faded away too as did the brave words of the newspapers.

The *Times* had editorialized upon the policeman's conviction. "The verdict leaves the Police Department of this city in a shameful position. . . . The result of the Becker trial . . . tends to confirm the worst reports regarding it [the police] and if the mayor does not now take prompt action to reform the police the people must take up the work for themselves."

In the time of the Becker-Rosenthal scandal, city hall was in the hands of Mayor James Gaynor, a virtuous but curmudgeonous man whose rasp-like tongue had often distressed even his friends. Although a Democrat, Gaynor had managed to keep himself reasonably free of the Tammany taint.

Against the wishes of the mayor, the aldermanic committee under Henry Curran assembled to sift the corruption dump uncovered by the Becker-Rosenthal case. The Committee had $25,000 for its purposes but was going nowhere until a retired brothel owner, Mary Goode, broke into anger because sitting in the church pew ahead of her was a police officer who had shaken her down.

Mrs. Goode in fractured syntax told the Curran Committee that there were 35,000 prostitutes working the city streets and bordellos and they all paid tribute to the police. She reported that "all the big houses that the citizens would notice, and know are running, Inspector Dwyer has closed with a great flourish. They have broken down the doors with axes and crowbars and thrown the girls out into the streets, and then an officer is there, and the girl comes after her clothes and they say, 'You have got to go and see the Inspector.' She doesn't go, of course, because she is too frightened. They [the police] come there warmly clad, warm underclothes, food, liquor, and cigars. And the rest of us are thrown in the street. They stay there for weeks and weeks. If they fancy a picture it disappears. If they fancy a tapestry, it goes."

"Don't you think that the Mayor and the Police Commissioner can stop the men from taking money from your class of women?" asked a Committee member.

"Never," replied the Madam. "There is not a mayor living can stop the police from taking money, and there is not a district attorney can stop it either." Mrs. Goode said that the "Becker pocketbook," a supposedly secret collection of money to save the lieutenant, had pushed the price of vice operations prohibitively high, that the bail bonds for arrested girls were exorbitant due to the requirements of the Becker pocketbook.

Mrs. Goode instructed Curran's group in the sociological aspects of her trade. "Every girl has a pimp . . . but . . . I don't think you will find an American or an Irishman pimp in this whole city of New York. . . . They [the panderers] are Italians and Jews, every one of them."

Someone asked, "You have been friendly with the Jewish women who run disorderly houses, and with the Jewish men who own disorderly houses or not?"

"I wasn't very friendly in 58th Street, because they insisted on going into the street and soliciting at night. They solicited some of the friends of the Paulist Fathers and it destroyed our neighborhood. You know you take a Jewish woman and it becomes a dull day, why she is wild, and she won't wait for trade to come back again. She goes right straight to solicit the people."

Mrs. Goode reported that although the mayor had ordered the police not to go into the rooms of the disorderly houses with the girls, they had not heeded him. "Is there any man so simple . . . to think that an officer comes into my house and he does not take a girl to the room? Is there a man within sound of my voice so simple as that? That he thinks he does not take a girl to the room?"

Asked if the police decline the service offered within the

room, Mrs. Goode delicately answered that he "stays there at his own convenience."

The answer did not satisfy the committee counsel, Emory Buckner, "Does he decline intercourse?"

"Certainly not," snapped Mrs. Goode. Buckner then advised the investigation that as a district attorney he had only heard policemen testify that the girl merely exposed her body after being offered a dollar and then the cop declined the service and made his arrest.

Among the innovations described by Mrs. Goode was what was labeled "the call girl." A proprietor kept a stable of women and sent them out on house calls in response to telephone requests. It made the arrests difficult because the girl worked on an appointment basis and at a place chosen by the customer. Mrs. Goode thought this system was most reprehensible since the buyer had no way of knowing whether his choice was diseased or not. She recommended to her audience that a city-sponsored vice committee be set up to supervise a number of disorderly houses. These would certify "clean girls" and "suppress those which did not or which catered to hoodlums or were not respectable."

A federal expert on white slavery testified that ". . . individuals of the Police Department, usually I believe in most cases, the uniformed men, and in some instances the others, would intervene between the pimp and a prostitute whenever she became obstreperous and refused to remain under his submission any longer and in that way would help him get her back to him or do some other thing like that." He reported that he knew of perhaps a hundred such instances.

Another professional, George Sipp, who ran a house in Harlem, appeared before the Curran Committee and implicated a police inspector then dying of disease. On his deathbed the inspector accused four captains who eventually were convicted of corruption charges. The aldermen ingenuously complained, "To our amazement, many members of the Department refused to sign formal waivers of immunity, and insisted upon claiming any freedom from prosecution which might arise from giving of incriminating testimony." A firm example had been set for these officers by Commissioner Rhinelander Waldo who refused to sign a waiver. Waldo's method of disposing of corruption charges was to feed the complaints to the accused, permitting them to investigate themselves. Even though the aldermen dredged up enough evidence to indict eight inspectors plus others, Waldo blandly announced, "There is nothing wrong with the police department except public clamor."

The Curran Committee demonstrated that Waldo's men practiced what was known as the "friendly collar." Only two percent of those arrested for vice in some areas were convicted, due to the failure of the policemen to supply proper evidence in court.

In his appearance before the Curran Committee, Mayor Gaynor advised the investigation to steer clear of Mrs. Goode's industry and not to "burn its fingers with this awful subject." After quoting from St. Augustine, he added, ". . . by the way, we have now places to lock up about a thousand of these women, . . . but if we could take the whole 25,000 of them and lock them up, their places would be promptly taken by others, as everybody knows." The Mayor then seized the opportunity for a stumplike peroration, ". . . to the merchants and storekeepers and manufacturers, to put it into their hearts to pay women wages that don't drive them on the town and into prostitution, and things like that we have got to do by slow degrees until the evil is done away with entirely. But for a man to pay a woman three dollars a week and then accuse me and say there are too many prostitutes in the city of New York is infamous, and there are people here who are doing just that thing." Applause rocked the hearing room and Curran had to gavel the spectators to order. Gaynor, who could not be accused of being a friend or profiteer of vice, suggested that localized vice areas gave the city far less trouble than reform movements that only forced streetwalkers to move out into the previously sanitary districts.

As in the past the revelations from the Becker trial and testimony before the Curran Committee temporarily unhorsed the political leadership of the city. New York, however, continued to live under the impression that only a few rascals stood between the city and the life of virtue.

CHAPTER XVI

A TASTE OF REFORM AND A DOSE OF ROTHSTEIN

The Becker case cost Tammany Hall the mayoralty election of 1913. Nominally a Democrat, John Purroy Mitchell ran as a Fusion Party candidate with the endorsement of Republicans and reformers within his own party. An intelligent, honest, well-educated man, Mitchell had presided over the board of aldermen in the Gaynor Administration and at thirty-four he was the youngest ever to take charge at City Hall.

Mitchell picked Yale-educated Arthur Woods to be police commissioner. His job was to reform the force. *Outlook* showed the urgency of Woods' efforts by quoting a popular definition of the police: "Police—(noun) a blackhander to whom the use of bombs is forbidden but otherwise fully authorized by the State. (v.t.)—to beat, club, shoot, bulldoze, threaten, or graft."

Outlook then quoted a "harness bull" who said, "Policemen are just folks. They've got feelin's an' families. They want to live clean and look their kids in the face when they get home. We've had crooks in the Department in years past but the men are finding you can't ever get the kink and smell out of a crooked dollar. When a man finds his ten-year-old boy won't go to school because he's ashamed that his father's a policeman, it's apt to get him thinkin'."

Woods made significant improvements within the 11,000-man force. His contributions included play streets, schoolroom talks by officers, improved training and a hard line against graft. But he obviously overestimated his success in the war on crime. He declared "the gangster and the gunman are practically extinct." The next two decades showed just how myopic a dedicated reformer could be.

The short-lived success of the Mitchell regime and Arthur Woods is tied to both the American role in World War I and the personality of the city's chief executive. Mitchell alienated labor with his handling of disputes. As a firm, early supporter of the Allies he fired up animosity among anti-British immigrants, the Irish, and Germans. Mitchell managed to antagonize Roman Catholics by calling for an investigation of their charities and using wire taps to gain evidence. Patrician in attitude, he also made the mistake of not using political patronage to insure himself of a strong base.

Like his superior, Woods was caught up in the fervor of the war. Even before the United States actually entered the conflict, Woods had organized thousands of his troops into what he called "a fighting force." When the Congressional declaration against Germany came, Woods mobilized his men to protect bridges and other strategic areas. The energy that might have focused upon police reform was channeled into the war effort. The Commissioner was not wholly misguided. Sabotage of American shipments occurred and a spy ring was actually located in New York. In 1916 the Black Tom explosion, a flaming eruption of two million pounds of munitions on a strip of land that jutted into the Hudson River from New Jersey, was probably an accident, but not until long after the war was it determined that enemy agents were not involved. German U-boats hung around the New York harbors torpedoing vessels within sight of land and they unloosed mines that floated into U.S. territorial waters.

When the 1917 election came along Mitchell had lost the Republican primary and rode only the Fusion ticket. He fought mightily against his opponent, John F. Hylan, a red-haired, red-moustached hack supported by William Randolph Hearst, the former Tammany foe. Hylan survived charges of being soft on the Kaiser and he was handily elected. Mitchell went off to enlist in the Army Air Force and died in a crash little more than six months after he left office.

The Hylan administration was one in which the Tammany Tigers again stalked the prizes of crime, corruption, and city business. The fester of municipal rot flared briefly into the open when several members of the Department were discovered in 1918 to have participated in a car-theft ring. And in 1919, a patrolman attempting to make an arrest called for help from bystanders. They laughed at him.

What really plunged the city back into wholesale corruption was the Eighteenth Amendment, ratified on January 16, 1919. The State of New York followed the nation with an even stiffer law against the consumption and manufacture of alcoholic beverages. But in the city the Noble Experiment failed on a colossal scale. Where 15,000 places sold drinks before Prohibition, 32,000 illegal establishments, ranging from hole-in-the-wall speakeasies to elegant places designed for the well-heeled, catered to millions of parched throats. The most venal law-enforcement system ever created was employed during Prohibition with political hacks and party regulars of no particular qualification hired as agents. Newspaperman Stanley Walker described the corruption: "It was a common sight in certain New York speakeasies to see a group of agents enter a place at noon, remain until almost midnight, eating and drinking, and then leave without paying the bill."

The two most famous local agents were Izzy Einstein, a fat forty-year-old postal clerk, and his partner Moe Smith, a clownish recruit from a cigar store. They relished disguises. They used burnt cork (to make themselves appear Negro), wore football uniforms, the suave apparel of society, or longshoremen's garb. Given their distinctive physiques and their burgeoning reputation it is hard to imagine how Izzy and Moe managed to fool illegal joints. But they were spectacularly successful, confiscating 5 million bottles of booze worth $15 million and making 4,392 arrests, 95 percent of which resulted in convictions. Finally, they fell victims of their own impish success. The sobersides of the Prohibition enforcement service decided Izzy and Moe made the agency a joke. In 1925, they were retired "for the good of the service."

No investigation uncovered the extent of city police involvement, but ninety miles away in Philadelphia a grand jury turned up cops with salaries below $4,000 who had bank accounts of $192,000 and $102,000. The worst record of all, of course, belonged to the prohibition agents. Some 1,600 were dismissed for bribery, extortion, theft, perjury, and forgery. The Assistant Secretary of the Treasury complained, "Some days my arm gets tired signing orders of dismissal."

The volume of business with which the police contended undoubtedly discouraged them. When Grover Whalen took over as Police Commissioner in 1928, he made a valiant effort to dam the flow of liquor. "Whalen's Wackers," as the raiders were dubbed, hit six hundred speakeasies at the rate of sixty a night. The Commissioner said he was responding to letters from wives, sisters, mothers, and others about men frittering away their lives, money, and health on illegal whiskey. But there is some suspicion that the zealous Whalen had fallen in a number of instances for tips from bootleggers who merely wished to crimp the competition's business. Whalen himself tired of the effort and began referring complaints to the federal agents after a month or two.

Federal Attorney Emory Buckner told a Senate committee that there were 180,000 complaints of liquor-law violations annually in New York. The arrests made by city cops in one month, said Buckner, would require the work of a federal judge for a year. Volstead Act violators often waited two, three, or even four years for their case on the court calendar, with the result that they were often dismissed without trial.

In 1931, New York Prohibition Administrator Andrew McCampbell said his men had raided 6,217 speakeasies, 386 nightclubs, 171 breweries, 94 cutting plants, and 64 drugstores. They arrested 17,513 people, destroyed 459 stills, and seized 400,000 gallons of whiskey and 122,150 wine bottles. The Prohibition era was a time of unparalleled criminality. Evasion of the law became more common than at any other time in U.S. history. The ugliness of the 1912 Rosenthal-Becker case had cast a pall over the traditional cozy relationship between politics, crime, and the police. The interregnum of Mitchell and Woods added more roadblocks to ambitious, unscrupulous cops. Politicians with a vested interest in corruption within the Department recognized that it was too hazardous to permit a member of the force to hold too much

power. In Bill Devery and Charles Becker, the urge to translate police power into personal political power had threatened the thrones
of Tammany executives. Simultaneous with the discovery of the
danger of ambition in a corrupt police force was the growth of organized crime. The man who welded a new arrangement for the or-
derly partnership of police, politics, and crime was the gambler,
Arnold Rothstein.

Leo Katcher, the author of a Rothstein biography, *The Big
Bankroll,* theorizes that the Tammany Boss, "Silent" Charles Murphy, after the Becker case selected Rothstein as the right broker to
serve as liaison between the underworld and the city government.

As a broker working between the underworld and the city
government, Rothstein organized a fruitful bail bond business. He
had performed this service on a modest scale starting in 1910, but
with improved conditions imposed by Boss Murphy, Rothstein
rose to new surety heights. It was reported that millions of dollars
in stolen Liberty Bonds and other securities passed from the hands
of thieves through those of Rothstein while on the way to new owners. Naturally, amounts stuck to Rothstein during the flow.

Rothstein, however, never abandoned the steadiest source of
income, gambling. He built several grand casinos on Long Island
and in Saratoga; these establishments featured fine food (with
black tie required) and high rollers crowded the tables. The gambler piled up huge profits in these places until local interests
squeezed him hard enough to force him to sell. Another rich harvest lay in "bucket shops," several of which owed their initial capi-
talization to Rothstein. These were a means of disposing of stolen
securities.

Suspicion centered on Rothstein as the fixer of the 1919
World Series when that scandal shocked the sporting world. He
steadfastly denied the charges and his only connection to the affair
was the involvement of his associate Abe Attell and two others.
Rothstein allegedly was offered the opportunity to participate by
Chicago White Sox players, but he turned down the proposition because he did not think it could be done without discovery. For all
of his innocence in the actual crime, Rothstein did not hesitate to
bet against the White Sox once he learned of their arrangement. He

won perhaps $350,000, although officially he claimed more modest winnings—less than $100,000. However, many people continued to believe A.R. did plot the Black Sox affair. When Scott Fitzgerald wrote *The Great Gatsby,* he inserted a gambler, Meyer Wolfsheim, partly modeled on Rothstein, and introduced him as the man who fixed the World Series.

The advent of Prohibition opened up another source of revenue for Rothstein. He was one of the first big bootleggers to bring in a shipment of whiskey from Scotland. Rothstein used large and fast speedboats to beat the Coast Guard, although he also managed to bribe some Guardsmen well enough for them to actually help unload one cargo.

Legs Diamond and associates rode shotgun on Rothstein's trucks as hijackers sought to pluck the fruits of bootleggers' harvests. Diamond and others were rented out to other bootleggers until they went into business on their own, hijacking and selling booze for themselves.

When Tammany Boss Murphy died in 1924, Rothstein was already in danger. Not only did a fight for control of Tammany menace him, but the gangsters that he had once ruled now were becoming powerful enough not to need him. In fact they threatened to take over Tammany ultimately. Jimmy Hines, later jailed for criminal conspiracy, wielded the political sceptre. Louis Lepke Buchalter, labor extortioner and murderer for hire; Lucky Luciano, dope and prostitution entrepreneur; Ciro Terranova; Albert Anastasia; and Thomas Lucchese (Three-Finger Brown) brandished criminal firepower.

Rothstein's end came in the fall of 1928. The circumstances surrounding his death illustrated the thick web of crime, corruption, and politics woven around the gambler. For the three days of September 8–10 a poker game raged. Nate Raymond, a West Coast gambler, Alvin "Titanic" Thompson, the legendary wager hustler, Meyer Boston, Joe Bernstein, and George McManus, a bookmaker and gambler serving as host, dueled one another and Rothstein at cards. The game, allegedly guaranteed by McManus for honesty, saw Rothstein using IOU's right from the start.

A.R. dropped $350,000 in the markers and to add outrage he

tore up the pieces of paper at the end of the game and said that he could be trusted without any evidence of his debts. Since some of the participants lost cash and only wound up with an oral commitment from Rothstein, the atmosphere in the gambling fraternity was tense.

For days the creditors waited for their money, but Rothstein showed no inclination to honor his IOUs. He had suffered financial reverses, but beyond that Rothstein knew his clients always needed cash and, under pressure, could be expected to settle for less than 100 cents on the dollar. An added complication, however, was the suspicion that the game had not been wholly honest. Rothstein's wife claimed that her husband told her he received two anonymous telephone calls informing him that the game was crooked.

A few weeks later, Rothstein was dining at his regular table in Lindy's restaurant on Broadway when he received a telephone call summoning him to a meeting. He left the premises and a short time after was found staggering in the lobby of the Park Central Hotel suffering from gunshot wounds.

Later the cop testified, "I says to him, 'Who killed you?' He says to me—'I won't tell you. I'm shot. Get me a taxicab.' "

At the hospital, Detective Patrick Flood interviewed the dying man. "What's happened to you, Arnold? 'I won't tell you,' he says to me."

The police did discover a room in the Park Central Hotel where George McManus had been living under an alias. While they searched for McManus, Rothstein lingered between life and death at the hospital. A lawyer who represented his mistress showed up and then departed with a new, signed will. Later, however, a nurse testified for Rothstein's wife that the lawyer took Rothstein's powerless hand and guided it over the signature.

The police, except for the single uninformative interview obtained by Detective Flood, made no attempt to see the wounded man. He died after four days.

Newspapers carried ugly editorials about the lack of progress in the Rothstein case. Sophisticated students of New York City corruption would have agreed with Fiorello LaGuardia's law clerk, Ernest Cuneo, who later wrote, "If Rothstein alive had been an unsavory article, Rothstein dead was a calamity. His activities had not been limited to the dregs of society; on the contrary, certain of his dealings had involved very eminent citizens indeed. . . ." Some people considered Rothstein's death a civic benefit. Alva Johnston wrote that this sentiment flourished "because Rothstein was regarded as a human tidal wave of crime."

A frantic search went on for Rothstein's records which hopefully would reveal the extent of his infiltration of the police and politics. Some officials hoped to find any records and destroy them. But Rothstein had been too shrewd an operator to leave any paper around that might have damaged him. Administrators of his estate attempted to collect over $400,000 in loans; another $650,000 was considered beyond reach since gambling debts could not be recovered under the law. Actually, the total amounts due Rothstein would nearly have doubled, had he survived the 1928 election. He had correctly guessed that Hoover would win and had bet a large sum of money on the outcome.

Some three weeks after the crime, George McManus telephoned that he was willing to surrender, and Detective Johnny Cordes picked him up. Even then some suspicions arose, for the procedures employed by Cordes and his associates in booking McManus did not follow the rules. Cordes and others received official reprimands for their failings.

Eventually, McManus was charged with murder, but it took a year for the case to come to trial. The prosecution witnesses proved easy to challenge, and McManus was acquitted.

Underworld citizens, in spite of the medical evidence of Rothstein's wounds, theorized that he had entered room 349 to be confronted by a drunk, who was half-crazed with anger about a debt. When they scuffled, the theory went, Rothstein was shot twice and then went staggering down the two flights of stairs to the lobby.

Gene Fowler insisted that he and other newspapermen had heard a number of rumors about Rothstein being marked for extinction. (More than likely such rumors had floated around town from the beginning of the gambler's success.) Fowler believed Rothstein had been in a floating card game and that one of the participants, full of bootleg whiskey, had scolded A.R. as a welcher.

Rothstein's habitual arrogance enraged the drunk, who drew a pistol, and fired a shot meant to scare him. Instead a bullet hit him in the groin. Fowler related that Rothstein offered some cool comment and then staggered from the room while the occupants all scattered.

Another commentary of a different nature came from Inez Norton, Rothstein's last mistress. For a Sunday newspaper supplement she informed the world of her devotion. "One year ago, this week, on the same day when Herbert Hoover was elected to the Presidency, the world lost one of its most thrilling personalities and I lost the tenderest lover, the truest friend, and the most fascinating company I have ever known. On that day, Arnold Rothstein died. . . .

"Please don't picture me as 'the gambler's sweetie' or anything of that sort.

"With that last gesture of his feeble dying hand—that hand which had dealt out and taken in so much and had been feared by the strong and blessed by the unfortunate, he attempted to scrawl his mark so that he might endow me with a portion of his millions." Possibly Miss Norton believed that her published memoirs along with the vision of Rothstein as Robin Hood, signing her legacy, might improve her chances of sustaining the new will in court.

She painted Rothstein as a man "who feared neither the law nor the lawless, who loved like a boy and punished like a czar.

"I would cook dainties that he especially loved with my own hands," she wrote. On that note Rothstein began to fade even from print.

Arnold Rothstein had begun his career in the freebooting period before World War I. In that era, thugs, gamblers, vice proprietors, cops, and politicians maintained an easy liaison with one another. Such a loose confederation was vulnerable to raids by reformers or easily rocked by the excessive greed of individuals. Money came from a myriad small private enterprises.

Prohibition welded the loose confederation into a much tighter organization. Prohibition also could not be circumvented by small cottage industries; to beat the Feds and supply the demand required big sums of capital, large numbers of employees, and protection on a grand scale. It was Arnold Rothstein who glued the organization together and his career illustrates the astonishing quick riches of the organization as well as its growing pains.

Rothstein survived only the first ten years of Prohibition's fourteen. But the time was enough to make pervasive, if not permanent, the partnership of crime, crooked police, and unscrupulous politicians. The cops who worked during the reign of Rothstein and Prohibition policed New York City into the 1950s and trained the men who now command the Department. And on the other side of the street, organized crime secured a large enough bankroll through Prohibition to give it permanent financial power and a working political structure.

CHAPTER XVII

THE SECOND GREAT INVESTIGATION

Rothstein's death cost the ailing Commissioner of Police, Joseph Warren, his job. The newspapers grumbled about his failure to find a killer or solve the maze of corruption that surrounded Rothstein. Warren's replacement was Grover Whalen, the former executive of a department store who had served as Commissioner of Plants and Structures for Hylan. Whalen made a conspicuous effort to get the Rothstein case out of the public's mind. In 1929, he created, with considerable puffery, a secret force of fifty men who were to live in the underworld. They wore no shields, never made arrests or even visited a station house. Instead, they were to rendezvous in clandestine places and turn over reports signed only with a code number. Several newspapers made unflattering comments about this melodramatic tactic. Whalen defended the unit with the claim that through the secret agents illegal immigrants wanted for a murder in Palermo, Italy, had been caught, a $200,000 bond robbery solved, a counterfeiter apprehended, and members of the Communist Party identified. Critics maintained that the last-named duty was actually the real purpose of the detail. Newspapers, unimpressed, still wrote about the Rothstein fiasco. Otherwise, Whalen was credited with improving traffic control and dressing the men in new uniforms.

The Rothstein chickens laid their first egg during the 1929 campaign for the mayoralty. A squeaky-voiced Congressman, World War I aviator, and political gadfly named Fiorello H. La

Guardia ran against that political sunburst and Tammany sprite, James J. Walker. LaGuardia zeroed in on Magistrate Albert Vitale for a start, revealing that the judge had borrowed $19,600 from Rothstein. The charge was not disproved, but Walker was too popular for LaGuardia and won the election, while Grover Whalen's men guarded Wall Street during the panicky days that followed the Stock Market Crash. Thus Tammany still held the seat of power in New York, and the Rothstein murder remained unsolved. But the Democrat in charge of the state at Albany, Franklin D. Roosevelt, found it impossible not to act.

Under prodding, Governor Roosevelt initiated an investigation of crime and city government in New York City. The chief figure in those investigations was Samuel Seabury. A minister's son, the portly Seabury had come of age just at the time of the Lexow hearings and the revelations of the day had made him an implacable foe of municipal corruption. (Another student of the Lexow material in the *New York World* had been the young LaGuardia.) Seabury's work in various reform administrations earned him a place on the bench. He came close to being governor and was even considered as a candidate for the presidency; partially because of his steadfast rectitude he was rejected by party powers.

Roosevelt picked Seabury because he was a Democrat who could never be accused of perpetrating a whitewash, and could be counted upon to conduct an investigation without a political carnival. Seabury shepherded three separate investigations: a study of the magistrates' courts, a look at the work of District Attorney Thomas Crain, and finally an examination of the entire city government.

The magistrate probe had been triggered by the behavior of Judge Vitale who not only had borrowed money from Rothstein but had also freed a Rothstein employee who was guilty of theft. Before the State Supreme Court Vitale admitted that he had an income of $165,000 over a four-year period, although his judicial salary totaled only $48,000. He offered no satisfactory explanation of the extra income.

Seabury revealed that Vitale's successor George Ewald had paid $10,000 for his appointment to the bench. During the Seabury investigations one of the shadier magistrates, Joseph Force Crater, disappeared so mysteriously that 35 years later supposed graves are still being excavated. "To pull a Judge Crater" is now a part of the American language. In Crater's dossier Seabury pointed to a tangle of inexplicable bank account entries as well as assorted love nests.

Seabury enlarged the investigation to cover lawyers involved in magistrates courts. Irving Ben Cooper, one of the counsel on Seabury's staff, said, "I was full of fight and inspired by the Judge. I would ride with a police car when a witness was being brought in to make sure that nobody was tipped off ahead. It was not exactly a safe occupation because you didn't know which cops were on the side of the law. This was brought home to me when I applied for life insurance during the investigation—and was turned down as a bad risk."

One of the specimens discovered was "lawyer" Joseph Wolfman, who had no legal training at all. But for three years he represented the accused in magistrates' courts, fixing cases in whispered colloquies with prosecutors at whatever price the traffic would bear.

The magistrates supplied power to crime and corruption at a pivotal point, the determination of whether to dismiss charges or hold for grand jury action. Magistrates could set bail, distinguish between felonies and misdemeanors, and in some instances of petty crimes try the case. The investigation pictured an interlocking of lawyers, bondsmen, political brokers, the cops, the underworld, and the courts, the very world framed by Arnold Rothstein at the peak of his career. One Seabury witness, May Palmer, for example, swore that detectives had planted $15 under her pillow and stole what was in her purse on the ride to the station house. She said bail bond fees and legal counsel cost her $575, although she was innocent and arrested only on the detective's planted evidence.

To avoid the eye of Seabury and his aides, a pride of magistrates resigned their posts, citing ill health and other excuses. Two fled the state and another quit, citing arthritis in a finger. Only Louis Brodsky who bore the curious label of New York's wealthiest magistrate managed to beat off Seabury. While on the bench Brodsky had run up a margin operation of $7 million. Brodsky went on trial before the State Appellate Division, but Seabury could not build up enough evidence other than the details of Brodsky's market speculations. The defense appears to have been limited to a speech which paid handsome tribute to dogs.

Seabury scored well against Magistrate Jean H. Norris, the first woman judge in New York City history—and a poor argument for equal rights for women. A former suffragette and loyal Democrat, she sat in untender mercy over the fate of prostitutes brought before her. She had pledged, "Poor unfortunate members of the weaker sex who appear before me will be dealt with in kindness, they will be handled with gloves of velvet rather than steel." Magistrate Norris handed out stiff sentences and few acquittals. A reporter noted, "More than one humble streetwalker incarcerated in the workhouse for one hundred days, was warmed and comforted by the knowledge she had been sentenced by a lady."

Seabury discovered that the lady jurist made her judgments on uncorroborated testimony from vice cops. Even worse, Magistrate Norris changed court records in order to hide her obviously prejudicial handling on one case. Unknown to Magistrate Norris, however, the court stenographer's notes had been preserved in full and Seabury had these in hand when he held a public hearing at which the doctored version of the court record was presented. Judge Norris on another occasion had a court attendant physically force a defendant to take the witness stand, a clear violation of constitutional rights.

The lady magistrate kicked up more mud on her judicial robes with the admission that she was a stockholder in a company that issued the bail bonds, which she then approved. And she saw nothing reprehensible in posing in her court robes for an advertisement that boosted the claims of Fleischmann's yeast as an aid to the digestion and sleep. The Appellate Division agreed with Seabury and removed Magistrate Norris from the New York City bench, in spite of a Tammany Hall battalion of defenders.

In the midst of the investigation of the magistrates, Governor Roosevelt commissioned Seabury to study the work of the district attorney of New York County, Thomas C. T. Crain. As the talk about the city courts began to raise the question of corruption in other agencies, Roosevelt was forced to extend the inquiries even further.

One item concerned Mme. St. Clair, a French-born black woman who banked a policy game in Harlem and cleared a quarter of a million annually. It was public knowledge that Mme. St. Clair paid off the police through one Mustache Jones who carried the $7,000 monthly bribes right to the West 123rd station house.

Another horror tale concerned a former assistant district attorney who collected regularly from bail bondsmen, lawyers, and policemen. He managed the dismissal of 600 vice cases and 1,000 immorality defendants. He reported, "The only time I went to the District Attorney's office was to get my salary check."

As always, a salacious murder scandal helped arouse public opinion. A good-time lady named Vivian Gordon had met with Irving Ben Cooper to discuss a prostitution shakedown being attempted against her. Before she could return to see him with evidence, she was strangled to death and her teenage daughter committed suicide. The details of Vivian Gordon's life shocked the public. She had introduced a young girl to a wealthy sixty-nine-year-old man. The girl received $25,000 in cash from her patron and turned the money over to Vivian Gordon for safekeeping. The girl then disappeared. In a letter to a friend, Vivian Gordon had threatened to tell a story of how she had been "framed," "railroaded" by her ex-husband and the police.

The role of the cops in the magistrate's scandal was poured out by a thirty-one-year-old professional stool pigeon from Santiago, Chile, named Chile Mapocha Acuna, celebrated in a limerick as "the human spitoona" after his testimony.

When the investigators first raised the subject of paid informers, Police Commissioner Edward Mulrooney had announced that the force never employed paid stool pigeons. But when Acuna took the witness stand six weeks later and pointed out his twenty-eight vice-squad partners, Mulrooney dropped any official doubt. Instead he appointed six lieutenants to guard the star witness with the threat that if Acuna died the officers would never reach the grade of captain. When Acuna began to testify, Seabury ordered women spectators removed because the material would be too sordid for their ears.

A tiny, 5-foot, 125-pound, curly-haired former dishwasher and counterman, Acuna was working as a waiter at the Broadway restaurant Reuben's in 1927. There, he said, he met two officers who were impressed with his command of Spanish and Italian, as well as English. Acuna said he agreed to feed information to the police, and in his first endeavor he received less than $100 for tips that solved a murder. Building his contacts, Acuna spent considerable time hanging around with segments of the foreign-language-speaking population. In 1929, a vice-squad sergeant asked for Acuna's help. He produced a list of four gambling houses and one place of prostitution. The raids earned him only $50 because the sergeant complained they were "cheap" places.

Acuna became a steady worker in the vice-squad vineyards and harvested $150 a week for his work. He furnished addresses of actual houses of prostitution and then received a share from the payoff that followed with a raid. Perhaps Acuna might have been dismissed by the public as simply a cog in a machine that siphoned off money from vice but the entrepreneurs in these ventures made little distinction between professional criminals and law-abiding citizens. Acuna told the hearings that when business slacked off, the vice squad hit Harlem apartments at random, preying upon partners in common-law marriages. The woman was accused of committing prostitution and given the choice of paying or a visit to court. Knowledge of conditions in the magistrates' courts, and fear of a trial for fornication or adultery, or ignorance, all made the shakedown business successful in such raids. Where no bribe was forthcoming the vice squad pointed to its arrest record as proof of vigilance. Another tactic was to have Acuna proposition women of any standing and have the police swoop down and make an arrest. Acuna admitted that he had played the role of the unknown man in more than 150 "immorality" raids in a single year, at $5 to $10 a hit. He also checked out tips from other sources on vice.

Acuna's appearance in Seabury's court was traceable to the knavery of his employers. In one instance the Chilean refused to testify against a middle-aged woman whom the vice detectives brought into court. And in fact he appeared in her defense. He was beaten in the station house and subsequently arrested on a charge of extortion for which he received a one-year sentence. In Court Acuna named Inspector Thomas Ryan. "He told me that I would have to be very careful and he gave me some instructions. The first thing I must do was to change my name. Then I must not let anybody know my real name or address. Then when I entrapped women I must give a false name and address ... I must play the part in a comedy, that I would be slapped around and insulted by the officer and that was the part of a stool pigeon but it was only a comedy.

"The main point the inspector said was that I should not go to court but that if I did go to court I should swear that I did not know the officers and had never seen them in my life." Ryan vigorously denied coaching Acuna.

The two men confronted one another in court. Acuna agreed that he'd never met Ryan. Later it turned out that Lt. Peter Pfeiffer had impersonated the Inspector.

Acuna instructed the court in the terminology of his profession. In a "jump" a stool pigeon performed his services. A "crash" was a break in by the police and "information and belief" justified a crash. One time the dapper Acuna trailed two men and two women to an apartment and chalked a cross on the door. When the police crashed, one girl pleaded guilty on the advice of a cop even though she had done nothing wrong. She accepted the penalty to avoid alerting her family to her problems.

Asked to tell the *modus operandi,* Acuna said:

"We usually ate about one P.M. and nine P.M. while the roll was being called in the station houses. Then we'd stroll around in front, where a detective friend would meet us. If we had any addresses, we gave them to him. He would give us five or ten dollars in marked bills. The we would all set our watches together. We would arrange it so I would just have time to give the marked bills to a girl and watch where she put them, so the detectives could get the evidence. Then when the policeman entered they would go through their little comedy with me. They would insult me and accuse me of everything they could imagine, and I would deny it all, insisting that the woman was my wife and I had been there for days.

"Then they would take me into another room and pound on the wall to make it sound as though they were beating me, but it was just more of the comedy. Finally, I would give them a ficticious name and address and hurry back to the station house. They would always bring in the girls as prisoners. The next day when the case came up in the magistrates' court the officer would testify that the man in the case was unknown and could not be found. I was always the unknown man."

"Did you always succeed in getting the evidence you went after?" asked an investigator.

"Oh, no," answered Acuna, "lots of times, thirty or forty times, there was no evidence."

Asked if he informed the arresting officer in those cases that there was no evidence, Acuna answered, "Yes, lots of times the police would come before I had time to get the evidence. Once I was standing in the doorway arguing with a woman when they came in. I told them I had not had time to get the evidence and gave them back the marked bills. They kicked me out and made the arrest anyway."

Variations on handing money to an innocent woman were detailed by Acuna. In the doctor version, the stool pigeon, posed as a patient and entered the office while the doctor was away. He put down some money, demanded an examination, and began to undress in front of the nurse. The police, working on a split-second timing, then entered and arrested the nurse for prostitution.

In the landlady racket, the informant rented a room in a boarding house putting up marked money as an advance. He then brought his alleged wife to the premises. The police arrived, seized the girl for offering to commit prostitution, and arrested the landlady for maintaining a house of prostitution.

Seabury subpoenaed records from the magistrates' courts in such cases. In some of them, innocent women were found to have been locked up merely on the word of the police. Seabury dramatized the effect of such incarceration with the case of a young married woman, dubbed "Betty Smith" by Seabury to protect her.

In 1929 Betty Smith was in her own apartment with a business associate of her husband, a real-estate agent. They were awaiting Betty Smith's husband for dinner. A pair of vice-squad cops burst into the apartment and arrested Betty Smith, not sparing her companion with their language.

Seabury reported: "I shall not mention the wholly disgusting indignities suffered by 'Mrs. Smith' prior to her trial. Suffice it to say that when she went on trial charged with committing an act of prostitution with one Joseph Clark, who was not produced at the trial, and who, according to the police officer, gave an address which would locate him somewhere in the midst of the Hudson River, the police officer took the stand before the magistrate and delivered himself of the case-hardened, stereotyped story customarily employed when a conviction was desired. Three witnesses testified to her good character. The vice officer changed his testimony and said that there were two men in the apartment when he made his unlawful entry."

In spite of this, the magistrate convicted Betty Smith and she was locked up. She apparently suffered a mental breakdown through the combination of unjust conviction and confinement with genuine prostitutes and criminals. It was two weeks before she was examined after her emotional upset and received six months probation. A court of special sessions eventually reversed her conviction.

Commissioner Mulrooney suspended every one of the twenty-eight cops identified, and they ranged from patrolman to deputy inspector. Departmental trials were held. Mayor Walker said he was "more or less shocked by the reports of the framing of innocent women."

A sour Heywood Broun remarked, " 'Some of these reports have been exaggerated,' says the Mayor. Suppose only one woman had been framed. And even suppose that lone case had concerned a notorious harlot. Even then I think we should expect from the Mayor something much stronger than 'more or less.' "

Seabury recommended that six women paroled after their convictions of prostitution be granted pardons and Governor Franklin D. Roosevelt complied.

From the trials of the innocent, Seabury moved on to people like Polly Adler, one of the city's more celebrated bawdy house operators. On the day she received her subpoena, a vice-squad officer happened to be in her apartment. She stalled the process server long enough for the policeman to scramble out a fire escape and walk down sixteen storeys without being spotted by officials or reporters.

Although Seabury and company pressed her hard, Polly Adler turned out to have a very poor memory, being unable to identify anyone who could be accused by the investigators. Not only did she avoid entrapping any of her many good friends, but she also was a direct beneficiary of the investigation. "The police," she later wrote, "no longer were a headache. There was no more kowtowing to double-crossing vice-squad men, no more hundred dollar handshakes, no more phony raids to up the month's quota ... thanks to Judge Seabury ... I was able to operate for three years without breaking a lease."

Acuna was not the only source of information and income for the police. He claimed thirteen others performed similar work. Harry Levey, Louis Taube, and Meyer Slutsky were named by Seabury. Once Levey asked his friend Louis Taube for a "good time." Taube gave Levey an address and then had the place raided and the girl involved was made to pay the arresting officer. Levey left town for part of the investigation to keep him from the witness chair. Vice policemen wired Levey a total of $700 in various cities to keep him moving. When he finally returned he told of having driven the speakeasy circuit with police, picking up $5,000 to $7,500 a month from the proprietors while officers waited for him in the car.

Police records, in spite of Commissioner Mulrooney's pre-hearing denial of fees to informers, showed an estimated $100,000 in payments to informers. At that there was evidence of padding the expense sheet. In one instance four separate detectives laid claim to paying one source for the same bit of information. Lt. Pfeiffer figured that his unit spent $50,000 annually on informers but he kept no records. The average bill from policemen in on the act was $35 a week.

The study of the municipal government in New York City turned up the same dismal portrait of non-feasance and malfeasance, as it ranged through a variety of departments including the police.

The Thomas M. Farley political club in 1926 was raided by a detective named Keller from the gambling squad. Farley's clubhouse had some interesting structural renovations, a peephole to scrutinize visitors and heavy steel doors and bars to prevent rapid-entry by holdup men or the police. A lookout spotted the detective and all Keller found was a crowd of domino players, and good samaritans packing balls, jumping-ropes, and Maypoles for an outing. Two days later Keller took more pains with his approach, coming over the rooftops and dropping through a skylight. He caught twenty-six gamblers, all of whom were bailed out by Thomas M. Farley who happened to be sheriff of New York County and a Tammany sachem. Farley proved a most unusual witness for Seabury. He had deposited $360,000 in banks. For all the stock certificates, real-estate deals, and paychecks he could show, his net income over six years should have been only $120,000 (granting him no living expenses at all). When questioned where the money came from Sheriff Farley said a "tin box" which he periodically visited to "put it in and take it out." Seabury suggested it was a rather magical tin box to produce so much money and the witness politely agreed "the good box I had . . . a wonderful box." Farley was removed from his post.

Another political hangout, the Harry Perry Club, was the scene of a murder, and two holdup men swore that they lost their $12,000 booty gambling in the Perry clubhouse. City Clerk Michael Cruise had turned his clubhouse over to Rothstein's erstwhile friend George McManus. The Registrar of the County, James McQuade, announced that he had "borrowed" the $500,000 traced to him in order to support thirty-three little McQuades, his own offspring plus assorted nieces and nephews.

The study of District Attorney Thomas Crain, a Tammany stalwart, uncovered no cupidity on his part, or at least nothing provable. He was allowed to serve out his term although Seabury considered his tendency to let those charged with major crimes plead guilty to misdemeanors, at the least, incompetent. Assistant DA John Westen, however, was accused of dumping cases for fees amounting to $20,000.

When the Seabury investigators focused on the police, they found some equally inexplicable financial statements. Officer Robert E. Morris, one of the two detectives who participated in the shakedown of Betty Smith, explained his assets by telling how he happened to bump into his Uncle George one day at Coney Island. Uncle George, who then lived in New Jersey, handed nephew Robert $40,000 in forty bills and then had the good grace to drop dead in California before his beneficiary was called to testify.

Another vice-squad detective, Charles Wund, deposited $70,000 in his bank accounts over a three-year period although his salary was only $8,000 total for those years. Wund attested that he made the money in the stock market but an audit of his transactions showed he actually lost $20,000. James Quinlivan swore that he won $9,000 on a horse named Flora Belle through a tip from a drunk jockey. No horse by that name could be discovered nor did the bibulous rider ever show up.

Quinlivan's wife left town when asked to testify. He "refused to answer on the ground that it may incriminate or degrade me." His refusal included an unwillingness to disclose his spouse's whereabouts. Lieutenant Pfeiffer, the impersonator of Inspector Ryan, banked $24,000 when the maximum savings he could have made from his salary was $7,500. Investigators wondered about Pfeiffer's five trips a month to his safe-deposit box. He said he liked to look at his insurance papers, often.

Lt. John Kenna and his mother had showed an income of more than $230,000 for a six-year period while the officer was in charge of 1,000 men in the Tenderloin. There were also supposedly 1,000 speaks in the district. Kenna was immediately transferred to Brooklyn. A year later he was promoted to captain, and Mulrooney said Kenna had suffered "a grave financial injustice." Police investigation showed Kenna's fortune flowed from income property, sales of securities, and inheritances. The study did not explain where or how Kenna's initial capital accrued.

When the time came to prosecute some of the charges raised

by Chile Acuna, the chief witness showed a change of heart. He agreed that seven of the officers whom he pointed out in the courtroom had never actually fabricated evidence. And he swore that another seven had "only honest business" with him. Acuna's retraction weakened any real purge within the ranks.

Commissioner Edward Mulrooney took some action. He demoted seven vice-squad cops because "their efficiency" had been impaired. Two detectives who shook down a woman and attempted to rape her went to Sing Sing because of the Seabury revelations.

To some observers nothing had been done to clean up the city. One of the constantly proliferating organizations for civic virtue, the Committee of Fourteen, issued a 1931 report: "Guerillas roam the streets soliciting men to houses where girls are kept behind locked doors." A white slaver told the Committee he imported his girls to Brooklyn from small Pennsylvania towns. A patrolman asked by a newspaper to comment answered, "We know there is some vice in this district. But what can we do about it. They spot a plainclothesman miles off." The gambling interests meanwhile had continued to flourish. Numbers banker Wilfred Brunder deposited $1,753,342 in his accounts over a six-year period and Jose Miro in three years put away $1,251,556.

A grand jury had written off the Committee of Fourteen report as worthless but Mulrooney agreed with its description of thriving prostitution. He defended his men, however, attributing graft to special squads such as the vice and gambling details "... temptations are so great there, some men fall and betray their trust."

There were honest police officials, like Keller and the head of the confidential squad, Lewis Valentine, who was a deputy inspector. But when Grover Whalen became commissioner he broke up Valentine's unit. "I see no necessity for having a gumshoe staff attached to my office nor for having any wiretapping done inside the department," said Whalen. He referred to the dangers of a confidential squad when run by a Charles Becker. Keller was transferred by Whalen to the Bronx and Valentine broken to captain and sent to Queens.

The quality of the leadership at City Hall is best described by an incident that occurred during these hectic days for Tammany. Mayor Walker and his mistress, actress Betty Compton, were sailing on a private yacht off the coast of Long Island. Walker suffered seasickness when a squall buffeted them and the boat put into shore. To pass the time they visited a gambling casino and Betty Compton went to the tables. She had won close to $2,000 when the County Sheriff and some aides burst in with the news that it was a raid. Walker slipped into the kitchen while his lady friend was herded with the other customers outside by the police. As the clientele passed through the kitchen on the way to the outdoors, Miss Compton saw her friend wearing a waiter's white apron and eating beans.

She demanded he do something but before she could say too much a burly deputy shut her off. Walker did not lift his eyes from the beans and a few hours later when Miss Compton was released she met him on the deck of the yacht.

Walker apologized for failing to come to her aid at the casino. "It might be a good idea if I didn't tempt fate at this moment by showing up in a rural hoosegow." Such resourcefulness did not save Jimmy Walker. Seabury wanted his scalp most of all. After his investigations the Judge went to Roosevelt for a marathon hearing on Walker's fitness to continue in office. Before the Governor could act, Democratic leaders, convinced that further trial of Walker could only hurt the party, forced him to resign.

Gambling corruption continued as an open sore in the police body even after 1933, in spite of Mayor Fiorello LaGuardia's stern admonitions and his inveighing against "tinhorn gamblers." Some of the more prominent bookmakers like Frank Erickson did shift their headquarters across the Hudson River to the friendlier clime of Jersey City, but the day-to-day handling of customers remained in the city.

A grand jury sat in study of Brooklyn's gambling in 1940 and concluded that it was understood that police in uniform made no arrests for gambling even if they witnessed the action. One patrolman had arrested a bookmaker who was subsequently convicted. The officer was then given a plainclothes assignment with "specific instruction that he confine his activities to violations ... relating to the disposal of garbage and the muzzling of dogs."

The Brooklyn panel uncovered a pattern of "unfounded" arrests that created "a record of apparent efficient enforcement," but with evidence produced in such a manner that no judge or jury could convict. Detective Joseph Isnardi arrested bookmakers but in his testimony invariably failed to state that he saw bookies put betting slips in their pocket or that he found any memorandums in the accused's pockets. Isnardi also testified at the initial arraignment that he had seen horseplayers consulting scratch sheets but when he appeared at trials he did not volunteer this information.

The gambling statistics for Brooklyn showed 2,275 arrests in 1935, 71 convictions; in 1936, 3,368 arrests, 181 convictions; in 1937, 5,163 arrests, 131 convictions; in 1938, 3,373 arrests, 482 convictions. The heat of reform began in 1939 and 2,181 arrests brought 753 convictions. In the next two years the percentage of convictions zoomed to over 33 percent. The low had been $2\frac{1}{2}$ percent. LaGuardia had fractured the linkage of vice and politics at City Hall. His was the first effort since Mitchell in 1914.

Commissioner Lewis Valentine took note of the outside influences on his department. "For a great many years many men in the Police Department ... have come to believe that racketeers, thugs, and criminals, especially those whose nefarious activities gained them financial and political standing, must of necessity be treated with kid gloves." Valentine ordered his men to get tough with these people but added it was not a call for "general police brutality"—more like specific brutality.

In Valentine, LaGuardia had found his kind of cop, tough, loyal to the Department, and above all honest, the very characteristics that the Mayor himself brought to his post. Neither man, however, had the talent or the power to really change the institutions that they governed. Whatever benefits the city received from their stewardship depended upon their personal efforts. Once they would leave office, the sins and errors of the police and the government would easily revive.

CHAPTER XVIII

THE TOUGH COP

Cutting the cords between silk-sheathed crime and corruption remained a political issue and a never-ending job for LaGuardia. The spoils of Prohibition had encouraged violence. While reform movements of the late 1920s and 1930s feasted upon revelations of police corruption, some officers were attempting to do their jobs and were dying for them. In the six years before 1930, 61 cops died in the line of duty. On the day that Detective Charles Wund was asked about his $83,000 nest egg two detectives died in a gun fight with a holdup man.

Indignation of the public and the press over gun play in the city streets had led Commissioner Mulrooney in an address before the Patrolman's Benevolent Association in 1931 to say, "I do not want you to have any hesitancy if you come upon a man who is a criminal or a racketeer and you have reason to believe he is armed. I want you to pull first and give it to him if he makes any attempt to get you. Do not be the last to draw."

Shoot-outs between hoodlums and police plagued the city through the 1920s and 1930s. Inevitably some innocent civilians, including children, fell in these skirmishes. While some people blamed trigger-quick officers for engaging in street fire, some policemen died rather than risk shooting in crowded streets. Patrolman Philip Clarius, directing traffic around a school, saw two bandits with guns drawn rushing down the street. Clarius unholstered his revolver, but when frightened youngsters huddled around him, he held his fire. The holdup men, unfazed by the presence of the children, fatally wounded Clarius.

In 1928 seven men were nominated for posthumous honors

for valor. Two died attempting to rescue fire victims; five fell in efforts to thwart holdups. Another thirteen officers survived gun battles with outlaws.

The violent 1930s created heroes in the ranks of the hoods and their image was reflected in films. Edward G. Robinson played *Little Caesar,* James Cagney, *The Public Enemy,* and Humphrey Bogart, an army of toughs, beginning with *The Petrified Forest.* The counterpart was the tough cop and interestingly enough every one of the "bad" actors eventually turned straight, with Robinson and Cagney in the ranks of the G-men and Bogart in the most satisfying role of all, the "private eye" who brought the manners of a thug to the side of the law. The real-life tough cops in New York were led by John Cordes, double winner of the Department's Medal of Honor, Barney Ruditsky, and, above all, John Broderick.

From the time George Matsell and some of his friends circulated through New York streets in 1843 beating up known hoodlums until very recent days, the tough cop was a New York City tradition. The birth of the professional gangster around the turn of the century and the crime boom that lasted through Prohibition undoubtedly endowed the treat-'em-rough school with even more popularity. During the 1920s, '30s, and early '40s, hoodlums and prominent racketeers actually sought public notice, favoring flamboyance in clothes, women, meeting places, and behavior. Their high visibility made them easy targets for police.

The epitome of the tough cop, John James Broderick, joined the force in 1923 and retired twenty-four years later. As a boy growing up on East 25th Street, the "gashouse section" of the city, around 1900, Broderick quit parochial school at twelve to drive a cart hauling bricks. He served a brief period in the navy and then joined the New York Fire Department but found that job dull. He also chauffeured labor leader Samuel Gompers for a short time.

In 1923 Broderick received an appointment to the Police Department. He entered under the favoring eye of Chief Inspector William Lahey; some years later Broderick was to call Lahey his "rabbi," police slang for a patron in high places who obtains for his protégé the kind of assignments that facilitate advancement. In five years, Broderick reached the rank of First Grade Detective.

During the twenties Broderick served as a detective on the Police Industrial Squad, the division of the department that dealt with strikes against fur manufacturers, the city transit system, the window-cleaning trade and other industries. Pickets and strikebreakers battled often, and racketeers lured by the money involved in labor-management fights moved onto the scene at the invitation of both parties. During the brawls between scabs and pickets, police waded in with night sticks, brass knuckles, and blackjacks. No Norris-LaGuardia Act protected strikers or legalized picket lines. The police, on the side of the taxpaying, political-contributing business-men, generally employed their power to break up picket lines and permit free passage of strikebreakers.

In 1927 Broderick and his cohorts became involved in the dispute of the window-washers with their employers. A newspaper account of one incident reports that Broderick, then a sergeant, followed a group of dissident window-cleaners because he was "warned by some sixth sense." The dissidents set upon a work gang and several cleaners tumbled from their perches.

Broderick, armed with a blackjack and fists, entered the mêlée. Someone allegedly fired two shots at him; he returned the fire and then gave pursuit to his assailant. The man ducked into a restaurant, dumped his pistol in a customer's bowl of oatmeal and escaped out the back door. When order had been restored, Broderick had suffered two broken ribs. That same year, a scuffle with fur industry combatants left Broderick unconscious.

During 1928, a tinge of scandal scarred Broderick's reputation. Stories circulated that Communist fur-workers paid Broderick $100 a week to stay away from the fur district when labor trouble broke out. A decade later, the tales of payoffs to Broderick and the Industrial Squad revived on a larger scale. A witness at a 1939 hearing on the relationship between Communists and labor unions testified that gambler Arnold Rothstein had lent the Communist Party $1,750,000 to carry on the fur strike. Bribes of $110,000 each allegedly went to three leading figures of the Industrial Squad—Broderick, Jesse Joseph, and Barney Ruditsky. But Broderick outrode this potential scandal, and he succeeded in dismissing the bribery tale as simply a cover-up for the disappearance or misuse of several hundred thousand dollars of funds collected for the strikers. Broderick's role as the bully-boy of labor disputes petered out with the legalization of union organizing tactics in the 1930s. But from the beginning of his career he had taken a physical approach to the problems of crime. His earliest recognition in the department had come from a prison break attempt at the Tombs Prison in downtown Manhattan in 1926. Three convicts overpowered a guard, armed themselves, and shot their way into the prison yard, wounding the warden en route. A call went out for police to recapture the men. Broderick charged into the Tombs Yard. The trio had taken refuge behind a coal pile when Broderick rushed toward them firing his pistol. One of the prisoners blew his own brains out while the other two surrendered.

The tough cop got star billing in the 1931 shoot-out against Francis "Two-Gun" Crowley, a youthful desperado holed up in a Manhattan apartment house on West End Avenue. Surprised by Patrolman Frederick Hirsch while making love to sixteen-year-old Helen Walsh in a parked car, Crowley had pulled a pistol and killed the policeman. The girl, a friend named Rudolph Dunninger, and Crowley then barricaded themselves in the apartment. Hundreds of police surrounded the area and the combatants exchanged some seven hundred shots before Broderick and two other cops burst through the door to grab Crowley, who had been wounded five times. Broderick got credit for being the first officer to lay a hand on the battered hoodlum.

The aggressiveness that sent Broderick bounding through Crowley's door brought him to the edge of trouble a number of times. The same year that he received the plaudits of the newspapers for the Crowley exploit, Broderick hurried to a hospital where a friend had been taken after an automobile accident. In the lobby, Broderick discovered one Charles Flebus, the driver responsible for the accident. The detective punched Flebus, then arrested him for assault and battery and for driving while intoxicated. A sobriety test showed Flebus to be cold sober.

Broderick enjoyed the hospitality of Madison Square Garden proprietor Tex Rickard for many years and the detective could be found at the Garden whenever a big event took place. The weekly boxing matches, the six-day bike races, and other extravaganzas drew a generous sampling of the city's underworld who were accustomed to wallow in Broadway night life. One evening a prominent hoodlum named Vannie Higgins paraded into the Madison Square Garden lobby prepared for a festive few hours at the fights. Broderick barred the way. Higgins protested that he had a ticket. Broderick took Higgins and his ticket and tossed him through a plate-glass window. The mobster left. On another occasion, Broderick became embroiled with some respectable visitors to the Garden, assaulted and arrested two men. Charges and counter-charges subsequently were dropped.

Such Madison Square Garden lobby battles brought complaints against Broderick and other police. Customers complained that the "specials" or house guards demanded tribute for the better seats, refusing them to the actual ticket holders. Citizens who demanded the seats indicated on their tickets without paying any further fee were allegedly turned over to the city police as disorderly persons. Again the matter was settled without any more unpleasant publicity.

Broderick's rising career received a setback in the wake of the 1933 investigation into municipal corruption. By order of the Commissioner he was relieved of his plainclothes detective post and exiled to Queens. Reporters got no information from the Commissioner on the reasons for the shift, which included a number of reassignments. Newspaper accounts suggest that authorities viewed dimly Broderick's ties with Tammany Hall, his Cadillac, his monogrammed silk underwear, and his lavish style of living on a $3,000–$4,000 salary. Ironically, a year before, five hundred people had attended a testimonial to Broderick for his good works as a detective.

For his part Broderick smiled and accepted his lesser position with good grace. Within a year he emerged from purgatory to resume his role of a Broadway detective. Back on the old beat, protests about Broderick's tactics were balanced by praise for his exploits. With a partner, Broderick in 1941 was on the lookout for a pair of bandits whose specialty was hotels. They spotted two suspects late at night. When approached, the pair drove off hurriedly. Broderick fired three shots at them and their car careened into a lady pedestrian. One bandit surrendered on the scene but the other fled on foot. Broderick traced him to his home, burst in, and felled him with a left to the face. In spite of his heroics, Broderick held only one medal, the Leroy Baldwin medal, won for arresting a maniac armed with a knife and pistol.

Broadway columnists made a cult of Broderick. After the detective had retired, Bob Considine, spurred by the growing, casual violence of the city, yearned in print for "Broderick, the beater" as an antidote to crime. Ed Sullivan boasted his eyewitness account of a Broderick incident. Sullivan recalled a night he visited Tex Rickard and the promoter expressed fear of a kidnaping. Rickard claimed that a car full of men had been "casing" the place.

Sullivan suggested a call to Broderick whose car "whipped into the curb about ten yards behind the 'snatch' car and hardly came to a full stop before Broderick was out and running. Four guys got out of the kidnap car. One apparently reached for his pocket. Broderick nailed him with a right-hand punch and catapulted him back into the car. The other three promptly reached for the sky." According to Joel Sayre in an ingenuous 1936 *New Yorker* profile, the Broadway cop even gave his name to a phrase of coppese— "To Broderick or to give the Broderick, to apply wild physical force." Cornelius Willemse, the police captain who wrote two books on his experiences, reported that he once assigned Broderick to smash the hangout at the Flanagan Bros. "As the chief strong arm of the police department today, Johnny Broderick still never drinks or smokes."

In *Beau James,* a biographical valentine to Mayor Walker, Gene Fowler skillfully added to the Broderick legend. Allegedly, an informer approached Broderick at the Paradise Café one evening and claimed that "Legs" Diamond was somewhere nearby, carrying a pair of loaded pistols, his announced object the ending of Broderick's career. Wrote Fowler, "The stalwart peace officer never carried a gun; his two hard fists were his only weapons." (Since Broderick on several occasions shot it out with thugs, Fowler obviously was embellishing the legend. Police regulations demand that a cop carry his pistol even when off duty.) Fowler claimed that Broderick sought out Commissioner Grover Whalen, who was at the

Paradise Café that evening in the company of Mayor Walker, band leader Vincent Lopez, and a reporter. Before these witnesses, Broderick asked Whalen for "carte blanche on Legs Diamond," to use Fowler's phrase. Mayor Walker offered the detective a free hand, but cautioned him that a gun would be advisable.

Broderick demurred, and invited all present to accompany him while he dealt with "this rat." Neither city official accepted the offer at first, but when Broderick located Diamond in a theater they went along. From across the street the party watched Broderick sally into the theater and then emerge with the body of a man in his arms. Broderick dumped Diamond in an empty garbage can and rejoined his small appreciative audience. Whalen asked about arresting Diamond but Broderick dismissed that on the grounds that "He'd only get a mouthpiece to spring him. This way he'll be so embarrassed he won't be able to face the boys." Not long after, competitors shotgunned Diamond to death.

The accuracy of this tale, with its reconstructed conversations, long after-the-fact, is hard for even a popular historian to swallow. But granting the basic facts, if not the dialogue, Diamond in such a circumstance would have known that any attempt to resist could only have resulted in his own death. In fact all of the hoodlums terrorized by Broderick realized that the detective always held the trump card, the right to use his pistol lawfully. They submitted to Broderick's humiliations, but there is little evidence that he ever made any dent in the revenues by which the Diamonds, Colls, Lepkes, and Higginses lived. The use of the tough-cop routine by the Brodericks of the department followed the tradition of containing crime and vice when they became noxiously conspicuous. This was Mayor Gaynor's line: the duty of the police was to "preserve outward order and decency." Any racketeer or Mafia chief who chose to behave quietly in public did not have to fear Broderick, although the hired hands who performed the necessary acts of violence did run the risk of being "Brodericked."

Shortly after World War II, Broderick's career on the force ended on a sour note. In the fall of 1946 he retired with twenty-four years of service. Rumors circulated that District Attorney Frank

Hogan forced the resignation, accusing Broderick of associating with gamblers most particularly Owney Madden.

Broderick quickly denied the story that he was forced to quit. He claimed that RKO had bought the film rights to his life story for $75,000 and he was now financially set. The detective's lawyer admitted: "Certainly Mr. Broderick knew plenty of gangsters. Plenty of gangsters knew Mr. Broderick in a fashion that could not please them. Broderick's only link to a gangster was a handcuff." Police Commissioner Arthur Wallander also lauded Broderick, whose retirement included a $2,325 pension. Except for an unsuccessful attempt to become a Democratic Committeeman in 1949, and for nostalgic references to his career, Broderick drifted from the public eye. He took up residence as a farmer in upstate New York and died peacefully in 1966.

Today's detectives, some of whom served with Broderick, flatly assert that the tough-cop syndrome no longer would be acceptable within the department, nor would it be very effective. Oblivious to news accounts that detailed Broderick's use of a pistol, some worshipful columnists still claim that he never carried a gun.

Cornelius Willemse, one of Broderick's first superiors, himself believed strongly in muscles and nightsticks. He openly admitted to beating up "Dopey Benny" Fein "where it wouldn't show" in order for the District Attorney to get "civil answers." Willemse also cited Inspector Dick Connolly's admonition to his men. "Don't forget that unlawful resistance covers a multitude of sins." Broderick had his own answer for those who objected to his tactics: "Legalismo is a lot of bunk." The tough cop had been one answer for an openly lawless period. But the tough cop had no influence upon hidden corruption. At best the Brodericks forced gangsters to be more discreet. At worst they fostered a tradition of official violence that continues to be a problem for the police.

CHAPTER XIX

MR. G., BILL "O," AND THE PREVALENCE OF VICE

The retirement of John Broderick signaled not only the passing of the tough cop but also of the era that created him. Broadway, the Great White Way of New York, no longer attracted a money crowd. The flash of Times Square may have beamed brighter than ever, but it couldn't dim the squalor of the streets. During World War II, soldiers and sailors flocked to this center of Manhattan to be serviced by a growing army of prostitutes and refreshed by bars and cheap restaurants. When World War II ended, the military disappeared but the whores, saloons, and hot-dog stands remained. The lowering of legal barriers brought sex book stores and "exploitation" films. However, Broderick's traditional enemy, the bejeweled hood, vanished. Those few underworld figures who had survived the gang wars of the 1930s, and who had also escaped Thomas E. Dewey's reforms and later Estes Kefauver's Senate hearings, tended to turn respectable and moved out to the suburbs. The henchmen who remained and who still employed guns, ice picks, and knives for the good of the Syndicate now worked with more discretion. Rarely does gang factionalism scar New York City. And when it does care is taken so that innocent bystanders do not get gunned down. The murders occur quietly, if possible.

The gangster disappeared from the streets in the 1940s but some carryovers from the earlier decades remained. Foremost was gambling. The introduction of pari-mutuels, the licensed, controlled system of at-the-track betting, had failed to eliminate the entrepreneur who catered to those who couldn't afford a day off to visit the track or who suddenly came up with a good thing.

Just how pervasive gambling had become in New York, and how heavy was involvement of the police, was demonstrated with the unmasking of Brooklyn's biggest bookmaker, Harry Gross. The tarnish of the badge started with some barroom talk overheard by Ed Reid, then a reporter for the *Brooklyn Eagle*. The word was, "A new boss has taken over the bookie joints in town. Guy called Mr. G. They say he was put in business by three top coppers."

Reid learned that in the first nine months of 1949 not one bookmaker had been sent to jail from the Brooklyn gamblers' court. Since Reid had secured information that there were 4,000 bookies in the city, he found the absence of Brooklyn convictions hard to justify. He did locate one man who had been arrested fifty times over a twelve-year period but never convicted. To the reporter it appeared to be a typical pattern of payoffs with arrests bungled to make sure that no one went to jail. Yet the raids silenced anyone who might say the police were not hounding professional bet takers.

Reid's series of articles declared that Brooklyn was wide open for gambling and flatly asserted that the police were accepting bribes. Kings County District Attorney Miles McDonald and Assistant DA Julius Helfand began an investigation. The eventual aim was the mysterious "Mr. G.," Harry Gross. To prevent any leakage of information through crooked cops, McDonald recruited twenty-nine raw graduates of the police academy to do his undercover work. The horrible implication was that only men who had not served in the department even for a few months could be counted as free from contamination.

The immediate target of exploration was the widespread betting on basketball games at the borough's colleges. McDonald's agents began hanging around Brooklyn College, Long Island University, Pratt Institute, and Brooklyn Law School. A smoke shop at LIU drew the attention of Patrolman Anthony Russo. He insinuated himself into the confidence of the proprietor and watched the placing of bets. McDonald raided the establishment and a couple of inconsequential arrests ensued.

Other undercover men picked up the scent of bookmaking close to the Brooklyn Navy Yard. But at the appointed hour for a strike, McDonald's operatives discovered the bookie hangout strangely deserted. A parked car with four men in it drew their interest. The four were seized and turned out to be city police with a list of auto license numbers that identified spies for the District Attorney. The incident confirmed newspaperman Reid and DA McDonald's suspicions.

The study now produced more positive evidence. Among the possessions of some bookmaking arrestees were found halves of a $2 bill. The owners admitted that this was a sign of paid up protection that could be flashed, should a policeman attempt to interfere with the gambling. Several high-ranking officers resigned as McDonald's information began to become public.

When the shadow of Harry Gross darkened New York, the City's chief executive was himself a former cop. William O'Dwyer was probably the last of the elected New York kings to have been born on the *ould sod,* a County Mayo cottage. He had an excellent scholastic beginning; both his parents were teachers and he himself studied for the priesthood in Spain. But for reasons never amplified, "Bill O" abandoned ambitions for a clerical collar and arrived in New York as a burly twenty-year-old in 1910.

Seven years later he went on the force. As a foot patrolman he suffered a severe beating when he attempted to quell a disturbance by some drunken sailors. And he accidentally killed a drunk who had yanked out a gun. With his penchant for book learning, O'Dwyer spent his off hours at law school, passed the bar, and then went into practice. Like many an ambitious young Irish attorney he trekked the route of clubhouse politics. And when Joseph McKee occupied James Walker's seat upon the latter's resignation, O'Dwyer shyly admitted, "Joe, I'd sorta like to be a magistrate." McKee appointed him in 1932.

He made a good record on the bench and even survived the LaGuardia clean-up of courts and offices. O'Dwyer plucked the election plum of a fourteen-year-term on the King's County judiciary in 1937 but he left the safety of that post to campaign successfully for the job of District Attorney in 1939.

In the late '30s, Brooklyn was firmly in the grip of the crime syndicate. The mob had reached the point of organization where territories and shares were alloted by a board of directors. Anyone who disobeyed was executed by a group of specialists in assassination, Murder, Inc., as headline writers described the disciplined platoon available to do the killings.

As a special prosecutor, Thomas E. Dewey had made great inroads into organized crime in Manhattan in the late 1930s. He got Lucky Luciano as a white slaver, put in prison Jimmy Hines, the city hall fixer for criminals, and exerted so much pressure on Dutch Schultz that the numbers king, against the authority of the Syndicate, marked Dewey for death. In so doing Schultz consigned himself to death. His fellow executives in crime saw that the murder of Dewey would bring even greater pressure for reform.

But the fires of reform turned to ashes somewhere along the way as Bill O'Dwyer ran for District Attorney. Immediately after election he dished out most of his first appointments to individuals selected by the party bosses. Even worse, he botched, through incompetence or design, an investigation that might have cleaned up the Brooklyn docks. Special prosecutor John H. Amen had been appointed to scourge the racket-run waterfront unions. O'Dwyer, as DA for the county, began his own investigation and Amen handed O'Dwyer all of his material and suspended his operation. O'Dwyer allowed the study to die of inaction.

The key figure in the Brooklyn waterfront was Albert Anastasia. His name cropped up often in the 1940 dissection of Murder, Inc. The State's star witness, Abe "Kid Twist" Reles, a killer in his own right with fourteen deaths credited to him, supplied the prosecution with evidence covering 1000 homicides in the U.S. and eighty-five murders in Brooklyn. Kid Twist's information dished up many thugs on a platter for O'Dwyer and he sent four to the electric chair, dozens to prison. However, O'Dwyer did not reach any of the leaders of the organization although Reles talked freely of Anastasia's participation in nearly thirty killings. But O'Dwyer never moved against him.

And when hired killers in 1957 pumped bullets into Albert Anastasia as he sat in a barber chair at the same hotel where Arnold Rothstein was shot, the order for the hit came from the Syndicate itself. Anastasia had made the mistake of attempting to muscle in on the organization's untouchable power broker, Meyer Lansky.

Reles himself met a strange end. Held in protective custody for twenty months at the Half Moon Hotel in Coney Island by a special squad headed by O'Dwyer crony Capt. Frank C. Bals, he fell, jumped, or was pushed from the window in 1941. The official explanation was that Reles had tried to escape by tying together bedsheets into a rope. However, since he was obviously marked for extinction by the mob, some students of crime find the theory of attempted escape hard to believe. Eleven years after Reles fell a Grand Jury confirmed death by accident but castigated O'Dwyer for not prosecuting Anastasia.

O'Dwyer added to his political capital by serving in the Army as a brigadier general during World War II. After the war it was relatively easy for the popular Irish veteran to run successfully for mayor on the Democratic ticket. His Democratic Party could overcome the revelation that top hood Frank Costello was on such intimate terms with the candidates that Thomas Aurelio, nominee for the State Supreme Court, telephoned him to thank him for helping to secure the nomination. Aurelio, nevertheless, was elected.

But City Hall did not turn out to be the pleasure Bill O'Dwyer anticipated. He told one reporter "There were times when I was mayor when I wanted to jump. . . . You would say to yourself, 'Good Jesus, it's too much for me.' " The city suffered particularly from a shortage of apartments. Strikes brought one emergency after another. The mayor collapsed once from nervous exhaustion and his romance with and marriage to Sloan Simpson, a divorcee, caused tension with the head of the "Powerhouse," Francis Cardinal Spellman, the autocrat of St. Patrick's Cathedral.

Still, O'Dwyer successfully ran for reelection. Hardly had he been sworn in for a second term when the Harry Gross bubble began to stretch to its eventual popping point. The mastermind had not yet been publicly identified when McDonald's investigation pointed fingers at the high and the low in the police department.

One captain called for questioning, Captain John G. Flynn, put a gun to his head and shot himself to death in the station house.

Although Flynn had been cleared by McDonald and his suicide seemed to have stemmed from other causes, O'Dwyer, deciding the Brooklyn DA was out to smear him, tried to turn public opinion against the probe.

The Mayor made Flynn's funeral a spectacular display of police hostility toward McDonald. Some 6,000 cops, without official orders and behind the Department's band playing a dirge, silently paraded to the Church of the Ascension in Queens, with the Mayor and Police Commissioner William P. O'Brien up front. O'Dwyer said of Flynn, "Nobody had the guts to say he was a clean man, but six thousand policemen walked by his children to tell them so. I am not opposed to the gambling investigation in Brooklyn, I have aided it when asked. But I am opposed to witch-hunts and the war of nerves made popular by Hitler!" However successful the gesture was toward appeasing resentment, the newspapermen, including Ed Reid who had triggered the investigation with his *Brooklyn Eagle* series, knew McDonald was not on a witch-hunt, and O'Dwyer's words later came back to haunt him.

In spite of official resistance to the scrutiny of police-gambling relations, the McDonald team began to pile up evidence. A stand-in who took an arrest for a bookmaker talked to the police after he had been released, because he felt the bookmaker double-crossed him.

The key to the gambling operation proved to be the mysterious Mr. G., now identified as Harry Gross, a heavy-set man with thick wavy hair. The quarry kept a room at Brooklyn's St. George Hotel, as well as a home in the borough. Theresa Scagnelli, a policewoman, secured a job on the hotel's cleaning staff while McDonald attempted to build a case against Gross. The head gambler played the game carefully, leaving very little of value for the policewoman to discover other than that he had a fetish for cleanliness. He showered three times a day and wore monogrammed silk shirts and undershorts. Miss Scagnelli managed to copy some names from a notebook left in the room.

However careful her surveillance, Gross became suspicious and he checked out of the hotel. The search for him began again. He was discovered at another hotel and observations continued.

Meanwhile, Patrolman Costello ingratiated himself with a well-known bookie, who was summoned to Helfand's office one day for interrogation. By chance Costello happened to check into Helfand's office at that very hour to file his weekly report. As soon as Costello spotted his gambler acquaintance he flamed into a rage at Helfand. The Assistant DA picked up the cue and joined the impromptu performance so convincingly that the bookmaker became absolutely convinced of Costello's trustworthiness. He gave Costello Gross's unlisted telephone number. McDonald installed a tap. Listening in, detectives heard an irate bookmaker complain that he'd just paid $350 to a new plainclothesman who said the gambler would still have to accept an arrest. After some haggling the detective agreed to accept a stand-in.

McDonald finally decided to make his move, and seventeen men including Gross and his brother were seized. McDonald claimed that Gross handed out one million dollars a year in protection money, while doing $26 million worth of business with thirty runners. Among Gross's employees was a former plainclothes detective, James Reardon. Favors done for Gross included reassignment of cops who refused to allow gambling operations in their bailiwicks. And on the day that McDonald smashed Gross's operation, two officers filed for retirement. Later they admitted to a grand jury that they had paid $50,000 for a Florida orange grove.

The trials of one hundred cops and Gross turned out to be just as bizarre as the inquiry. Inspector Frederick Hofsaes hauled his 320 pounds before a grand jury and refused to answer questions about a TV set delivered to his home in 1948. All that could be determined was that Hofsaes never paid for the set nor ordered it. It apparently just arrived one day and he accepted it without question. Two other arraigned officers committed suicide. One, a decorated hero, had been a $100-a-month employee of Gross. Another detective leaped out of a courthouse window.

The trial of eighteen more officers was scheduled for early September, 1951. Gross, apparently, had agreed to perform as a friendly witness for the state against his former employees on the force. However, while in protective custody, Gross managed to slip out of his home and pick up his brother's automobile which was parked nearby. One of his guards, disregarding orders, had gone for something to eat. For twenty-four hours Miles McDonald and his associates sought Gross and pondered the ease with which he escaped attempts to pick him up.

The missing man turned up just as nonchalantly as he had vanished. In Atlantic City, a race-track policeman recognized Gross, a feat made less difficult in that the fugitive still wore a tie clip with the initials H.G. engraved on it. Gross admitted his identity. "I'm not running away," he insisted. "I just came down here to play a couple of hot ones." (Successful bookmaker though he was, Gross himself lost big sums of money betting horses—unlike his spiritual father, Arnold Rothstein.) "If I were trying to beat it," added Gross, "I wouldn't hide at a track. Did you ever get fed up? I had these two cops around all the time. It got embarrassing. My friends wouldn't come near me. So I just wanted to get away." Actually, until shortly before his vanishing act, Gross had been under only continuous surveillance instead of protective custody. However, his wife Lila had received letters, ". . . If Harry testifies, . . . your children will never live to grow up." Adding to the Gross discomfort, one of the guardians had left his pistol on a bedroom shelf for a moment. A six-year-old Gross offspring picked up the weapon and fired a bullet into a wall.

Late one afternoon of the September trial, Gross suddenly broke from the witness chair and scrambled for the exit. Attendants restrained him but for all Gross was worth to McDonald he might just as well have kept on running. For the star performer refused to bare his breast. With no ammunition to blast the eighteen accused cops, McDonald watched helplessly as the Court scrubbed the indictments. The judge hammered Gross with 1800 days for contempt and a $15,000 fine. According to McDonald, a $75,000 silence fee had been raised for Gross and in twenty-four hours after his disappearance, persons who wanted Gross to keep his mouth shut had reached him.

Gross, however, attempted to make some amends by talking freely at Department trials of his former associates. In the wake of Harry Gross, 110 cops sank from the force—36 retiring or resigning before testifying before a grand jury and 74 after the Department trials. The departures included a chief inspector, an assistant chief inspector, three deputy inspectors, four inspectors, and three captains, all in all, a high percentage of top officers. One of them, O'Dwyer's crony Frank Bals, had formed a special squad to harass bookies, but they complained it was simply an enormous shakedown. Bals was considered so greedy by fellow cops that he was forced to retire.

The bookmaker himself received a twelve-year term for his activities and he served seven years. Then, in 1955, the Federal Government attempted to collect $7.4 million in back income taxes. While fending Internal Revenue people off with a bankruptcy plea, Gross became mixed up in a scheme involving a $27,000 steak house, motel, and legal gambling den in Mexico. He was acquitted. Pending another trial for a used-car swindle, Gross got into deeper trouble in California in 1959 when a brawl with his eighty-one-year-old father-in-law ended with the old man's death. Harry Gross received a five-year-to-life sentence at San Quentin for manslaughter.

Harry Gross went out of business in New York. But one of his partners, James Reardon, who helped raise the bank for Gross when the gambler's operation was temporarily interrupted by his brief hitch in military service during World War II, stayed around. Reardon had left the department in 1947 but Reardon's brother Michael had remained on the police force, and he too was a part of the Gross operation. It was Michael Reardon who refused to name ten other policemen present at a bacchanal of whiskey and women thrown by Harry Gross in 1947 in gratitude toward his helpmates.

Federal agents arrested James Reardon in a $450-a-month Greenwich Village apartment in 1967 for a bookmaking operation with a new twist. Reardon had employed Westchester housewives to take his telephone calls, using a code which enabled him to call back the bettors from pay phone booths. The tactic forestalled use of a tap. Some of the suburban matrons thought they worked as an answering service for an insurance broker. Others were more sophisticated but for $50 to $100 a week they did not ask questions. Reardon paid cash to women on welfare for this work—an arrangement with mutual benefits.

In the Gross era, Reardon was known as the Squire of Connecticut. He lived in Westport, an unusual address for a policeman, but Reardon's assignment had been to the Chief Inspector's Confidential Squad, a sensitive post for any attempt to buy police protection. For his role in Harry Gross's business, Reardon sweated out a three year and eight months sentence on a perjury charge. Henry Morgenthau, Jr., the U.S. Attorney for the Southern District (of New York State), claimed that Reardon's 1967 gambling involved $1 million a month. Reardon had also branched out to legitimate business. He presided over a frozen food corporation with an annual gross of between $3 and $4 million.

Corruption of the Gross stamp continues to plague the department in spite of increased vigilance, higher salaries, and the rise of a more professional spirit among the policemen. One continuously erosive force is the public's demand for gambling. The ambiguity of the public position on wagering cropped up in 1954 when Deputy Chief Louis Goldberg of the Brooklyn Morals Squad was torpedoed while attempting to shut down church-run bingo games as illegal gambling. The word around the Department was that church bingo operations were not to be disturbed unless known hoods were discovered running the games (a common arrangement in charity affairs and street carnivals).

Goldberg drew no support for his action from any part of the public or the press. The *New York Herald Tribune,* normally a scourge of gambling enterprises, editorialized: "Being practical about bingo, all the law should do is draw a distinction between church bingo and Harry Gross corrupting hundreds of cops." (The statutes of the state and city made no such distinction, but Commissioner Francis Adams did. When Goldberg insisted on closing down the ecclesiastical games of chance, Commissioner Adams busted him to captain for insubordination. Goldberg retaliated by retiring at his former rank.)

The Brooklyn Morals Squad came under heavier fire in 1959. Sgt. Joseph Luberda, who had been a member of the unit until his retirement in 1956, was arrested for drunken driving in upstate Rockland County. In the car, Rockland police discovered $18,495 along with a list of known gamblers. The subsequent investigation uncovered a bookmaker who complained that three policemen had set up an illegal phone tap and used it to shake him down. When the District Attorney arrested the bookmaker he complained, "I might as well go back to pressing pants. Just yesterday I got hit for $500 from a deputy inspector."

The tide of corruption rose beyond the Morals Squad. Among those involved was an employee of the New York Telephone Company, William Hussey. If police secured a legal tap on a telephone they were obliged by law to notify the telephone company whose wire they had been listening to. Hussey worked in the security office of the utility and the information was available to him. At the time he was seized, Hussey blustered, "I've been the father to five-hundred cops and telephone men. If I go down, I won't go down alone, but will drag them with me." The investigation never went much beyond the initial splash and no wave of dismissals, such as those that followed the Harry Gross case, disturbed the police department. Cases of police corruption continue to come up. In 1968 an eight-year grand jury study indicted 37 members of the gambling ring, including 16 former cops and three men still on the force.

More cancerous signs of corruption have fingered policemen as traffickers in narcotics and, in at least one case, partners to murder. One case of police "heroism" during the 1950s which brought the death of a holdup man has since been explained as murder: an off-duty cop riding shotgun for a bookmaker killed an unlucky soul who was attempting to rob him of his fat bankroll.

Ghetto residents are firmly convinced that members of the narcotics division have profited from the sale of drugs. One periodic shakeup in 1968 indicted three top narcotics detectives for allegedly going into the business on their own. Unlike gambling, narcotics offers lower echelon officers the potential of large cash payoffs for failing to act or for serving as a partner in a transaction. The nearly $1 million allowed to the police department for "investigative expenses" largely falls to the 700-man narcotics division for use with informers and to make the necessary buys in order to catch peddlers. Detectives on this detail know full well that some of the money given informers is used by them to maintain their personal supply of heroin. While the idea of city money being used to support a drug habit may shock city fathers, no one has come up with a superior system for the arrest and conviction of dealers. The police consider the indirect effects of narcotics addiction one of their most serious problems. A high percentage of the city's murders, muggings, thefts, and holdups stem from the need by addicts for money to support the narcotics habit.

But addiction is one more offense for which the police receive little support from the public. Residents of a neighborhood may complain about a crowd of addicts hanging around dirtying hallways or hanging around a street corner, but the public has been unwilling to face up to the connection between syndicate-supported gambling and the narcotics trade. It is from illegal bookmaking and gambling, and the lawful enterprises at Las Vegas, Grand Bahama, and Nassau that Syndicate executives amass the capital necessary to finance the expensive importation of narcotics to the United States. The investment includes payoffs to permit the traffic to slip past customs, and evade federal, state, and local police restriction.

On a pettier scale there is police payola from merchants, saloons, hotels, and other commercial enterprises attempting to avoid days in court for minor offenses. What had been common practice since before the Lexow Committee made the front pages of newspapers again in January, 1968. A detective dropped one of those incriminating sheets listing establishments with figures beside them. The payers ranged from hotels such as the Waldorf-Astoria down to some of the lesser bars. An experienced cop explained, "Say you have some trouble in a place. A bartender sells a drink to somebody he shouldn't have or there's a fight. The police can make it very tough for the owner and all he wants is to avoid trouble. So he makes a regular Christmas payment. And when something happens in his place he hands out more money. Take a big hotel. When they have a problem, they want fast action. So they take care of the people in the precinct and they get good service when they need it. And if an arrest must be made in such a place it will be handled discreetly, without handcuffs, the prisoner leaving by a back door."

Many places operate on the fringe of legality. An unescorted woman customer having a drink at the bar may turn out to be a prostitute. A good customer may use the telephone to make book. A steady pair of male customers could be homosexuals. The one drink too many may lead a man to vehicular homicide (the law makes a saloonkeeper responsible for selling drinks to an intoxicated individual). One Queens bar claimed its police bill ran to $4,000 a year. While the owner swore he ran a shop devoid of illegality, a detective sniffed, "He must have had some joint to be willing to pay out that kind of money."

The Queens man told an interviewer that when he opened his bar twelve years before, men from the local precinct started dropping in. "You should meet the captain," said the best man. "And make me and yourself look good. Give him a hat." The price of hats varies with the state of the economy and in 1968 was supposedly worth $20 while a "suit" sold for $100 and a pack of cigarettes for $5.

Those who take this kind of money have their own justification. A retired captain recalled his career during the Depression. "I never took a cent until I had a kid with lobar pneumonia. The pediatrician, that thief, asked for $45. I didn't have it. I ran over to the nearest saloon and borrowed fifty bucks. I told my wife then that's the last time I'll ever be without money. In Queens, a guy offered me $3,000 a month for a crap game. I had twelve detectives and they would have grabbed the money. But I said no. I had promised the borough commander—no crap game. Then the guy said, be sensible—at least let me buy you a hat. I said, if I catch the game I'll take it with the bank, which was seventy-five big ones. To catch a game like that you'd have to get a call at four in the morning and get five guys from way out in leftfield and don't tell 'em where you're going."

An enthusiastic patrolman from the Tactical Patrol Force, who completed his tour with that unit, moved onto a detective squad. Within a few months he quit the Department. "It was all a matter of who you knew and would you take part in the payoffs. You had to have a rabbi (influential friend). I just couldn't take it after the TPF (an organization not known for its sensitivity on social problems but generally considered less corrupt than others)."

A uniformed cop working Manhattan's upper West Side was

offered an opportunity to become a plainclothesman. He rejected the ostensible promotion. "You have to become a taker. If you don't accept the graft then you get sent out to the boondocks. It's a system and you can't stay out of it once you put on plainclothes."

A young, black, college-educated cop was asked about reporter David Burnham's recent *New York Times* story on widespread police corruption. "I don't see anything wrong with taking money from gamblers or even prostitutes. I never took a cent but people want to gamble or buy a woman and I think that will be with us forever." Asked about payoffs to police by narcotics pushers he responded, "If I had a partner who took money from a pusher I'd tell him don't ever do that with me again. And I'd get a new partner. Then I'd bust that pusher so he'd get the idea that he can't pay off cops. But I wouldn't turn in the guy who took the bribe."

High officers know this attitude and officially decry it. Said a precinct commander, "If we don't stop it, it will ruin us." A deputy inspector gloomily observed that well over a century of corruption had "institutionalized corruption." He thought, "a generation of absolute honesty" was necessary if the tradition were to be ended.

Yet, not all the police work the payoff system. A youngish inspector, still active, speaks with cold contempt of accepting money from hotels, saloons, and businessmen. "It's like being a doorman and taking a tip. It's unprofessional." Late in 1970, Manhattan District Attorney Frank Hogan estimated as many as 1,000 cops on the take. He considered the figure not excessive in view of the temptations and size of the Department.

A senior officer points out how insistent citizens bearing gifts are: "Many policemen have to be nearly insulting in refusing gifts, but it's in the law not to accept them."

Reformers who have temporarily assumed command of the Department often abruptly cease inveighing against the police as the bulwark that supports vice and gambling. Inevitably, the new regime also speaks of the social evil and the willingness, indeed the desire, of the public to gamble or frequent houses of prostitution. Professional cops who work their way up through the ranks to the top posts have known this all along. During stressful times such as the early 1930s, when newspapers and public opinion railed at the police as the chief culprits responsible for the prevalence of illegal gambling, the professional cop would answer the critics and also assuage the injured or guilty feelings of his men. Commissioner James Bolan said, "It is difficult to say what particular laws a community takes seriously and what laws it is inclined to regard lightly." Bolan of course spoke at a time when most of the country participated in a gigantic conspiracy to break the Eighteenth Amendment. Continued Bolan in his indictment of the civil populace, "It is too simple and hypocritical to assume that all graft and crime are the acts of willful and wicked persons entirely set apart and distinguishable from the superior rest of us, and that the police can—if they so wish—separate this class and by vigorous application of the criminal law, eliminate crime at its root by incarcerating all evildoers." Boland added that the police represent "a simple cross-section of the public," and that same public offered no aid controlling gambling although it condemned the crimes arising from it.

The extent of police acceptance of corruption in gambling, prostitution, and narcotics is connected with Bolan's premises. Beyond that, some recognition must be given to even more basic attitudes from which policemen take their cue. Dick Croker had pointed out that if city officials were plundering the taxpayers through arrangements with contractors and businessmen he could ill afford to deny the lower echelons their petty booty, although he might consider it dirty graft. For that matter, the elements of New York that deplored the Dick Crokers found them profitable men to do business with. A policeman risking his neck for relatively little money reads every day in his newspaper that large respectable corporations engage in price-fixing and sweetheart deals, and bribe officials of cities such as New York. He can be blamed for accepting a payoff but it must be understood that he's following an ethic that had been institutionalized in the expense account. His experience is that society does not wish or expect the vices of gambling and prostitution to be totally extirpated. "Law-abiding" citizens show little alarm over betting and make jokes about prostitution. The courts demonstrate no concern over these infractions of the law, turning loose practitioners with punishments that do not merit the effort that must go into an arrest. Payments to police to permit gambling, prostitution, and immunization against nuisance charges reflect an imperfectly functioning economic and social order greased with minor lawbreaking to ease the frictions. The narcotics problem reflects graver societal ills but the peculiar characteristics of the drug trade make for enormous profits and difficult control. It too will continue to flourish as long as its economic and psychic benefits surpass the desires to wipe it out.

CHAPTER XX

CIVIL DISORDER

In dealing with vice, the police face activities that serve as a safety valve for the pressures generated within a society. The customers of vice (as opposed to the operators) are a part of society; they do not wish to see society destroyed and pose no threat to the police themselves. Civil dissent, whether that of the economically depressed, the racially oppressed, or the politically disenchanted, does threaten the social system. To the police, who see themselves as the first and last bastions of the social order, dissent directly threatens their own existence.

In the volatile development of the United States, civil dissent has vexed the New York City Police Department since its inception. The major troubles after World War I began with the Great Depression of 1929. Attempts to unionize local manufacturing widened the unrest.

Labor difficulties kept Johnny Broderick and his Industrial Squad busy. As soup kitchens formed and breadlines lengthened, the police found themselves interposed between the unhappy unemployed and those with a proprietary interest in maintaining the status quo.

Leaders of workers and dissidents in 1930 started to talk of a massive rally to protest the lack of jobs and the failure of the city government to provide adequate relief. When discussions of the demonstration first arose, Police Commissioner Whalen summoned three Communist leaders to his office. He informed them that city ordinances required a permit three days in advance of any outdoor event. The Communists refused to apply for a permit and stalked out of the meeting. Later, Whalen said, "I doubt if any police commissioner has ever been more openly defied." He had very little sympathy for radicals and was once quoted on Communists: "These enemies of society were to be driven out of New York regardless of their constitutional rights."

Crowd estimates of the 1930 Union Square rally vary from 35,000 to 50,000. It was certainly the largest affair of its nature ever put on by the Communists, whose actual membership fell well short of these figures, according to the police. Whalen's undercover men figured the exact number of Reds in the city was 9,567. To limit attendance, Whalen had arranged for the subways to make no stops in the vicinity of Union Square.

As orators whipped up emotions, the Commissioner in typical sartorial splendor, wearing a dark overcoat and homburg, watched the proceedings from a police booth. Newspaper photographers and silent film cameras got free rein but the Commissioner barred talking pictures. "I saw no reason for perpetuating treasonable utterances, and I don't mean to engage in censorship. But why glorify these people?"

The Union Square talk reached a fever pitch with the notion that the crowd should march to City Hall and demand help from Mayor James J. Walker. Whalen gave orders that no mass parade was to be allowed, and he rebuffed a request for permission from the Red officials. However, the Commissioner offered to drive some representatives to City Hall, but his offer was unacceptable to the higher spirits of the demonstration.

William Z. Foster, later U.S. Communist Party head, shouted out, "Are we going to stand for that?" His answer was a surge of people toward the streets leading to City Hall. A police emergency service truck immediately blocked the thoroughfare chosen by the crowd. The police met them with flailing nightsticks. Miss Sadie Van Veen was seized for kicking one officer in the stomach. A Negro was observed being beaten unconscious with blackjacks. One man claimed he was just a passerby who asked a patrolman how to escape from the mob. The cop reportedly shouted, "Give it to him," and several nearby detectives pounced on the civilian. One patrolman was seen holding a girl while another officer smashed his blackjack into her face three times. The editor of *Outlook Magazine* watched from his publication's office window as a dozen cops worked over two unarmed men. Some of the Communist Party hierarchy put colored cards in their hatbands to pass as reporters. The police were observed playing the same game. Scores of people suffered injuries; one cop went down when hit with a paving block. The Communist leaders were arrested.

The American Civil Liberties Union reviewed the police performance at the Union Square exhibition and gave the cops low grades. Commissioner Whalen had made the mistake of talking to the *New York Times*. "I thought I would crack my sides laughing at some of the undercover men who figured in the Union Square demonstration last Thursday. They went there as Reds, singing the *Internationale* and other Revolutionary songs of the Communists. They carried placards and banners demanding overthrow of the government and made just as much noise as the genuine Reds. But the fun started when one of the undercover men started to razz a cop. He got a terrific punch in the eye and was knocked down before the cop was pulled off." Whalen added that he had assigned men to this duty because of a Communist attempt to subvert school kids. Whalen even managed to suppress the newsreel films of the Union Square battle.

The Commissioner's interview embarrassed him considerably when defense attorneys for five arrested Communist leaders brought up the subject in court. Whalen denied that he laughed at anything that occurred in the demonstration or that an undercover agent carried a banner. However, he never made a public denial of the *Times* account.

Court proceedings also provoked the ire of the American Civil Liberties Union. The men arrested at Union Square were taken before Judge William McAdoo on misdemeanor charges. Judge McAdoo refused to take action for hours, thereby keeping the men in jail. He did not set any bail at first although it is mandatory in a misdemeanor. When Judge McAdoo finally did name a figure it was exorbitant and not until he was threatened with legal action did McAdoo set a figure for William Z. Foster.

The police department wielded billies with abandon against Communists or groups identified as left-wingers, but the cops were not unsympathetic to the problems of the poor during the 1930s. Men from the department contributed $35,522 a month to relief programs. Officers making less than $2,500 a year gave a dollar a month and those in the $5,000 bracket put up $5 monthly. Headquarters ordered the cop on the beat to look around the neighborhood to find the destitute and the hungry and to locate jobs by talking to storekeepers. Police records show that 71,145 people received help from the police in a two-week period.

Far more troublesome for the police than the commotions of the proletariat have been eruptions resulting from racial tensions. During the Depression, one of these disorders briefly boiled over in Harlem. On March 19, 1935, in a Harlem branch of the S. H. Kress store that employed blacks only in menial jobs, Lino Rivera, a sixteen-year-old black boy, was seen by store manager, Jackson Smith, a Southerner, shoplifting a knife. Rivera was grabbed and Smith and an assistant began to haul him out to the street. During the scuffle, Rivera bit them. A policeman named Donahue arrived. He brought the youth back into the store and asked if some arrest was desired but Smith demurred. For some inexplicable reason, Donahue then took the boy down to the basement and released him from a door opening out to the back alley. A shopper however began to yell that they were taking the boy into the basement to beat him.

Out front an ambulance pulled up, apparently called by mistake because of the bites Lino Rivera inflicted. No patient entered the ambulance, but a passerby noticed a hearse standing nearby. Rumors spread that the boy had been killed. Some women searched the store looking for the corpse and found nothing, but the rumors attracted angry crowds.

The store shut its doors and a speaker harangued the people in the street. Police dragged the orator off and began arresting his audience on charges of unlawful assemblage. Rioting now broke out, including "larceny" (now known as looting), according to the *N.Y. Times*. A dozen men were charged with attempted arson.

Two Harlem groups, the Young Liberators and the Young Communist League, circulated leaflets that Rivera lay near death from abuse meted out by the cops. These flyers, however, reached the streets long after violence had hit a crescendo in Harlem. Some of the steam went out of the disorder with the publication of a photograph of Lino Rivera with Lt. Samuel Battle, a black police lieutenant, who had been the first black man to join the department, in 1911.

An investigation after the riots summarized: "We find much to criticize in the conduct of the police." The report said "widespread hostility" on the part of the law-abiding element "among the colored people toward the police is proof positive there is something wrong in the attitude of the officers toward the people, whom they are there to serve and to aid, not to browbeat."

The investigatory panel cited a witness who reported, "I said to the policeman, can't you tell us what happened?" The answer was "If you know what's good for you, you better get on home." People who had been arrested at the street corner meeting shortly after the rumors about Lino Rivera's death began circulating claimed that police had beaten them, and that the police denied access to attorneys and served no food for almost twenty-four hours.

The one fatality of the riot died in a fog of doubt. Patrolman John McInery shot and fatally wounded Lloyd Hobbs, sixteen. The officer reported that the Hobbs boy had been looting an automotive supply store of a horn and a socket wrench. A witness denied that the youth had been stealing and also swore that no warning shot had been fired. The panel concluded that the shooting was inexcusable and the failure of a grand jury to indict McInery was due to "mayoralty pressure" on the DA.

Actually the turbulence boiled in Harlem for days after the initial disorder, according to the investigation. On March 23, Patrolman Zabutinski went to arrest a drunk, Edward Laurie. The drunk died from a fractured skull. Thomas Aiken, waiting for food from the relief bureau, objected when police shoved him out of the line he had waited in for three hours. He lost an eye as a result of the skirmish.

The inquiry into the causes of the 1935 riot focused in part on police abuses. Critics pointed to the practice of entering private Harlem dwellings on almost any pretext to search for policy slips. In their defense the police argued that they had a right to search and seize if they had a reasonable suspicion of a felony. But lawyer and civil libertarian Arthur Garfield Hays pointed out that the penal code permitted such an entry only if the law enforcement forces knew a felony had been committed, not if they merely thought so.

Samuel Battle appeared as a character witness for the department. Ironically, Battle, a magnificent physical specimen in his youth, somehow had not been able to pass the physical examination when he applied for an appointment to the force in 1911. Only through the political intercession of a powerful black politician of that era, Charles Anderson, did Battle get on the force as the first Negro. Years later, for the Schomburg Collection of Negro history, Battle recorded memories of his early days on the force when sightseers came to Harlem for the novelty of a black cop and children yelled, "There goes the nigger cop, there goes the nigger cop."

But in spite of Battle's protestations of police and governmental virtues, one witness at the inquiry cried, "If there is another riot in Harlem, we'll blame the Mayor's Commission for it. You're not dealing with pussyfooting Negroes now...."

Summing up, the Committee recommended an advisory group drawn from Harlem citizens discuss complaints about the police, and described a policeman who kills as "somebody who becomes at once, prosecutor, judge, jury, and executioner." Nothing changed in Harlem as a result of the riot or the study. Not so coincidentally, however, that spring a black detective became the first member of his race to win the department's highest award, the medal of honor, after he shot it out with an extortioner.

The summer of 1943 brought the simmering ghetto of Harlem to a boil once again. At a sleazy hotel, a twenty-six-year-old off-duty black military policeman, Robert Bandy, scuffled with white patrolman James Collins, who was arresting a woman for disorderly conduct. The soldier allegedly grabbed the cop's nightstick and the patrolman wounded him in the shoulder with a bullet. The violence brought 5,000 police into Harlem, five people died, and 500 blacks including 100 women were arrested for looting.

Major outbreaks of disorder rocked the ghettos of New York in 1964, 1967, and 1968. The first began with an encounter between a seventeen-year veteran of the Department, Lt. Thomas Gilligan, and a fifteen-year-old black youth named James Powell. Gilligan was thirty-seven and lived in an all-white middle-income housing project in lower Manhattan. He had an excellent record including nineteen citations. In 1958, he wrestled with a prowler on a roof and in spite of a broken wrist shot his assailant when he attempted to flee. On another occasion, a youth breaking into parked automobiles near Gilligan's apartment smashed two of the lieutenant's fingers with a fire hose nozzle when the cop grabbed him. Gilligan shot him. On at least four occasions Gilligan disarmed suspects; he had rescued a woman and some children in fires, saved a man trapped in a basement from an explosion, resuscitated an unconscious person through first aid, prevented a would-be suicide, and used mouth-to-mouth respiration to save the life of a woman with an overdose of barbituates.

James Powell at fifteen had already brushed against the law four times in his short life. He had been cleared of attempted robbery, breaking a car window, and boarding a subway train and a bus without paying the fares. In July of 1964 Powell was a summer school pupil on East 76th Street in Manhattan. He lived in a low-rent Bronx housing project.

Along with other school kids, Powell had gotten into an argument with a building superintendent near the summer school. The youths often sat on the stoop of an apartment house, sometimes discarding litter. After words passed between the super and the youngsters, the former sprayed his adversaries with a garden hose. The boys began tossing garbage can lids and bottles.

Gilligan was off duty and in a radio repair store nearby. Hearing the commotion, he rushed out and attempted to quell the disturbance. He confronted Powell. Agreement on the facts ends at this point. A companion of Powell, Clifton Harris, later testified that Powell had left home with two knives. Harris said Powell handed the knives to friends to carry and obtained one back from Harris just before facing Lt. Gilligan.

The police officer swore that the youth advanced on him with a knife in hand and did not halt either on command or after a warning shot was fired. Eye witnesses said they indeed saw Powell raise his hand but either saw no knife or insisted it was only a gesture of trying to ward off a blow. Gilligan fired two shots that killed Powell, and as the boy lay on the pavement Clifton Harris rushed up to ask if the officer should call an ambulance.

Allegedly Gilligan replied, "No, this black —— is my prisoner. You call an ambulance." Later the police produced in court a knife which they asserted had dropped from Powell's hand when he was shot. Ghetto residents claimed that it was a plant. Adversaries of the police maintain that cops habitually carry items that can be attributed to opponents and justify the use of force.

The shooting occurred on a Thursday. On Saturday a demonstration in the streets of Harlem turned into a parade to the 28th Precinct house at West 123rd Street. Police blocked entry to the station house. Bottles and other missiles rained down upon the officers who then seized control of the neighboring roofs and began to make arrests.

Using a bullhorn, the police ordered the people to go home. The blacks of Harlem answered, "We are home, you go home." A phalanx of TPF, the Tactical Patrol Force, shock troops of riot duty, charged the throngs outside the station house, breaking up knots of people who then shattered store windows, began looting, and set fire to paper-filled trash receptacles.

In the early hours of the trouble the police had not even employed their clubs but as the situation worsened they not only resorted to nightsticks but started to fire pistols into the air to drive people off the roofs from where they had showered stones and bottles down on the bluecoats.

The gunfire, according to some reporters, convinced the black people that a massacre was imminent. A man telephoned the *Herald Tribune* and inquired as to the quickest means of reaching Governor Nelson Rockefeller since "the Goldwater thing had started." Another caller begged the newspaper to print accounts of the disorders so that people outside of Harlem would know what was being done to the residents.

Reporter Bill Whitworth heard an aged lady say, "They want to shoot all of the black people." Someone else commented, "They wouldn't do all this gunslinging and clubbing on 42nd Street." For all the bullets (about 2,000, according to the official accounting), only one man was killed and thirty wounded.

The disorder raged on, spreading to the other large ghetto, Bedford Stuyvesant in Brooklyn.

For the first time, white reporters who had long enjoyed an immunity from violence while covering outbursts in the black sections discovered they too were subject to the rage of the community. Several were beaten and it took black newsmen to rescue others from the threats of people on the streets.

Black policemen probably suffered the most pressure. A woman was heard to holler at one, "If you were my husband, I'd beat you to death." The authorities, recognizing the effects of the continuous taunting and strain, rotated their men with fresh reserves frequently as some police began to react to their antagonists with the kind of force that only spurred the hysteria.

Mayor Robert F. Wagner was in Europe; the head of the City Council, Paul Screvane, broadcast an appeal for order and hinted that subversion lay behind the disturbance. When Wagner returned he ignored the notion of conspiracy and spoke soberly of the need for reconciliation, order in the streets, and improvements in the way of life of the minority people. By then the fury of the few days was spent.

Police commanders in Bedford Stuyvesant as well as in Harlem attempted to get "community" leaders to halt demonstrations but no one could control the mobs, nor for that matter could the precinct people single out effective leaders.

Fred Shapiro and James Sullivan wrote in their book *Race Riots, N.Y. 1964:* "Negroes were beaten, some brutally, in Bedford-Stuyvesant that night. Yet, for the most part, New York City police operated under the greatest restraint and discipline ever imposed on an American police department, and did it creditably."

Other reporters agreed that restraint keynoted most police efforts, although in the ghetto opinions varied. Incidents of overreaction were cited. "Sure we made mistakes," said Commissioner Michael Murphy, an officer who had risen from the ranks. "You do in any war." The death toll in other cities that year and later supports the impression of restraint.

A grand jury subsequently found Gilligan innocent of any wrong-doing as did a departmental investigation. To illustrate the complexity of the situation in 1964, policemen could point out that when Bedford-Stuyvesant residents went to police headquarters to protest, local whites pelted them with garbage, bottles, and obscenities. As a final note to 1964 the police reported that during the height of the riot scene, a cop cornered a man waving a knife in Times Square. The officer drew his gun, but held his fire for fear of wounding passersby. As a result the cop was badly slashed in the neck and barely survived.

Detroit was still burning in the summer of 1967 when Manhattan's Puerto Rican district was seared by riot. The match was lit in the course of a street fight between two youths over a girl. They slashed at one another with knives until a patrolman wounded one who had turned his fury on an officer, cutting him on the arms. Word spread that the police had killed the blade-wielder without warning. Later, the boy did die in the hospital.

Window-smashing, looting, and some shooting at police followed, and the helmeted Tactical Patrol Force drove crowds off the streets. Mayor John Lindsay hurried to town from his summer home on Long Island to walk the streets and talk with residents. His aides with contacts in the community also circulated through the East Harlem area trying to keep peace. One of them answered a distress call from a young man in the not-too-tender clutches of the Tactical Patrol Force. The cops switched their attention to the Mayor's assistant and he had already received a clout on the head when Commissioner Howard Leary, on the scene, halted the beating with the cry, "He's one of ours."

The residents complained to the Mayor about the presence of the TPF. "They don't know us; they aren't with us; they don't understand us." Then they praised Lindsay. "At least we've got a sympathetic mayor. At least we've got a way of reaching those damn cops."

When quiet was restored, two Puerto Ricans had died of bullets fired by police, and an inquest determined that the young victim whose eventual demise started the uproar had actually been fatally wounded by the knife during the fight that had brought in the police in the first place.

The 1968 disorders followed the assassination of Dr. Martin Luther King. Only four hundred people were arrested, no fatalities were recorded nor did the police fire any shots. For this effort the ACLU praised the police but a number of merchants sued the city for failing to defend their property effectively. Critics of the administration said that the Mayor had tied the hands of the police and kept them from proper action. Officials in Newark, Chicago, and Los Angeles scoffed at New York for allegedly having managed to cover up a major disorder.

The end of what was a relatively quiet summer in 1968 threatened to turn into a volcanic outburst. Shortly after three Cleveland police died in a shoot-out with black militants, and while Huey Newton, the California Black Panther leader, was on trial for the murder of an Oakland officer, two Brooklyn policemen answered a routine request to intercede in a domestic quarrel. In the early hours of the morning, the pair walked toward the entrance to a building in the turbulent Crown Heights section. A shotgun ambush blasted both of them.

While the officers recovered from their wounds, the Brooklyn Assistant District Attorney announced that his office had reason to believe that the trap had been laid by three members of the Black Panthers who were being sought. The group, however, denied any involvement and a city official later agreed that there was no evidence to link the Black Panthers with the affair.

A few days later, firemen fighting a blaze in Brooklyn were pelted with rubbish. It had become so common for ghetto residents to bombard fire trucks that all companies in troubled areas had built shields to protect the men riding the trucks. Police near the Brooklyn fire site attempted to arrest three Black Panthers on the accusation that they had participated in the attack on the firemen. The trio resisted, and when they were arraigned in court, the charge of assaulting policemen led the court to set high bail.

Defense attorneys sought another court hearing to get lower bail. The courtroom was packed with off-duty cops and in the hallway of the Brooklyn Criminal Court another large contingent of off-duty officers and their friends awaited the judge's decision. An elevator let off a handful of Black Panthers with some white allies. A witness said that a large man in a beige polo shirt with a tell-tale bulge over his service revolver shouted, "There are the Black Panthers, let's get them." The whites, presumably police, surrounded the small number of Panthers. Outsiders, beyond the hurly-burly, saw blackjacks whipping in the air. Uniformed police broke up the mêlée, but without making any arrests, and they gave the Black Panthers a safe escort for a few blocks. A reporter who attempted to get names or information from the assailants got no answers to his questions, though he received a steady tattoo of kicks in his shins. One Black Panther dripped blood from a scalp wound, and a white girl also was bloodied.

Some of the off-duty policemen (Commissioner Howard Leary who ordered an investigation agreed that police had participated) wore Wallace for President buttons and shouted "White Power" and "Win with Wallace." Mayor Lindsay denounced the behavior of the participants.

A splinter organization, known as the Law Enforcement Group, had recently surfaced as the voice of right-wing adherents in the Department. It had originally been formed after several thousand policemen signed a petition protesting Judge Michael Furey's tolerance for alleged raucous behavior by Black Panthers and their supporters in his court. The first demands of LEG included the end of any civilian complaint review board even within Department control, the elimination of civilian employees in precinct houses, an inquiry into the fitness of Furey to hold his post, support for senators opposed to "the Warren Court," and higher standards for candidates to the force.

A leaflet, ostensibly signed by LEG officers, had urged that policemen stand up and be counted at the trial of the Black Panthers. Defense counsel for the accused called the appearances of the off-duty cops in the court intimidation. A patrolman who served as executive chairman of the group denied that LEG issued the leaflet. The organization also fought the suspension before Departmental trial of a patrolman accused of beating and kicking a suspect.

After formal incorporation, LEG dropped the demands for an end to the civil complaint bureau, the elimination of civilian employees, and the imposition of higher physical standards that Puerto Ricans claimed would discriminate against them because of their smaller stature. The group also stopped its attack on Judge Furey.

Members of the Department took a cautious attitude toward the upstart organization. A lieutenant called it a policeman's parallel to the New Left that attracted youth. LEG satisfied the younger men in the Department who felt frustrated by the hostility of the community and the restraints placed upon officers. The *Times* interviewed a number of officers who saw some justification even for the courthouse attack on the Panthers. "If you felt it was the only way to get things done . . ." Sentiments for George Wallace were echoed by men on post. "He [Wallace] usually backs the Police Department." "He seems more or less to have a principle of live and let live." A deputy inspector said, "I don't see why anyone is surprised. Eighty-five percent of the police voted for Goldwater in 1964." William Kunstler, the attorney for the Black Panthers, seized the occasion to file a suit for community control of the police along the lines of the controversial school decentralization program.

The birth of LEG indicated that unanimity did not rule within the Department's lower ranks. Even John Cassese, president of the Patrolman's Benevolent Association, denounced LEG, and he could hardly be labeled soft on criminals or procedures that in the eyes of cops protected malefactors. Cassese was supported by PBA delegates in a resolution that threatened any policeman who supported LEG or "radicalism or extremism" with having to forfeit his rights. Although he said he was not convinced that any police had taken part in the courthouse brawl, Cassese was firm that officers could not take the law into their own hands. From the other side Cassese received a challenge from the Traffic Patrolman's Association objecting to his earlier call for total enforcement of the letter of the law. Some of the opposition of this group was said to flow from Cassese's failure to invite their adviser to a PBA convention.

Even without the Black Panther opposition, the police in 1968 had reason for anxiety. Well before the summer, rumors circulated of plots by black extremists to attack police. A sergeant at a New York National Guard training unit told one of his fellow part-time soldiers that police intelligence had learned of a scheme whereby, on signal, members of police families would be gunned down. The reign of terror would force every cop to stay at home to protect his wife and children, leaving the city without police. As a practical scheme for disrupting the city, it had some obvious flaws. But the fact that members of the force actually believed this alleged plan suggested the anxiety of the police.

In the immediate aftermath of the Black Panther mêlée, the Mayor's office attempted to mediate. Members of the black group met in a Manhattan office building with some high officials of the Department. The cops sat and listened while the Panthers told them the "pigs would have to stop their racist actions or they would be driven out." The black-bereted, black-jacketed young men, however, continued to be arrested by police for disorderly conduct and other minor offenses. All across the country the Panthers drew attacks from law-enforcement agencies with charges that included murder, and twenty-one were indicted in New York, accused of plots to bomb stores and government offices. On the other hand assaults and sniper attacks on cops have steadily increased nationwide.

The supplement to the initial report of the National Advisory Commission on Civil Disorders includes an opinion survey of attitudes by whites and nonwhites. Part of the sampling came from New York City and it is therefore reasonable to equate the findings with opinions about and by New York cops.

The Kerner Commission in this supplement said, "We asked several questions about the effects of race on treatment and discovered only limited support for the notion that replacement of whites by blacks will make any great difference to most Negroes. With regard to whether black policemen treat Negroes better than do white policemen, 73 percent of the sample could not see any difference; the rest were divided somewhat more in favor of white policemen than Negro policemen." The survey came up with negative sentiments on black storekeepers as fairer or more respectful to

Negro customers. The study showed support for more black cops but mainly as a source of jobs rather than because black police would be more sympathetic to black problems.

Better than 50 percent of the white respondents thought that Negroes did not suffer unnecessary roughness or disrespect from police compared to the treatment accorded to whites. About 20 percent of the male black sample (10 percent of the female) said they had personally experienced insulting treatment from police and better than 43 percent believed that police treated blacks badly. Another complaint was that the cops failed to show up quickly enough when summoned. (This was the opinion of 51 percent of the blacks but less than 30 percent of the whites.) Roughly 25 percent of the blacks said they had experienced delays themselves; from 31 to 35 percent knew of them happening to someone they knew.

Almost three and one half times as many blacks as whites (42 percent to 12 percent) believed police frisked or searched people without good reason. The charge of roughing up people unnecessarily was made by 37 percent of the black males, 32 percent of the females. For both sexes, the percentage of those who actually suffered such treatment fell well below 10 percent although more than 20 percent said they knew someone who had experienced physical abuse.

When it came to perception of Negro experiences, one occupational group, the police, on their part were less conscious of anti-black discrimination than were members of other occupational categories (merchants came a close second to the police in holding this attitude). Political workers, social workers, and educators all perceived more discrimination against Negroes than did employers, merchants, and police. Police, more than any other occupational group considered black progress too rapid. The Commission concluded, "The same occupational groups who tend to see that the Negroes in their city are relatively well off, progressing well over the past five years, are also the same groups who feel that Negroes are pushing too fast for improving their position."

The black cop has suffered an ambiguous role in the Department from the beginning. New York, like almost every city, shows

a disproportionately small percentage of black cops in comparison
to the number of black people living in the community. Not until
1965 did a black man get command of a uniformed precinct. Statistics from the National Advisory Commission on Civil Disorders
shows that in New York, with 16 percent of its population nonwhite, 5 percent of the police are nonwhite.

Former patrolman Gene Radano in a book of reminiscences,
Walking the Beat, reported locker room talk. "I'm standing on
116th Street and Lenox Avenue (Harlem). The place is boiling. We
had orders not to use force. Anyway there's these five colored guys
on the corner. I go over and say, 'I'm sorry men, but you can't
stand here. You're going to have to move on.' They look at me with
contempt and ignore me. I repeat to them, 'I'm sorry, fellows, but
you can't stand there.' They still ignore me. Now I don't know
what to do."

"I'd lay the stick across their backs."

"You couldn't. That would start a riot. . . . Suddenly a well-
built Negro cop shoots by me with his stick half-raised. 'Move you
black bastards,' he says, 'or I'll cave in your skulls.' They grumbled
but they moved."

"If it was us we'd be up for brutality."

"To tell you the truth, I was sure glad he was there."

A veteran black cop reaches into his memory to show how it
was. "A Negro cop used to get lots of insults. Once I was sent to
break up a family fight among some Irish people. The woman who
called for a cop said, 'What the hell are you doing here? Go back
and tell that sergeant to send me a white policeman.' " Nor were
brother officers easier on him. One day two white cops stopped
him, simply because he was driving a Cadillac. And of course there
is the animosity of his own people. "Some blacks feel a Negro commander should let them break the law because they're black."
Ghetto people flayed black policemen attempting to control civil
disorder with comments about their manhood and selling out soul
brothers. For the cop assigned to riot duty on his home turf the
emotional pressures squeezed hard. Says one, "You can imagine
my feelings when they brought the ammunition cars into my home
area. There were people [police] shooting indiscriminately. In the

summer of 1967, I was standing next to a police car when a call came in that there was a sniper on 117th Street. Three guys piled out of the police car and started shooting wildly."

During the 1968 school decentralization fracas in the Ocean Hill-Brownsville sector of Brooklyn, black Inspector Lloyd Sealy was threatened, "We know where you live." When Sealy protested that the police did not initiate the confrontation a voice yelled, "You nigger, you're next."

The police abuse of minorities reflects the basic division of America into white and black societies. As a white-oriented group with strongly ingrained lower-middle-class sentiments the police will continue to be in conflict with nonwhites, until the nation's racial problems become resolved. As defenders of the established order, the police once visited their abuse on another out group, the labor movement. Unions have achieved respectability within the U.S. (to the point where the police themselves practice collective bargaining) and the conflict between labor and the police in New York has disappeared. For all of the courses in human relations given to New York City police, race will continue to be a focus of abuse until color of skin loses its importance in the U.S. At best, indoctrination in racial harmony, coupled with strong discipline that punishes racist-inspired abuse, can lower the temperature of the city. But it cannot eliminate the fevers.

CHAPTER XXI

DEMONSTRATIONS AND DISSENTERS

Although the third degree has lost its vogue and complaints of police abuses directed against minority groups dropped in the first year of the Lindsay Administration, dissenters and demonstrators came to believe that open season had been declared against them. A member of the New Left insisted that the word from the Mayor's Urban Action Task Force was "take it easy on the blacks but beat the crap out of the hippies."

Demonstrations by dissenters have sporadically troubled the city, but only in the last few years have they become a consistently irritated boil on the body politic. And as the picket line or protest march lost power to effect immediate changes in policies, the mood of the demonstrators has become more and more fractious.

Even when the mass protest has been physically placid, the police, goaded by the invective hurled at them by the protestors and by the protestors' ideas, have come on strong. Hippies, dropouts from the middle-class folkways that are ingrained in the police, have on several occasions aroused a show of police force.

At Tompkins Square on May 30, 1967, a band of hippies had secured a Parks Department permit for a musicale. Nevertheless, police attempted to break up the sessions which featured bongos and guitars and a cacophony of chanters. The hippies refused to disperse when ordered, and arrests as well as clubbing followed. In court, the judge threw out the cases because there were no reasonable grounds for arrest. In his decision, the judge wrote, ". . . it is not inappropriate to state that one officer testified that the sergeant told him to arrest five people. When asked by the Court 'Any five?' his answer was 'Yes, any five.' "

A far more excessive performance occurred at Grand Central Railroad Station on March 22, 1968, when a variant group, the Yippies, attempted to celebrate the vernal equinox. The New York Civil Liberties Union put together a report for the Mayor from witnesses present that night.

"David Lyle, a magazine editor, arrived at 11:45 P.M. 'The main waiting room was filled with people. Most seemed to be recognizably of the sort I expected to find—those who had responded to the Yippie call. Also present were the sort of midtown standers-around that one encounters in any quasi-public place. There were also a few apparent train travelers, and there were police.'

"Roger Vaughan, a writer for *Life* magazine, said, 'The place was already very crowded, enough so that movement across the floor of the station was slow and difficult. There was a festive spirit in the air. Many people had brought balloons with them, and had set them in motion by tapping them into the air. . . . At about 1:00 A.M. the spirit of the gathering was a bit more chaotic than it had been at midnight. Large segments of the group would decide to sit down for a while, usually centered around some kind of activity (a guitarist, for example). A few conga lines started, but were short-lived because of the density of the crowd. It was tough enough to move slowly as an individual, let alone moving rapidly in a group dance. Occasionally chants started, sometimes accompanied by a coordinated movement to jump up and down in rhythm to the chant. These activities too were short-lived.'

"Manfred Wolkeiser, who was passing through the Station said . . . , 'The police made no effort whatsoever to bar . . . persons from the station or to discourage them from entering. I was under the impression that they approved of the demonstration. The crowd was festive, a girl gave me a flower, and many were singing.' Around 12:35, Wolkeiser saw 'Inspector Garelik standing in front of the policemen in civilian clothes. At about 12:45 I saw a larger group of people climbing on the Information Booth. I would guess about nine or ten. At that point, Inspector Garelik called a uniformed policeman over and said that he should get these people down from there.'

"Some time after 12:45, according to David Lyle, more people began to mount the Information Booth and move the hands of the clock. Roger Vaughan says that 'In short order, the hands of all four clock faces had been removed. Now I would say that this was the first (and only) action I saw which was a legitimate cause for arrests to be made. It is not the reason for police action that I question, but the way in which that action was carried out.'

"Several persons, on or around the information booth at the time of the first police charge, say they heard no warning to get off the booth, nor were they arrested while on the Information Booth, but rather while trying to run from the station.

"According to David Lyle, the police rushed toward the Information Booth at almost the same time that people began to leave it. The perchers had almost all hit the floor before the police reached the booth. Roger Vaughan adds, 'People actually started getting down from the information booth before the police charged. But the police charged anyway. There was no warning whatsoever. Having taken a number of trains from Grand Central, I know there is a public address system but this facility was not used at this point, or at any point up until I left the station at 2:30 A.M. The police didn't use bull horns, and no attempt at verbal communication was made that I could detect. The police simply formed a column of twos, as they say at Ft. Dix, and with night sticks flailing indiscriminately, charged the Information Booth as though it was a pillbox containing a machine gun. There were perhaps forty to fifty police in that first charge. People standing quietly as much as sixty to seventy feet from the Information Booth, people who had nothing whatsoever to do with the defacing of the clocks, were slammed into unmercifully and without warning by the sheer force of the police charge. People who had no idea what was happening felt the crack of clubs on their heads as the police made for their objective. These could have been Yippies, commuters waiting for their trains, women, girl members of the press—anyone. On the first charge I saw at least a dozen people go crashing to the marble floor of the station.'

"Josh Edelman, a high school student, says, 'About one o'clock, when the cops took the Information Booth, I remember seeing people being beaten on the floor with clubs. In addition, the people nearest the cops were shoved and hit in the back with clubs, as they ran.' David Lyle saw 'the police cut a swath to the booth by wielding their night sticks at anyone or anything in their way . . . Attack is the word of choice.' Dwight Bayne, a student at the New School, saw '. . . with no prior notice or warning, a wedge of maybe thirty to fifty cops charged from the 42nd Street side towards the Information Booth forcing a path with their nightclubs. In the mêlée that followed, people were thrown, or clubbed, to the ground, trampled upon and brutalized. Panic existed for a moment as a wave of cops surrounded the booth and threatened to charge the crowd.' Monte Stettin, a student, was 'walking towards the 42nd Street exit at about 12:50 when the police started massing in large groups with their night sticks ready for use. Being a photographer, I naturally tried to move towards the center of the floor, as the police broke into a series of wedges and commenced violent clubbing on any and all people in their immediate vicinity . . . At this point I began to run towards the exit.' He was arrested at the 42nd Street exit.

"Leo Barnett, Director of the Computer at L.I.U. Brooklyn Center, describes what he saw of the police behavior. 'At about 12: 45 A.M., without any warning at all, the police came charging into the main waiting room from the 42nd Street side, in a 'V' shaped [inverted] phalanx formation. They were running at full speed, swinging their night sticks. They grabbed people in the crowd and dragged them into the 42nd Street waiting room. This was repeated three or four times. Later, [when he was] on 42nd Street, the police came charging through the doors onto 42nd Street, creating panic among the bystanders, again hitting people at random and arresting people for no apparent reason.'

"Peter Stander and his wife were both arrested. His wife describes what happened after the first police charge, when she returned to the Station to look for her husband and her handbag. 'The first thing I saw was a man, lying face down, and three policemen over him, beating him with their sticks. He was in shirt sleeves. . . . I did not associate him with my husband because my husband was wearing a jacket . . . but when the policemen got off him and started dragging him by the belt and by his hair toward the 42nd Street exit, [she recognized him]. I started to follow them. At the first doors leading to 42nd Street I was stopped by a policeman . . .' After a brief exchange she was allowed to pass. She next saw her husband in front of the second doors to 42nd Street. 'He was being beaten up by a policeman in plainclothes; a uniformed policeman was looking on and holding my husband's jacket. My husband was bleeding profusely and looked quite unconscious. I walked towards them and said he was my husband. The policeman in uniform handed me the jacket and left. The plainclothesman went on beating my husband and dragging him towards the exit.' She followed them out onto the street, where she was put into the police wagon with her husband. She was informed at 4:00 A.M. at the 17th Precinct that she was under arrest. Mr. Stander describes the incident. 'I was struggling through the crowd in the direction I last saw her [his wife] when I was stopped, shoved and prodded by a policeman. I automatically grabbed the wrong end of the night stick that was buried in my abdomen. It was snatched out of my hand and my abdomen and brought down on my head. I think I must have lost consciousness for a moment. The next thing I remember I was lying in a sea of blue legs and being kicked. As I struggled to my feet I was clubbed and punched. I fell again and was kicked and dragged along. One cop grabbed my belt and hoisting me by it dragged me along on my face. I remember only hands and fists and feet after that, and the recollection that first my jacket was pulled off, then my sweater and finally my shirt was pulled up over my head. The next thing I remember outside of a long drag, was being in the Paddy Wagon. At the station house I was left to bleed for over an hour until the police had collected an ambulance full. One trip saves all that energy.'

"Mrs. Boyd Zinman, the wife of an exporter and former stockbroker from Yonkers, New York, was passing through Grand Central on her way from the opera with a friend. She was quoted in the New York *Post* of March 26th as saying that as she was walking behind the track doors, she saw four cops drag a youth behind the gates as their commanding officer looked on approvingly. 'They had his arms pulled up behind him and they were giving him a terrible beating. I walked up and I said, "Does it take four your size to beat one kid?" The captain then walked over, he was only about three feet away, and he said, "You want to be pulled in lady? Mind your own business!" Then he asked me where I was going. I said I was waiting for a train. He said, "Well, get on it or I'll pull you in." '

"After the first police charge there were repeated charges, apparently in an attempt to clear the Station completely. However, there was still no use of the public address system, bullhorn, or any effort to get the crowd to peacefully leave the station. At some point after the first police charge, Abbie Hoffman, a member of YIP, attempted to negotiate with Barry Gottehrer from the Mayor's office to use the Station's public address system. He was told that it was too late, 'It's already a police action,' and that further intervention on the part of the Mayor's office was impossible.

"Marthe Schiller saw a young man at the bottom of the stairs as the police wedge approached. 'He stumbled on the steps before the policemen as they were marching up the steps. He could not get himself away from them fast enough to escape getting hit on the head with a night stick by the two leading policemen. He was hit continually as he was trying to get up the stairs. The two policemen were taking turns hitting him on the head. He was bleeding profusely.' The name of this young man is Edward Perlmutter, treasurer for the Social Service Employees Union. In his words, 'I had to go back into the station [after the initial charge] since I had left a female companion at the stairwell and was, frankly, quite concerned as to what might have happened to her. As I was walking on the floor of the station, I spotted a detective and indicated to him my indignation toward the use of force by the police. He was very discourteous and told me he was too busy to talk. As I was walking back toward the stairway on the left of the station, suddenly people started running as about ten policemen attempted to push people up the stairway—at the same time, they were swinging their sticks at everybody. I tripped going up the stairway, which unfortunately slowed me down. As I backed up the stairway one policeman was swinging a stick on my right leg continuously. I made the mistake of turning to my right in an attempt to get a view of his badge number. He noticed my attempt and clubbed me over the top of the head. I left Grand Central bleeding, assisted by some individuals who hustled me out of the Station before anyone was able to arrest me. I ended up in Bellevue Hospital where they stitched up my head.'

"Nicholas Von Hoffman, a reporter for the Washington *Post* who was present at the YIP-IN, is the only person to report that the police 'at first were pretty nice about trying to clear the station.' However, he adds, 'but then something happened to them and they began to use their clubs. They drove the kids up the inclined ramp of the 42nd Street entrance banging them in the knees, the groin, the stomach, and the head. They pushed one boy head-first through a glass door. Almost none of them fought back as they were driven up the cattle-run to the street.'

"John Putnam, a magazine art director, walked up the 42nd Street ramp. 'I saw police officers violently pushing, clubbing, and arm-twisting young people as they were forcibly rushed out of the station through the 42nd Street ramp. I was allowed to leave the station unmolested, and stood right by the exit door. From this vantage point, I saw the forcible ejection of at least thirty persons through the exit doors. Peering back into the inclined ramp, I clearly saw at least twenty brutal beatings by uniformed policemen with the TPF insignia on their collars. These men did not escort the ejected demonstrators, but they waited for them to appear and beat them with nightsticks as they ran the gauntlet. On four occasions I observed as many as six police officers throw demonstrators to the ground, kicking and beating them.' "

There was no official reaction from City Hall or the police to the Civil Liberties Union report.

One recurrent criticism against police tactics with demonstrators and dissenters has been the attempt by the police to avoid identification. Members of the Communist W. E. B. DuBois Club were attacked by neighborhood toughs in 1966 after Attorney General Nicholas Katzenbach had announced he would investigate the clubs to determine if they were subversive. During the battle of the civilians, the police arrived and managed to arrest only DuBois club members and none of the outsiders. TV cameras, on hand because of Katzenbach's statement, clearly showed police roughing up the DuBois people. Complaints to the Department about the behavior of the officers collapsed because, said the Department, "none of the allegations could be substantiated. . . due in part to the inability of those assaulted to identify any police officers as their assailants."

Street fights or a night stick attack permit little time to catch a good look at an assailant's face. Five-digit badge numbers are even more difficult to remember in the turmoil. Some uniformed men have been known to remove their badges or to cover the number with tape before entering riotous engagements. The practice is defended on the grounds that badges provide targets for snipers but the tactic has been employed where no such threat existed.

Plainclothesmen wear tiny colored buttons on their lapels to identify themselves to one another, and they refrain even from showing their badges in these confrontations. Occasionally this anonymity works to their disadvantage and a detective may wind up hitting a colleague, but basically the small button adds anonymity with protection in crowd situations. Critics contend that the purpose is to hide identity. Where badges have been worn, police have been known to harass those attempting to record the numbers.

Another gimmick has been the wearing of raincoats to cover badges, or turning the badge upside down. The controversy over hidden identification and the use of plainclothesmen in place of uniformed patrolmen added fuel to the confrontation of rebellious students and police at Columbia University in the spring of 1968. After several weeks of protesting over the erection of a new University gymnasium that would use a piece of city park land on the edge of the Harlem ghetto, some three-hundred Columbia students seized Hamilton Hall, a building that housed some of the University administration offices. The students received support from some ghetto groups such as CORE, the United Black Front, and the Harlem Committee for Self-Defense.

The youths captured Hamilton Hall where they held a dean as an involuntary guest for twenty-four hours. Some activists attempted to disrupt work at the gym site and tore down a fence but a squad of patrolmen, swinging clubs, drove them off. On the second day of the engagement, the students invaded Fayerweather and Avery Halls as well as President Grayson Kirk's offices. Black militants took total control at Hamilton. Some whites haggled over the segregation but leaders justified the racial split. Columbia canceled classes. The *New York Times* with a generous sprinkling of Columbia alumni and trustees in its ranks reported, "Many students were openly resentful of the demonstration." The *Times* estimated a crowd of two-hundred milling about the campus protesting the protesters.

City officials began to worry about the effects of the Columbia scene upon neighboring Harlem, only a few weeks over the shock of Martin Luther King's assassination and the disorder that followed it. Representatives of the Mayor met with Kirk and uniformed and plainclothes cops appeared on the University grounds. They could only do so at the invitation of the school, for in the absence of a felonious act the territory is a private preserve. (Opposition to police on school property was not new; back in 1894 the Lexow Committee had heard from aggrieved students of an invasion of police.) A *New York Times* editorial scolded the students for hoodlum behavior and "vandalism."

On the third day, a group of Columbia teachers tried to interpose themselves between the police and the students still occupying buildings. At President Kirk's request, more than twenty plainclothesmen, armed with night sticks, attempted to liberate the President's office. One professor, who was blocking their approach, was struck on the head with a club. Sid Davidoff of the Mayor's office stepped into the fray to announce that no one in the buildings had been arrested. The plainclothesmen retreated.

On the eighth day some 1,000 police were mustered on the campus. As night came on it became obvious that an attack was due. Originally scheduled for 1:30 A.M. it was moved back an hour. A police spokesman candidly admitted the change was to make certain that Harlem was asleep when the action began.

At Hamilton Hall a bullhorn asked the people inside to come out quietly. With perfect discipline, those in Hamilton filed out to be arrested. Not a single nightstick was swung, because none of the police there had clubs. Nor was there a report of any individual being manhandled or injured.

Somewhat similar experiences were recorded at two other buildings. But at Avery and Fayerweather the picture was entirely different. There the officers had night sticks. Many were not in uniform; they had put their badges in their pockets. When they entered the buildings, pushing, shoving, punching, kicking, and club-swinging followed. One reporter overheard a cop breathlessly ask another if he had hit anyone yet. "It was definitely a class thing. You could feel these cops wanted to get those smart-ass kids," said the reporter.

The night ended with 720 people arrested on charges of criminal trespass and 148 injured. The casualties must be considered high in light of the fact that in several of the buildings such as Hamilton the lawbreakers received no wounds at all.

Many complaints were filed on police brutality. Members of a volunteer medical corps said officers prevented them from ministering to the bloodied heads. Several members of the press, with their credentials prominently on display, got roughed up including one representative of the *New York Times* who was buffeted down a flight of stairs. Later a city hall official justified that beating by explaining that the reporter had recently been on an assignment to write about hippies and his hair was long.

The *Times* insisted that veteran reporters who had covered civil rights confrontations across the nation regarded the night stick work as gentle. Undoubtedly the violence did not match that of the Yippie session at Grand Central; or that of Selma, Alabama, in 1964 or the 1968 Democratic Convention in Chicago. But although no one spent a night in the hospital, the beatings dismayed a good portion of the campus, including neutral students and faculty.

The Mayor announced that a committee would investigate to determine if excessive force was used. Meanwhile the Department issued its own statement saying, "Police were punched, bitten, and kicked, with many attempts to kick policemen in the groin. A pattern was seen in the use of females to bite and kick the policemen."

(This was an excuse for clubbing girls.) "Violence against the police was on a large scale."

While the campus seethed because of the building bust, mediators attempted to get classes started again. But the students and the administration continued to be adamant in holding out for their positions. The police drifted off the campus but four weeks after the initial arrests another running battle broke out on the campus.

The trouble began with another seizure of Hamilton Hall. Ten hours after the demonstrators took possession, helmeted police arrived on the campus to drive the students out. The campus residents had attempted to seal off the university gates with barricades but to their ultimate chagrin they only remembered to bar the main entries and left some side gates untended.

The police massed a large force on one side of the campus, drawing the attention of the opposition and the curious. Then a force of uniformed officers entered Hamilton through one of the tunnels that connect the Columbia buildings underground. The activists came out quietly. "Our desire is to get the building cleared with no violence," announced Dr. Grayson Kirk and so far as Hamilton Hall was concerned the goal was accomplished.

But while the police were evacuating the building a rowdy mood of hostility built up, and students began throwing bricks at policemen, while the Barnard girls shouted obscenities that matched the cries of their male friends. Several small fires broke out in buildings, and fistfights engaged counterdemonstrators. Columbia asked the cops to clear the campus.

Suddenly, the police charged a large group of kids milling around the Sun Dial at the center of the twenty-eight-acre campus. Clubs swung freely. Newsmen saw a TPF man lope after a student and fell him with a club. While he lay on the ground another officer hurried up and added a blow. Other witnesses saw repeated assaults upon fleeing students. One leader of the student groups showed up the following day with multiple wounds of the head and face. An assistant dean was whacked by a cop when he failed to move swiftly enough.

Although the police statement after the first Columbia raid indicated that uniformed men should be employed where possible in such raids, the battle of the Sun Dial featured plainclothesmen. A shortage of uniformed troops could hardly be blamed for this deployment since stolid phalanxes of uniformed men stood motionless on a stretch of campus ground throughout the imbroglio. The net result of the fight was 135 arrests, 51 student injuries, and 17 police injuries.

Some observers believe that the bloodier battles of Grand Central and Columbia might have been avoided by better tactics and command. "We made a big mistake letting the Yippies into Grand Central," said one official. "We should have kept them in a park or somewhere out in the open, someplace where you didn't have to climb over a dozen people in order to get at the one guy who was making trouble." Grand Central also presented the classic example of a crowd confined in a small area without adequate means for escape by those who wanted to avoid any confrontation with the police. Means of escape for demonstrators being driven in a direction by police would have eliminated jam-ups that spurred the police to beat laggards.

At Columbia, a police expert said that one mistake was in the failure to first clear away the kids and materials blocking movement of the police. "By the time the cops got through to some of the buildings they were absolutely on their own without any supervision." A fact-finding commission said ". . . two conclusions are beyond dispute . . . police engaged in acts of individual and group brutality for which a layman can see no justification unless it be that the way to restore order in a riot is to terrorize civilians. . . . Second, some students attacked the police and otherwise provoked the retaliation. Their fault was in no way commensurate with the brutality of the police."

The behavior of the Chicago police during the 1968 Democratic Convention drew censure not only because of its brutality, but also because the police appeared to have arrogated to themselves the roles of judge and executioner, determining who was to be punished and then administering chastisement. The traditional role of the officer, making an arrest for a violation of the law, was disregarded. In dealing with hippies and political protesters, the

New York City police have occasionally committed a similar error.

A series of antiwar parades in December, 1967, resulted in mass arrests in which the marchers were carted away from the United Nations building, Rockefeller Center, and the Army Induction Center in lower Manhattan. In the latter incident a sit-down in the street was labeled disorderly conduct and the participants were lawfully arrested. In contrast, around the UN nearly a hundred people were seized, taken away, and then released without ever being charged. In the case of the forty people arrested while peacefully picketing near Rockefeller Center all charges were dismissed. In fact, during a three-day period, 279 people were arrested in connection with antiwar activities. Of these, five pled guilty, one was convicted after trial and the remainder were acquitted or had their cases abandoned.

Paul Chevigny, in his book *Police Power*, decided that the most serious abuse is not the excessive or unjustified use of force but a pattern of behavior that prevents civilians from obtaining redress and protects the policeman who abuses his authority. As a lawyer for the New York Civil Liberties Union, Chevigny concluded that the police habitually cover a false arrest or illegal action with a charge of disorderly conduct or resisting arrest. Particularly since the "no sock" provision was enacted have the cops been protected through the use of a resisting-arrest complaint. A second grievance by civil libertarians is the tactic of mutual protection. That officers support one another when a civilian carries a complaint against a cop to the Department should not be surprising. All professional organizations tend to show an inner loyalty and an antagonism toward outsiders. Physicians testify against fellow doctors in malpractice suits with great reluctance. Military units habitually resist investigations by civilians into misconduct by members of the armed forces. It is, in a sense, a mark of the professionalism of the police that they believe in cleaning their own house. On the other hand it is also a mark of professionalism for an organization to react to every suggestion of misconduct by individual members as a threat to the group.

CHAPTER XXII

PROFESSIONALISM

It would be hard to date the birth of professionalism among policemen. For the first seventy-five years of its life, the Department demanded little more than a letter from a political power and a minimum of physical strength. Cornelius Willemse reminisced about his appointment in 1899 when some fellow officers could neither read nor write, although Theodore Roosevelt insisted applicants were required to take a written examination.

In 1885 a one-month period of training had been established. In 1895, regulations of the Department required each man to be armed with a .32 caliber pistol. Grover Whalen, as commissioner under James J. Walker, ordered the heavier caliber .38 to be the standard armament. In the first years of a revolver-armed force, the men did on-the-job practice with their pistols, popping away in deserted areas.

Under Mayor John Purroy Mitchell's commissioner, Arthur Woods, in 1914 the standards for officers became sharply higher. The schooling of recruits was entrusted to trained instructors, men who had learned how to teach police tactics, and the course lasted twelve weeks. Currently, newcomers endure a four-month program that covers physical training, firearms, and academic work. The physical conditioning includes lectures on, among other matters, the parts of the body vulnerable to the night stick, practice in leg throat chokes and side headlocks, and film situations depicting when to shoot and when to hold fire. The academic instruction not only includes intensive study of the penal code and the duties of an officer but such materials as "Crime and Race, Conceptions and Misconceptions." For years cops participated in higher education through courses at the Baruch School of Business and Public Administration at City College. In 1965 the College of Police Science, now John Jay College of Criminal Justice, opened its doors.

Headquarters for sixty years has been a massive eyrie on Centre Street in lower Manhattan built in 1906. Commissioner Francis Adams (1954–1955) called it "The Victorian Foxhole." Dark and forbidding inside, it is matched by many station houses built forty and fifty years ago. One of the first items to go in every capital budget paring seems to be a new headquarters building, and new station houses are another sacrificial lamb to budget austerity.

Thomas Byrnes had created the rogues' gallery. In the beginning, it operated on a rather spontaneous basis with prisoners being taken to a well-lit streetcorner for the picture-taking. The Bertillion system of describing suspects by physical measurements and proportions was adopted in 1896, but only ten years later it was superseded by the new science of fingerprints. There are four million now on file. In 1906, too, the old gray bucket helmets were discarded finally in favor of caplike headgear.

The shield worn by New York City police received its final design in 1898. Aside from the number that will mark a man's entire career, the shield bears a number of symbols appropriate to New York: an eagle, the Western hemisphere, beavers (an important item of trade in the New Netherlands), a windmill (a common power source in the early Dutch and British colonies), flour barrels (an export granted exclusively to New York by the British in colonial days), an Indian, a bow, and a sounding lead. The shields cost around a dollar to manufacture but in 1964 the police were shocked to discover some 1,500 forged copies in a Brooklyn warehouse. The purpose of the counterfeits was never discovered.

Traffic control officially became a police responsibility in 1908, but the Department gave up the job of cleaning the streets in 1881. Until the police took over traffic control, teamsters settled disputes over the right of way with fists and clubs. For several years bicycle cops coped with thieves and other culprits who moved more swiftly than men on foot.

The first policewoman signed on in 1888 and the first Department medal of honor went to Captain John Saunders for the rescue of a drowning man. The first black cop, Samuel Battle, was appointed in 1911.

Two technically professional units, the Air Service and the Emergency Service Division, were set up under Grover Whalen in 1929 and 1930. The first triumph of the air-borne police involved following a carrier pigeon back to the hideout of an extortionist. A more heroic effort was recorded in April, 1933. Acting Sgt. Joseph Forsyth and Patrolman Otto Kafka rescued five Navy men from the non-rigid blimp J-3 which crashed while searching for survivors from another air disaster. The police air force now consists only of helicopters. These are suitable for traffic control, for security precautions during the visits of dignitaries, for rescue of small-craft users, for quick transportation of the mayor, and are a potential weapon in time of civil disorder. The Department no longer requires fixed-wing aircraft.

Emergency Services possesses the tools for dealing with subway accidents. This includes serious derailments as well as the occasional youngster who manages to jam himself into a turnstile. The Department also handles gas leaks, plane crashes, and all sorts of engineering problems not covered by the Fire Department. At one time Emergency Service also handled riot control but the Tactical Patrol Force now serves as the manpower pool for that type of endeavor. Emergency Service, using lubricating oil, freed a 375-pound lady stuck in a bathtub, and the men employed 200 feet of rope and a 25-foot ladder to get a would-be suicide down from the George Washington Bridge. Such rescues are almost routine.

For many years, particularly during the Depression, the number of applicants for police appointments far exceeded the openings. In 1938, 3,500 women applied for 27 job openings. The number of eligible male candidates generally ran two to three times the number of available spots. The high-water mark was 1946 when 23,418 men applied.

By 1955 the candidates had dropped sharply in number and in ability. Only 13,300 applied and the city announced it would grade examinations leniently. The passing score was lowered. Still the number of men seeking to join the Department continued to decline. In 1962, the city waived the customary $5 fee charged and gave the examination to 325 Pennsylvanians in Pittsburgh. Programs to get policemen away from desks and out on patrol began in earnest in the 1960s. Teenage cadets took over some of the routine clerical work with the hope that when they matured they would enter the Department. More and more civilian employees manned desk jobs. By 1969 of 7,328 candidates, nearly 25 percent came from minority groups. The high percentage was attributed to an intensive recruiting drive in the ghettos.

The modernization of the communications system began under Arthur Woods. The first prowl car with a radio rolled through the streets in 1917. It carried a thirty-foot mast. This was strictly a one-way system with the men on patrol able only to receive. At that it was a vast improvement for previously men could only be dispatched from the station house after a phone call or alerted to trouble in the area through a police call-box. Two-way communications were installed in 1937.

An inspector of detectives in 1968 credited the improvements in his line of work to technology. "We've made great strides in detective work through a fabulous system of communication. We've got three-way communication, city wide. You dial 911 and you get headquarters. The dispatcher's call can be heard by adjoining cars to the one selected, and we've got car-to-car communication as well as central to car."

The inspector was boasting of communications in cars by 1968. But it still took approximately ninety seconds to dispatch a car from the moment a call was received. Calls from civilians for police aid were relayed by the man answering the phone through pneumatic tubes to radio car dispatchers. Beyond that initial minute and a half lay the inescapable time lag caused by traffic conditions. It was long enough for a man to die of a heart seizure, or for holdup men to escape, or for a family argument to turn into a fatal brawl. On occasion, the high volume of requests for police help, an average of 15,000 a day, clogged the telephones and callers got a busy signal.

The continuing rise in the number of serious crimes forced the police to speed up their methods. A study of Los Angeles crime problems by the President's Commission on Law Enforcement and

Administration showed that the time lapse between receipt of a call and getting a man on the scene averaged 6.3 minutes for cases in which the police were ineffective while the time for cases where the police met with success averaged 4.1 minutes. When police responded within one minute the arrest percentage hit 62 percent; after five minutes it dropped below 50 percent.

Full computerization of the communications system—electronic handling from the receipt of a call through the dispatch of officers—saved ninety seconds in Los Angeles. New York got the message and in 1969 installed a computerized system, the Special Police Inquiry Network known as *SPRINT*. Where formerly calls could have jammed up in a particular borough, now no one will ever get a busy signal while calling for help. No longer does a switchboard operator have to pause to determine who is free to receive the incoming call; it goes automatically. Non-emergencies can be funneled off to a secondary listener who can advise the caller what to do about such problems as the loss of a social security card or of an army discharge.

When a call comes through a colored light tells the operator which borough it comes from. As the pertinent information comes over the phone, the operator fills out an IBM card, and in from four to nine seconds a conveyor belt whisks the card to a dispatcher. The latter, sitting before a map of his sector can see streets, parks, and patrol sectors clearly color-marked and, most important, he can see where cars on duty are at the particular moment, and who is free to answer the call. From here on, it is a matter of the time it takes for a car to move through the streets to the site of the incident.

Total computerization will eliminate the conveyor belt system. When *SPRINT* is perfected, the operator will be able to feed the information from the call directly into the computer which determines the precinct, patrol sector, the nearest three cars, and the nearest hospital. The information will light up on a screen in front of the dispatcher who passes it immediately to the proper prowl cars. While they are already on the move any additional information received by the operator can be funneled to them. The computer will also memorize and feed back instantly data on stolen cars and previous records of suspects.

Men on foot are now more accessible to command through walkie-talkies; 14,000 police-fire squawk boxes will eventually put every citizen within one block of a direct communication to police central communications.

One of the more exotic professional police operations is the New York bomb squad. This force was created in 1914 because of a rash of anarchist bombings that culminated in an attempt to get J. P. Morgan and other Wall Street luminaries which killed 35 people in the street. Ordinarily the bomb squad is a boring duty with long stretches of inactivity broken only by the studying of manuals dealing with the technology of explosives.

The unit worked on an informal basis without any special training until 1940 when a bomb rigged at the Polish Pavilion in the 1940 World's Fair went off on July 4, killing two members of the squad and badly injuring a third. Since then, bomb disposal has been approached more professionally. Some members of the twelve-man group graduated from army ordnance units, but the types of explosive devices they must deal with are generally homemade and neither reliable nor predictable pieces of ordnance. "We've had to pioneer," said Lt. Kenneth O'Neill, the 1968 commander. "You don't have many people in this business. Since the 1940 tragedy we've gone in for equipment and research." Recruits now spend ninety days training, constructing and taking apart all types of dummy bombs.

After World War II the two biggest problems for bomb deactivators were the efforts of George Metesky, and anti-Castro forces. Metesky, the so-called Mad Bomber, mildly terrorized the city for the seventeen year period of 1940–1957 with contraptions. Metesky exploded or hid forty-seven bombs around the city in the course of his unique career, all because of a peeve against Consolidated Edison whom he believed had cheated him out of his rightful pension. In fact, it was the pattern of targets against the power company that eventually led to the identification of Metesky. Another and more serious threat was a 1968 series of blasts that tore up consulates and offices of nations dealing with Cuba. Two members of the bomb squad, Andrew Sweeney, a fifteen-year veteran of the unit and his partner James Dooley, with thirty-three years at the same job (their longevity in itself testifies to their skill) dismantled in 1968 an explosive creation hanging on the door of the French Tourist Office in Rockefeller Center with a bare two minutes leeway. The bomb squad experienced a boom in business as extreme radicals turned to explosives as a way of bringing revolution. While unfounded bomb threats in 1969 hit 2,500, 93 devices actually exploded and 19 others failed to detonate.

In 1959, the city went through a protracted siege of youth gang warfare. One weapon developed to curb this form of lawlessness was the Tactical Patrol Force, a unit of men specially selected for brains, brawn, and a willingness to work difficult situations. While the gang problem yielded to a number of forces, including the TPF, police authorities in the city saw in a special force of this nature a flexible weapon to employ in a variety of situations. Early publicity built them into an elite of better-than-six-foot, college-educated officers, supercops if not superhumans. But the nearly one thousand men are not all massive physical specimens or candidates for Mensa. Blacks and Puerto Ricans constitute 10 percent of the TPF, compared with 4 percent of other units.

Not all of the public saw in the TPF unmixed virtue. Several times, ghetto people accused them of swinging too free and eager a club, precipitating wider violence than might have normally occurred. "Head-beaters" is a common label applied in the ghetto to the TPF. The men in the unit, naturally, defend themselves against such charges. "Every complaint against the TPF has been exonerated," one patrolman said proudly.

The majority of men in the group have spent only a few years on the force and as one officer points out, "Particularly in the first few years a cop is inclined to be suspicious. His training all points toward this, looking for the violations and the lawbreaker." This same official describes members of the TPF as men "at the peak of ambition. The TPF has served as a manpower pool for the Department's detective division, and most men aspire to plainclothes assignments."

A patrolman serving in the corps boasted, "Generally in the

TPF you find men a notch above average. They have pride. The morale is much higher than among the average patrolman who puts in eight hours, a long time in a slow post or a quiet precinct. You can see in a steady precinct job how the work can stagnate a man." Elsewhere in the Department TPF stands for Truth, Purity, and Fidelity or among those who ridicule their immunity from the temptations of office, Tall, Poor, and Foolish.

The basic element of the TPF functions that makes the unit a sore point with some areas of New York is, in the words of an official, that "it places more emphasis upon enforcement." TPF cops pile up a generous number of arrests but become a focus for cop-haters and people who see in the police the symbol for an oppressive system. "The lower class," says a TPF man, "where most of the crime takes place [and where the TPF efforts are concentrated]—they hate the cop. If you're courteous to people generally they're courteous to you, except in certain areas. But we're the symbol for authority and the Establishment. Whatever isn't being done for them [the poor and the black] we get blamed for."

Beyond apprehension of criminals, the TPF suffers a bad name whenever street demonstrations, picketing, or civil disturbances occur, because its members serve as shock troops and as the first barrier of containment. Some observers believe that the emphasis upon "enforcement" for the men of the TPF promotes a tendency for them to swing their nightsticks too soon. These critics feel that TPF behavior turns tension into street battles.

Within the Department there is considerable debate over the worth of the organization. "The single most important element in keeping the peace during 1968," insisted a captain. "It was the TPF that precipitated the trouble," said a black officer after 1967 summer disturbances. A Brooklyn desk lieutenant spoke for much of the Department when he told one reporter, "They're more gung-ho than elite. Why every time I hear they're being sent into my precinct I know I'll be writing up arrest cards all night. They arrest anybody. They're all looking for nice fat arrest quotas. One time I sent two of them out to quiet down a little Friday night family dispute, and they came back with two arrests."

The TPF's chief asset in times of civil disorder is discipline.

Among the unit's officials there seems to have been some feeling that the discipline broke down at the Grand Central Station mêlée and that the men used their night sticks there with an unprofessional abandon. On other occasions, however, the TPF's discipline and restraint in group situations stood out against that of other units.

During the 1968 disturbances in Manhattan's East Village, much of the local hostility focused upon the presence of the TPF. Roman Catholic Rev. Matthew Thompson said, "The TPF, I believe, is the catalyst behind all this trouble." "People do not want the TPF governing their area," said an eighteen-year-old youth who worked for a community action group.

At the same time, merchants who have stores in the East Village, but not homes, welcomed the TPF, claiming that the Fifth Precinct men did nothing while vandals smashed windows and looted.

Said a TPF deputy inspector, "We never cause a riot. When we are brought into a situation all else has failed. Rapport has broken down, community relations aren't working. Shots have been fired, bricks and rocks thrown, windows broken. We're not there to engage in a community relations effort. Once we have restored order then other programs can take over."

A superior officer faults the TPF for its excessive zeal. He rejects force as the deterrent and stresses the precinct man as the key to peace, particularly the black cop in the ghetto. "When a white cop gets a call about youths on a street corner disturbing a neighborhood with rowdy, obscene talk, he tells them to scram. They argue with more obscenity and he locks one or two up and we've got a real picnic.

"A colored cop can go up to that corner and say 'Listen all you cats. The captain's been bugging me about the neighbors' complaints.' He may exchange a few obscenities with the youths; and he'll take ten or fifteen minutes to clear the corner. A white cop, he's already nervous about his surroundings and he wants those kids to move right away. That's why he has trouble. The TPF is like the white cop in the ghetto. Guys who don't give a damn for nothing.

The absence of selective enforcement of the law, however, betrays a lack of regard for the way of life endured in parts of the city. In the steamy tenements on hot summer nights people of all ages live on the streets until the early morning hours, gamble on the sidewalk and the vacant lots, consume beer and other alcoholic beverages on the city streets. Particularly in the black communities where the social values often differ from those which created the city penal code there are differences that, in the eyes of a strict enforcement officer, mean arrest. During the summer of 1968 a zealous cop broke up a crap game in the tenement area of Coney Island. In the course of the altercation someone bounced a brick off the officer's body and he arrested the alleged missile launcher. Rumors spread through the community that the offender was being manhandled down at the station house and the tension that precedes a rock throwing, fire-bombing episode stretched near the breaking point.

Alerted to the situation, members of the Mayor's Urban Action Task Force arrived on the scene, rounded up some local community leaders, took them to the precinct house where they could see for themselves that the prisoner was not being mistreated, helped secure a defense lawyer and arranged for representatives of the community to stay with the captive until he finally went off to be arraigned in court. The hostility slackened in Coney Island. Later, a city hall official termed the arrest "stupid. A couple of blocks away there are people playing poker and sipping Scotch in their air conditioned home. These people in the slums can only move out into the streets."

One of the more novel departures from traditional police activity was the creation of a Family Crisis Unit with eighteen men selected for a month of intensive schooling in psychology. The aim is to train men to handle one of the most persistent headaches of police work, the family quarrel. A blunder in dealing with a husband and wife squabble can turn both disputants into violent assailants of the police, and a precipitous arrest of one party may send the neighborhood looking for the blood of cops. Also, out of domestic battles come most of the homicides that police must face. (The national figures show that one-third of all murders and one-tenth of all assaults are committed by one family member against another.)

From a political and administrative standpoint the professionalism of the Department reached new levels under Mayor Robert F. Wagner, Jr., who commanded City Hall from 1954 to 1966. The patrolmen assigned to work with juveniles received better training. Some attempts were made to deploy men more efficiently, and Wagner added nearly 7,000 men to the force. The first glimmering of a board to review civilian complaints was created, although control remained strictly inside the Department. And after the Harlem riots of 1964 the first black commander of a precinct received his appointment, Lloyd Sealy in Harlem. To be sure, Wagner commissioners had given rank to black policemen before the disorder but this was the first post with authority over uniformed men.

The most important aspect of these years was the determined effort to get political influence out of the Department. Wagner's staff said that before Wagner assumed control $100 bills to the Democratic Party used to precede appointments to posts above the rank of sergeant. So strong was the effort to get the police out from under the thumb of City Hall that people began to complain that the Department had become an independent duchy, responsive neither to the elected officials nor the community.

The chief architect of Wagner's reform was a career officer, Stephen P. Kennedy, who had earned a reputation for fierce, bookish honesty under Lewis Valentine and as a result found himself exiled to civil defense paper-shuffling in the early 1950s. Wagner's first police commissioner was Francis Adams, a lawyer without a working knowledge of the Byzantine maze within the police organism. On the advice of J. Edgar Hoover, Adams plucked Kennedy from obscurity and made him his chief inspector. From there it was a simple promotion to the top job when Adams resigned.

Kennedy held his post six turbulent years in which he enhanced his reputation as a zealot of rectitude. He ordered a severe campaign against traffic violators and actually reversed the rising tide of accidents for several years while drivers howled about the persnickety cops and the latter grumbled about the P.C.'s demands.

For it was the police who heard first from irate motorists. The mid-town tow-away program still irks cops who bear the brunt of the outraged yells from car owners.

The same vigorous enforcement of the rules of the Department cost Kennedy the affection of the men. For although he was by career the first of their own since Lewis Valentine, he was, like Valentine, strict in his demands for absolute adherence to the pre-scribed codes of behavior for cops. Roving shoo-flies enforced Kennedy's standards.

When it was suggested to Kennedy that he was too strict he snapped, "When I find a crooked cop or drunken bum on the force who might some day use his gun to kill some innocent person, I get rid of him as fast as I can. If that's inhuman, I'm inhuman, but I'm not going to be pressured into neglecting my first duty, which is to protect the public. We are not children playing a game. This is a se-rious business. There can be no substitute for integrity and fidelity and for moral and spiritual courage." Civil liberties champions felt that during his reign there were fewer instances of abuse of police power.

Like all men of steadfast virtue, reformer Kennedy became a headache to almost everyone. He stoutly defended wire taps as the best means of getting at the Syndicate, and could not be dissuaded by potential dangers. "There is frequent invasion of individual free-dom in the common interest."

With the ghetto areas getting roily, Kennedy refused to ap-point anyone to a post or promote him simply because he was black. A "turning back of the clock to what has been described as the 'black precinct' concept would be to admit defeat. We must continue to fight for a truly integrated city."

The Commissioner roused a tumult during the 1960 visit of Nikita Khrushchev and Fidel Castro to the United Nations. In the emergency of security for the guests, Kennedy denied time off to Jewish policemen to attend Rosh Hashonah services and remarked that they got religious only when it meant a chance to miss a couple of days work. Mayor Wagner apologized for the alleged slander and said Kennedy would also beg the public pardon, but the Com-missioner did not. Another issue on which Kennedy stood firm was moonlighting. He constantly battled to get higher pay for his men but he fought just as hard against any suggestion that they might be permitted to supplement their income with outside work.

Kennedy tried hard to eliminate the customary Christmas gifts to cops and won no love from his subordinates for his unyielding opposition to this sort of gratuity. On the other hand it was his unswerving demand the city grant a flat $600 raise to the police and maintain a pay differential over the politically potent firemen that led Robert Wagner to pick a new commissioner.

The Wagner police commissioners reduced corruption, united political influence, and improved some traditional police tactics. The Lindsay Administration continued the tough approach toward corruption. Under Leary, the Department became a part of the electronic, computer age. The patrolman's discretion, his traditional right to make "street decisions" was reduced by written instructions and continued discipline from superiors, including the Mayor. But Leary was not as tough as Steve Kennedy when it came to political influence. When some honest cops complained about corruption, city hall officials, sensitive to any attack on the cops and conscious of Mayor Lindsay's uneasy relationship with the politically strong cops, ducked the evidence. Policemen also chafed over political influence exerted by ethnic groups, particularly blacks and Puerto Ricans.

Again, one of the most effective methods to lessen the tension between police and civilians in such confrontations has been the interposition of the Mayor. On a number of occasions members of the Urban Action Task Force have been present at demonstrations and parades attempting to maintain communication between the police commanders and the organizers of the action. The *New York Daily News* accused two members of the Administration, Barry Gottehrer and Sidney Davidoff of interfering with the police by exercising restraint over police action. Commissioner Howard Leary, however, scoffed at the assertion. "Nobody interferes with me," said Leary shortly after the *News* as well as the opposition political party grumbled over the restraint of the police when 1,500 youths showed up at City Hall and wrecked several automobiles while petitioning for summer jobs. "There are young fellows around City

Hall who like to push themselves out front. In the City Hall matter we exercised the principle for handling militant groups. You can't extend yourself unless you have sufficient police force."

City Hall considered Leary an outstanding asset, a man who had managed to win both the confidence of his men and acceptance in the community. Leary had owed his appointment to a willingness to live with the Lindsay review board. (His predecessor Vincent Broderick was rated by the less enthusiastic observers of police procedures to have been excellent in civil liberties matters but he was unable to accept the Review Board.) When the referendum on the Review Board arose Leary managed to convey to the members of the Department an impression that if he could live with it, he could also live without the civilian-controlled board. In his promotions and the tactical uses of his troops he proved himself a professional. He has sought a new breed of officer, better educated, more devoted, attuned to modern problems. And in the troubled areas of the community he managed to convince people that at least at the top of the Department there was a man responsive to the aspirations and needs of minorities.

Leary corroborated some of the findings of the National Commission on Civil Disorders, which reported that almost every riot, whatever its long-evolving causes, was triggered by a police action. "Police in large cities," said Leary, "have learned much, a great deal of what hasn't happened [speaking of the year after the 1967 disasters] is because of what police learned. Thousands of incidents occur in which police are involved. These are things that aggravate and exasperate a community. The police choose on their own volition not to do something and a bad situation is avoided."

Leary and City Hall were convinced that the upper echelons of the police recognize the value of restraint and discretionary action. But in the ranks the policy has continued to be a debatable one and Leary believed external pressures make his men uneasy about restraint. "We've had the resurgence of the Negro. There is the social revolution, the international scene, the juvenile explosion. The police are on the front line, absorbing it both ways [from the proponents of change and the foes]. The policeman thinks as a professional he's done well. He goes to a bar on an off-night and some says, 'What's wrong with you guys, are you cowards?' The cop finds himself a loner. He may blame 'court decision, the bosses,' for his behavior. But if a Department can bring a city through a time of crisis it's done a good job."

As an example of newspaper pressures, Leary cited a series of disturbances in lower Manhattan that had been blown out of proportion by the reporters. "It was nothing. The first consideration was to contain it. You don't want it to spread. If we kept the problem in the East Village we were better off than having it all over the city. By holding the status quo, do nothing aggressive or obnoxious, we would eventually win out. The decisions were made by captains and inspectors," said Leary. "To be aggressive is no problem. After a few days the community itself would express itself. They want law and order. Public opinion turns against a demonstration. Mr. and Mrs. Nobody in the ghetto have a good deal of sophistication. They're not easily taken." On this occasion, as on others, Leary's theory of restraint proved out.

The Commissioner was quite strict on the use of police pistols. "When police start shooting without discipline we have trouble." Leary clamped down on indiscriminate use of pistols after he came upon a cop firing down an alley into an intersection one troubled summer night in 1967. When asked what he was firing at the cop said he didn't know. Leary ordered the pistol holstered immediately. "Bottle-throwing is no excuse for using your gun," he announced. In the event of a sniper Leary planned to withdraw regular units and bring in specially trained officers to handle such a threat. "This is not the wild, wild West."

The Leary strategy of restraint has been construed by some as a policy of permissiveness. But when his regime could muster sufficient men to control the situation there has been little evidence of unwillingness to use force. The outbreak of violence around New York immediately after the sniper death of Dr. Martin Luther King went beyond the bounds of local police control. Shopkeepers and property owners bitterly attacked the city for failing to provide protection, but Leary and company believed that excessive force, especially the use of bullets, would have worsened the situation, and restraint is often exercised to protect the working cop.

He quoted a Chicago policeman who remarked after that city's Mayor Daley ordered that looters and arsonists be summarily shot, "I have six bullets in my gun and two-hundred people rioting and looting. What happens after I shoot the first six?" Added Leary, "We will never have enough police to maintain law and order and tranquility through police action alone. That is where we need the support of the community. Does the community want us to shoot looters?" He expressed doubt.

Leary put a great deal of faith in a man who has worked the ghetto, echoing the traditional theory that a cop who has worked in Harlem can handle anything. "There's a real difference between a professional who's worked the ghetto, and a cop whose understanding comes from pure theory or less troubled areas."

Leary's resignation in 1970 provoked new questions on the relationships between City Hall and Centre Street. Leary had been unhappy over Mayor Lindsay's criticism of police failure to act when hard-hat workers assaulted college anti-war demonstrators. He was pressured to deny publicly that sniper attacks on cops represented national conspiracy. And he was trapped into political considerations on promotions, assignments and investigations by City Hall residents.

Professionalism in the police showed an interesting ambivalence in 1970. The TPF represents the acme of old style paramilitary force, a mobile attack unit under strong discipline. The TPF prevents crimes through its presence or it efficiently makes arrests. The TPF approach accepts lawbreaking as an unpleasant but expectable element in society. Simultaneously, there has been growing recognition by men like Howard Leary that police actions in themselves can trigger criminal acts and that there is even a responsibility for the police to help eliminate the conditions that breed crime. Some black cops have begun to speak out against the abuse of fellow blacks by white policemen. The monolithic police attitudes have started to crack. The question is whether the forces for heightened professional behavior can work together or if the community service cop will eventually confront the TPF cop in the street.

CHAPTER XXIII

THE SPIRIT OF
THE FORCE

As the ultimate force behind the law, the police support the status quo. The nature of their job inevitably pits them against change. Whether natural selection eliminates individuals who might be more open to change or the job itself transforms even those who are liberally inclined, cannot be ascertained. One police administrator observed, "Police are innately conservative. I know I was more liberal ten years ago. The Department pushes you toward conservatism." In a sense the organism that is the New York City Police Department exerts enormous pressure towards conformity. The tendency to conformity involves the often observed dominance of Irish-American Catholicism.

The "Powerhouse," St. Patrick's Cathedral under the late Cardinal Spellman, generated a conservatism that covered a broad spectrum of issues: tax money for parochial schools, church bingo, abortion, and divorce law reform. The powerhouse warred on Communism, upheld censorship of films, books, and plays, and for many years made no effort toward racial harmony. Until Sanford Garelik, a Jew, was appointed to the post of Chief Inspector by the Lindsay Administration in 1966, men born in Ireland or the descendants of Irish immigrants occupied all the executive positions within the Department in an unbroken string running back to the early 1900s.

The conformity extends to black policemen, whose reputation in the ghettos often matches that of white cops. Said a Negro patrolman, "When I hear one of those black militants sound off, I want to smash him in the mouth." A policeman learns almost immediately that it's them (the civilians) against us, no matter what his previous experience has been.

One reason for the conformity is the disciplinary structure of the department. Not even a soldier experiences the all-encompassing control over his life that envelops a member of the force. On post the patrolman must notify the precinct every time he relieves himself, ring in regularly, and inform control when he starts and finishes a meal. Aside from the techniques of military courtesy, the salute and the deference to rank that he shares with the soldier, the New York City cop finds that the Department regulates him twenty-four hours a day. Employment during off-duty hours has been permitted since 1967, but there are certain jobs which are forbidden. A soldier who gets intoxicated while off duty can be arrested and fined by civil authorities, but no punishment from the military need follow. For a policeman a breach of conduct on his own time can subject him to departmental discipline. Men have been dismissed from the force for such social misadventures as adultery, an infraction that society no longer considers worth prosecuting. Association with members of the underworld, some of whom might have been childhood friends, is another cause for dismissal. Then there is always the threat of the judge or politician. In spite of all of the barriers set up to keep City Hall away from the force, it is still possible for the influential to reach down and tap a friendly captain or lieutenant who will see to it that an offending patrolman gets punished.

Discipline within the Department starts with the sergeant who can impose heavy pressure upon a patrolman through humiliating assignments, onerous duties, and small penalties. The disciplinary courts within the Department offer very little in the way of appeal for the patrolman who faces charges.

A high-ranking police officer remarked, "The difficulty is that other professions have a place for the maverick, very often from the maverick we learn; but police don't tolerate a maverick." Most likely, few mavericks ever enlist. Those who might be ignorant of the rigid discipline actually exerted, must recognize the uniform and the surface behavior as the antitheses of individualized behavior. A top officer, representative of the new better educated, more socially perceptive breed, said, "After all, why does a man want to be a policeman? The gun, the badge, the authority. These help to prove to himself what he is." Men who must rely on externals to prove to themselves who they are cannot be counted upon for unorthodoxy. The challenge to that identity, the failure to recognize the badge and uniform, the decision to resist with firearms is the trauma that creates physical abuse and police riots as exemplified in dealings with hippies, dissenters, and black militants.

Within the New York City Department, the devotion to standardized behavior has meant that the police have traditionally been associated with right-wing political movements. For all the talk about John Broderick and other officers being in the pay of the Communists, there was little doubt about where the sympathies of the Department lay and the performance at the 1930 May Day fracas spelled the attitudes out clearly.

Historically, the New York City police have belonged to the Democratic Party and supported the local organization, with Tammany the chief beneficiary of their devotion. Neither the public nor the city officials care about what other organizations enjoy the support of individual policemen—with a few exceptions. Americans, including police, have shown themselves joiners in a myriad of fraternal, civic, religious, professional, social, and political organizations. Recognized by the Department are nearly a dozen police fraternal and religious clubs.

Mayor Fiorello LaGuardia sounded the first real tocsin against membership in some political groups during the 1930s when the question arose about possible infiltration of the Department by Communists. Textile manufacturers claimed that Communists abducted twenty-five workers while the police stood idly by saying they could do nothing. The businessmen swore that the Communists shouted, "The cops are with us." LaGuardia thundered, "If I find a policeman taking as much as a Cremo cigar from a Communist or anybody else, I'll fire him."

In the spring of 1940, with Nazi Germany beginning its sweep through Europe, LaGuardia and other New Yorkers became aware of police participation in right-wing pro-Nazi activities. John F.

Cassidy, leader of the Christian Front in Brooklyn, was on trial for conspiracy to overthrow the government and to steal munitions. Cassidy testified that five hundred applications for membership in the Christian Front came from Brooklyn cops, and he intimated that the police membership numbered in the thousands. LaGuardia's police commissioner, Lewis Valentine, produced figures showing that 407 police belonged to the Christian Front. The Patrolman's Benevolent Association objected to LaGuardia's attempt to ascertain the involvement of police in the Christian Front on grounds that this infringed on civil liberties. LaGuardia declared the Front off limits to the police, saying that meetings had evolved into "demonstrations" and police who had to act could not be a part of the demonstrating group. LaGuardia added that the police as a whole behaved impartially and that only twenty-seven officers retained their Christian Front membership. The right to membership was never legally tested; World War II destroyed the Christian Front.

The political sentiments of the police became an issue again during 1965. Prowl car radios inveighed against mayoralty candidate John V. Lindsay, pledged to the creation of a civilian review board for complaints of abuses by the police. A few days before the election exhortations for Conservative William F. Buckley blared anonymously over the police car radios. There was no possible way that central communications could determine which cars were doing the political electioneering. Considerable furor arose over a Catholic Holy Name Society police breakfast at which William F. Buckley defended the actions of Alabama Sheriff Jim Clark when faced with Martin Luther King's attempted march through town. A newspaper reporter who attended the breakfast printed excerpts and noted that the 5,000 police present applauded Buckley's statements.

Later, the Conservative insisted that the reporter wrote down the remarks out of context but in 1965, support for the actions of Sheriff Jim Clark turned the fury of editorial writers on the police. A reporter who happened to be in a Harlem precinct at the time of the Selma march remembered a white sergeant turning red-faced with anger at the press's distortion of the truth. He shouted that the front-page photograph of Clark standing over a black woman and brandishing his club failed to show that moments before the woman wrested the club from Clark and had threatened him with it. Police, in that period of history, often warned reporters that the demonstrations by civil rights groups in the South and the North could only lead to a catastrophic breakdown in law and order.

John Birch Society membership became a matter of contention. At first Commissioner Howard Leary ruled that members of the Department could not belong but when he was advised that such a prohibition denied the civil liberties of the police, Leary withdrew his order.

The link-up of the police with the conservative forces in the American system can be attributed to an occupational predilection for the status quo rather than innate right-wing political leaning. Political orthodoxy receives police support in any state-dominated economic system. In both fascist and Communist countries the police generally take the most illiberal line, for there, as in America, the police serve as a bulwark against change.

John McNamara's study of New York City police recruits' background and training concluded policemen through training come to view the law "as fixed and immutable." Officers "defend themselves from criticism through knowledge of the letter of the law rather than its spirit."

While the organism that is the Department attempts to mold the membership into 32,000 standard units, a certain amount of variety flourishes. There is a diversity in avocations that covers a narrow spectrum of the arts, sports, and part-time employment that might also be applicable to any other group of lower-middle-class Americans. Officers also approach their vocation in various ways. Some men pile up big arrest records, others avoid trouble. Said a police captain, "We had a cop who stood on the corner of 116th Street and Park Avenue [in Harlem]. He was always on his post, wore white gloves, never failed to salute, and he never made an arrest in twenty years. A block away on Madison Avenue another cop had the highest number of felony arrests. He would ride around in his own car or go on a roof and watch for hours, looking for some suspicious activity."

A modern authority on police called the work basically "voyeurism." A working cop said, "You're always looking to see what's wrong. You don't notice all the law-abiding people." Looking at life through jaundiced eyes, the reactions of cops to incidents can take ominous turns. In the 1950s a study by the New York Institute of Technology explored the work of 800 cops involved in 8,000 incidents and decided that police habitually misperceive and overestimate the danger.

One of the more perceptive appraisals of the police personality was done by a former New York cop, Arthur Niederhoffer, in his book *Behind the Shield.* Niederhoffer ran his own battery of tests on his colleagues and browsed through the skimpy studies done by others. One 1950 investigation of New York Police used Rorschach tests and among the twenty-five subjects the study found the "more maladjusted tended to be more satisfied with their work than the less maladjusted," a disquieting thought considering the potential power of life or death held by the individual cop. *Behind the Shield* also cites a 1944 survey that defined the authoritarian personality. The qualities included conventionalism, authoritarian submission, authoritarian aggression, anti-intraception or the barrier against outside prying into affairs, superstition and stereotyping, power and toughness, destruction, cynicism, and projectivity. Niederhoffer believes the syndrome fits many policemen. He theorizes: "The police system transforms a man into the special type of authoritarian personality required by the job role." Sociologist Niederhoffer warns that the cop is now being asked to be a social scientist instead of a head-splitter, and the system is not geared for such a transformation. He sees the values within the Department as in transition. "The old police code symbolized by the 'tough cop' is waning. The new ideology glorifying the 'social scientist police officer' is meeting unexpected resistance."

Niederhoffer mentions the tendency of police at ceremonial occasions to compare their work with a religious calling. Supporting this vision, a minister who works a simmering section of lower Manhattan once listened to the local police captain expound: "You know, Father, you and I are alike [the police officer was absolutely in error in his assumption]. We came to a point in life where we had to decide, either to become a priest or go on the force. I chose to be a cop but," he added the final note, "if it weren't for men like you, we'd have to conquer these people." Niederhoffer points out that the exalted view of the job generally belongs to higher-rank or special assignment officers. For the patrolman, the vicissitudes of his daily job are enough to convince him he does not bear the aura of a clergyman.

The feeling of personnel experts in the field is that the best patrolman material comes from working-class families that live in the city rather than middle-class college-oriented ones. The offspring of blue-collar city dwellers are more likely to have already sampled street life and know the population with whom they are most likely to have great contact as cops. On the other hand, the college-bred individual may bring to the job more sophistication about the causes of crime and civil disorder. Significantly, one study found that the greatest attraction of the force is job security. Obviously, individuals who are security-oriented would be antipathetic to dissenters and critics of the social order.

Life at the police academy does more than train a man in how to use his night stick and pistol or teach him the rules for an arrest. It is like basic training in the army—the period in which the hierarchical discipline is instilled. Consequently, the built-in conventionalism of class buttresses the professional training. The orthodoxy of the uniform and total discipline carry over to off-duty hours. Rules demand that recruits "wear a conservative business suit with matching coat and trousers" when in mufti. "Hair must be trimmed in conservative style. High pompadours, and long side-burns are prohibited."

"The job takes you out of the mainstream of life," admitted a narcotics detective. "When I talk to people I have to readjust myself in my train of thought. I keep pulling conversations apart, trying to figure out 'what did he mean by that?' "

"You live two lives," said another detective. "People complain that policemen are conservative and clannish. I admit I find it difficult to socialize with other people. I go to a party and a guy asks me what type of work do you do? I tell him and right away he starts to tell me about a cop stopping him for speeding and asking for a payoff. I'd like to know what really happened, how much he offered the cop. I don't know what it is, but people you meet always want to talk about cops and tell you all their bad experiences. That's why after a while cops stick with each other."

A young, uniformed cop said, "My friends are all cops. You find you don't have much in common with civilians. They live in a pink cloud."

While few police carry for long any romantic illusions about their work they don't deny the excitement. "When you get a call," said an inspector, "the adrenalin starts to go. When you become immune that's trouble. You have to approach everything as if it's a dangerous situation." That attitude protects a cop from being caught unaware; it can also lead to over-reaction. That double-edged threat, danger for the officer responding to a call and his potential to over-estimate the seriousness of the threat, can possibly be reduced by training and discipline. But the hazards can never be reduced to zero.

Old line officers talk about "street decisions" made by a cop and almost to a man veterans believe that a policeman has the intelligence, discretion and the right to make street decisions, some of which mean the death of another human. A retired officer who uses terms like "nigger," "spade," "guinea" says that a cop must always be able to bring up his wrath. "Up on the roof, if you lose that anger, you're nothing but a body. I remember once we had a call about a prowler on a roof. We went up there, I saw some fingers hanging on the edge. 'I see a cockroach,' I said and I rapped with my club. He [the prowler] went down the chute and we told the desk sergeant 'unfounded' when we reported." Such summary distribution of justice, if it can be graced by such a name, is rarer today as the department grinds toward more and more discipline and control.

Former patrolman Gene Radano in his book "Walking the Beat" recorded the diatribe of an "old timer." "Everybody wants to judge us these days! . . . What the hell do they know about a mob? No bastard knows anything except the poor cop whose ass is on the line. A mob is the ugliest animal in the world. You just try to quiet them by quoting something out of a book. They'd run over you like a herd of cattle. And you haven't got time to wait for the Supreme Court to make a decision. You only got five seconds to decide whether to run like a dog or stand up like a cop. Five seconds; you, God, a mob and no reference books. So you hold the club short and you hit the first son-of-a-bitch on the head—bang! three stitches! If the bastard keeps coming—bang! three more stitches! And that makes you a fascist! For weeks they'll argue whether you did or didn't use too much force! For weeks! And you had only five seconds! . . . I say the cop who stands up to the bums does more for law and order than a roomful of judges."

Commissioner Howard Leary musing on the political schism among his men in 1968 attributed the strength of George Wallace support to the climate around the cops. "They're reflecting the community. They are responsive to what they believe the community wants." Leary attributed some of the police disenchantment to the now-habitual grievance against the courts for what is considered coddling of criminals.

If one listened to John Cassese it was simple to deduce the cause of support for George Wallace. Cassese told the *New York Daily News* long before the former Governor of Alabama began his campaign for the White House that in certain ghettos patrolmen were told to "turn the other cheek or make out you didn't hear it. In a different section of the city, if the same obscene language was used against the officer he could make the arrest."

Cassese reiterated his belief that members of minorities were getting "a few extra privileges." Later when a near riot in City Hall Park by youths seeking jobs aroused comments about seeming lack of police action, Cassese pronounced his membership as "sick and tired" of being butts of abuse from minorities and having their night sticks muted by City Hall. In the past the police defended only indirectly the status of the white lower-middle class. Mainly, the Department contended with individuals or criminal gangs who desired the same things as lawful elements did: money, material goods, and perhaps a certain amount of power. Even labor unions, except for Communist-dominated ones, did not reject the system; organized workers simply wanted a bigger slice of the pie for themselves. Today, however, the cops face up to an active minority, white and black, that rejects the system and in so doing attacks the whole range of values belonging to policemen. Unfortunately the tactics suitable for dealing with old-fashioned forms of crime are not suitable for dealing with dissent.

CHAPTER XXIV

THE DEBATE OVER PHYSICAL FORCE

In July, 1968, a *New York Times* reporter, David Burnham, explored the question of violence committed by the police, through a series of interviews with cops, former cops, social scientists, and experts at the Brandeis University Lemberg Center for the Study of Violence. Burnham concluded, from these talks, that "there is less police violence in New York today than there was in the third-degree days of twenty or thirty years ago when such policemen as the late John J. Broderick won wide acclaim for beating up persons they decided were thugs, and a gun fight was the quickest way to be promoted to detective."

Police force was divided by Burnham into several categories. The first of these was that force authorized by the State in order to make an arrest. In 1967 New York State passed a statute that sharply limited the number of occasions in which a cop could employ deadly force, or use his gun. The law stated that deadly force could only be used by a cop to defend himself or someone else from what he believed to be the imminent use of deadly or physical force. The law was in part a response to the bad reputation the police had acquired when stray bullets killed teenagers joyriding in stolen cars, and when unarmed burglars or thieves were shot while stealing items of negligible value. Under the old statute, an officer was entitled to fire away at a thief carting off more than $100 worth of goods, while a theft worth a dollar less did not allow a cop to shoot.

In addition, restrictions were placed upon the rights of a private citizen. Even in the presence of a prowler in the house, a civilian was no longer entitled to blast away with a shotgun unless his life were threatened. A vigorous campaign by the police and by parties favorable to their position caused the State Legislature to reverse itself in 1968. Both homeowners and cops received the right to shoot felony suspects, even if there were no danger to themselves.

A rider to the law added insult to civil libertarian injury with the provision that a citizen may not resist an arrest by an officer no matter how blatantly illegal the police action may be. Known as the "no-sock" provision, it in effect reversed a ruling by a Court of Appeals that overturned the conviction of a citizen. He had attempted to punch two detectives who illegally attempted to arrest him and then charged him with resisting that illegal detention. In the ghetto, the measure was interpreted as a license for policemen to harass blacks and Puerto Ricans with impunity.

The second form of police violence listed by Burnham is that "tacitly authorized by either public or police tradition to handle such offenders as the sex criminal or the 'cop fighter.' " One patrolman interviewed by Burnham said, "If you catch some terrible punk raping an old woman you want to sock him and you may sock him. This isn't the reaction of a patrolman or detective, that is the reaction of a human being. The cops identify completely with the disgust most people feel about a real bad crime."

Two other types of situations that the police felt encouraged by the public to punish involved homicide and homosexuality. "If there was a real bad murder, you would get the feeling that the public wanted the killer and they didn't care how we caught him," said Burnham's patrolman. "We also used to have the feeling that the public wanted us to keep pushing homosexuals and other perverts."

Still the most intensive kind of police violence follows an assault on a policeman. "An attack on a cop is viewed by the police as the most serious thing in the world," a city detective told Burnham. "When there is a 1013 call [New York's Code for a policeman in trouble] all hell breaks loose and patrol cars from all over the city respond.

"The rightful worry about our own safety leads to a belief that any kind of physical response—sometimes even an angry word—is a cause for a crack across the head or a few punches. I've seen an old drunk being creamed for having taken a harmless swing." Other police confirmed the detective's observations. It is agreed that the professional thug, aware of the police attitude toward resistance, ordinarily becomes quite docile once he feels escape hopeless.

The third source of force lies in the sadistic personalities of some policemen. Some officers insisted that no psychological misfits served, "only a few weak or stupid men who distort the hell out of the way police normally operate." Another detective, however, recalled "in my training company, two real psychos who just shouldn't have been there. One guy was always playing with knives—he later stabbed someone—and another guy who took every word as a personal insult. Neither should have been cops."

The danger of the unstable personality armed with a badge and gun came home to the police in the summer of 1968. A patrolman, allegedly drunk, caused a traffic jam on a parkway. When a rookie, just a few days out of the police academy left his auto to learn the trouble the patrolman began an argument which he climaxed by fatally wounding the recruit. A third officer, a detective, arrived on the scene, ordered the killer to throw down his weapon, and when the latter refused the detective was forced to shoot him.

One of the significant statements to Burnham came from a graduate of the New York City Department who now heads the police in another city. "It is a fact that until very recently a patrolman who got in a gun battle was immediately rewarded with a promotion to detective. And it is unfortunately a fact that the tradition of rewarding the man who winds up in violent confrontation is still a very real part of the New York Police Department and most other departments too."

Until the late 1950s the traditional word from the Commissioner has been an invitation to treat cop-fighters and racket musclemen rough. Mulrooney had told his men not to hesitate to draw their weapons, and his successor Lewis Valentine ordered that the police "muss up" thugs.

Murder of a cop is of course the extreme challenge to the police authority, and the N.Y. State Legislature has retained the death penalty in such cases, although other capital punishment has been abolished. Authorities in the field of civil liberties believe that police "brutality" in New York City now centers around challenges to police authority, challenges ranging from verbal insults to dangerous physical assault.

Self-control evaporates in a cop killing. In the early 1960s two thugs mortally wounded a pair of policemen. Detectives seeking information learned of a small-time Brooklyn hood who might have some knowledge about the killings. He was never considered a participant but after his interrogation by the police, suspects were captured and subsequently convicted. Later, the defendant's lawyer filed an appeal claiming that the witness had been coerced into revealing the vital information. As part of the appeal court record, the defense lawyer showed that the police had stabbed out cigarettes on their informant's testicles in order to get him to talk.

The Appeals Court refused to reverse the conviction but the Brooklyn District Atrorney did attempt to bring the policemen responsible to trial. Simultaneously the police department organized its own review of the procedures of the case. The hapless witness spent six terrified hours at the police trial and refused to press the matter. The District Attorney's case vanished when the tortured man refused to identify the policemen before a grand jury.

A member of the New York Civil Liberties Union described this incident as the worst he knew of. As for the witness, he was perfect game. "Given his habits of life, he was not so wrong to be terrified."

Sufferers from police abuse rarely come from the respectable white middle-class. And when an officer does make a mistake and misbehaves toward upright citizens, the Department, says the ACLU, can be expected to come down fairly hard on the offender, so long as no defiance has been offered.

The question of abuses of police power has periodically rocked the Department, the city government, and the citizens as far back certainly as the nineteenth century. The Wickersham Report revived the debate in the 1930s but it was not until 1953 that there was any real attempt to reform the entire system of police power. The unlikely sire of reform was none other than J. Edgar Hoover. Before a House Judiciary Subcommittee, then U.S. Attorney General James P. McGranery and several FBI agents said they had been told by the FBI chief that "his agents could not interrogate the police" in New York City.

The man in charge of the New York office for the FBI, Leland V. Boardman, said that Police Commissioner George Monaghan had directed, "It is the decision of the New York City Police Department to make police available to no federal law-enforcement agencies for questioning." The House Investigation followed a New York newspaper story that revealed that the Department had failed to take any disciplinary action against five policemen who had cost the city $152,000 in damage suits by civilians.

Hoping to capitalize on the poor publicity attendant upon the case, the NYCLU suggested that the police set up a Civilian Complaint Review Board. The department quickly accepted the proposal but modified it enough to eliminate features deemed necessary by the New York Civil Liberties Union. Most important, the police department created the board as an internal body, thereby retaining control over any investigation.

During the 1950s and the early 1960s, however, complaints mounted against alleged abuses by the police. These ranged from simple absence of respect toward minority group members to out and out physical beatings, including several incidents that ended with the deaths of civilians. One particularly nasty matter involved a pair of Puerto Ricans who were picked up in a prowl car and driven to an area not on the way to the stationhouse. Somewhere en route the civilians were shot to death. The policemen swore that the pair had snatched at their pistols and had to be shot in self-defense. Community leaders and minority group members did not accept this version.

The Thomas Gilligan case which triggered the 1964 racial uprisings in Harlem and Bedford-Stuyvesant further spurred the demand for some sort of external watchdog over police actions.

In 1964 one of the best publicized confrontations between the pro-review board people and the antis centered around the Devlin-

Cruz case. Detective John Devlin had staked himself out in Chinatown where a number of Chinese-Americans claimed they had
been mugged by Puerto Ricans. One victim, Chew Lie, had died
from the blows he received. Devlin started watching a housing
project on the strength of a tip that the assailant's car was parked
there.

Gregory Cruz, a clerk who matched the physical description
of the mugger, walked out the entrance to the project and Devlin
accosted him. From here on the versions of the story differ. Devlin,
a 200-pounder, claims he identified himself and that Cruz, who
weighed 130 pounds, then slugged him with a pair of pliers, and
fled. Devlin then chased Cruz and fired three times, hitting Cruz in
the stomach and arm. For his part, the civilian swore that Devlin
never identified himself and that he thought the cop was a thief and
lashed out in self-defense.

After five months, Cruz had four stomach operations and was
lame in his right arm. Devlin was certified by the Department as
unfit for duty during this period because of his head wound.

Two other men were subsequently arrested and charged with
the death of Chew Lie. While Chinatown bore a banner, "Chinatown thanks Det. John Devlin for his efforts ... and supports his
fight against crime in our community . . ." a grand jury investigated the action. It found nothing in the conduct of either man
worth an indictment. Commissioner Aloysius Melia held a Department trial of Devlin and acquitted him with the remarkable statement, "It would be most unfortunate for Cruz, Devlin, the community, and this Department if it not be clearly understood how two
well-meaning men going about their business both innocently became embroiled in a tragic occurrence."

Whether an independent review board could have found any
differently is impossible to determine. But for a part of the community the police finding of innocence could not be accepted with
confidence. This stemmed partly from the rising tide of rebellion
against the Establishment by both minority groups and dissenters.
And partly it came from the tradition of self-protection that has developed since the beginning of the police in New York and elsewhere.

The rank and file of the Department considered the independent review board proposals another challenge to police authority. The head of the Patrolman's Benevolent Association, John Cassese, talked of Communists and Communism as the forces behind a civilian review board. In the campaign against the independent review board, Cassese announced he was "sick and tired of giving in to minority groups with their shouting and their gripes." The review board became a major political issue in John Lindsay's drive to become Mayor in 1965 and he promised he would establish such an institution if elected. He kept this commitment after winning the mayoralty. John Cassese denounced the members of the board appointed by Lindsay as "pro-civil rights," an odd sort of disqualification.

When the Guardians Association, the black police fraternal organization, came out in favor of the Board, Cassese accused them of disloyalty. "They put their color ahead of their duty as police officers."

The police and their allies reacted quickly to Lindsay's creation and backed a referendum to ban such review boards. A bitter campaign followed with leading political figures from both political parties, including Lindsay and Senators Javits and Kennedy among others, plugging to save the board. Governor Rockefeller stayed out of the fight entirely. Proponents of the review board painted a lurid image of the need for a review board. Opponents suggested that continuation of the review board meant open season for rapists and muggers. Sensational advertisements that showed an innocent white girl about to walk into terrifying night toward dark shadows pandered to latent and overt racists. The thrust of the campaign was that a review board paralyzed the hand that wielded the night stick and the finger on the trigger.

Under previous procedures in which the Department had control of civilian complaints, about two hundred accusations of police abuse were filed each year. Lindsay's board received roughly one hundred a month during its short life. Although most officers fought the new system, it had offered some advantages to them. Until the board began to handle squawks from civilians, even unsubstantiated charges against a cop were entered on his record. The external board did have the power to order any such unfounded claims erased from the policeman's record. In addition, the civilian review procedures slackened the omnipotent control over a patrolman by his superiors, whose decisions often reflected what they felt was good for the discipline of the Department as a whole rather than the rights of the individual officer.

Adherents of the new board failed to win enough votes to defeat the referendum. The number of instances of gross misconduct were too few; they involved largely the minority element of the population at a time when white backlash was beginning to sting. A two-to-one majority destroyed the independent review board.

The campaign for the board ignored the basic reason for independent review, the creation of confidence in the operations of police and in their treatment of civilians. Privately, John Lindsay had recognized that the review board was more of a symbol than an actual tool against repression. At its best the board lacked the tools for thorough investigation; the final decision on discipline still lay in the hands of the commissioner. The Mayor remarked, in the words of Felix Frankfurter, "the appearance of justice is just as important as the fact of justice."

The police continue to be up very tight over the potential of civil disorder, the modern big city riot in the ghetto. A patrolman who worked the nights immediately after Martin Luther King was killed says, "When you see from building line to building line filled with screaming people, shit flying at you, you're scared. If you put in a show of force you can nip it in the bud.

"But the minute you break down the morale of the police, the cops will stand by and see stuff taken, why should I jeopardize my job? A guy with an armful of suits walks out. You can't just ask the man to explain what he's doing. But you won't take a chance unless police brass backs you up. I don't mind doing anything if you have a man behind you with the balls and gumption to back you up.

"Who's to know what is necessary force when you're out there?"

The short-lived existence of the Civilian Review Board did accomplish a few things. For one it gave John Lindsay enough time to convince many people in the ghettos that he would make the attempt to make the police more responsive to the community. His appointments in this period and the performance of the police also helped to improve the climate of opinion involving the police, at least in the matter of abuses towards minorities. The new police leadership made an intensive effort to indoctrinate and instill a discipline sensitive to the abscess of race hate. Lindsay also eased some of the hostility towards the cops by interposing himself between the people and the police. With his widely publicized walking tours he gained the confidence of the people and through his Urban Action Task Force he sought to improve communications and to provide better service to the citizens. Equally important, an outlet for frustration and for satisfaction of grievances beyond the police department was created.

CHAPTER XXV

TOWARD THE FUTURE

The American city is in trouble, trouble such as it has never faced before. To air and water pollution, the continuing erosion of housing into slums, the growing inadequacy of the public school system, a swelling number of welfare recipients, and a shift of the traditional rural poor into urban poverty has been added the pervasive feeling that the city is a dangerous place to live. Because the city offers its inhabitants entertainment, arts, anonymity, proximity to work, higher wages, and vitality, people have put up with pollution, slums, bad schools, and poverty. But the fear that now hangs over city streets, that denies an individual his freedom to pursue the pleasures of the city, may drive out all but those who are forced to live in the city because they can't afford to move out, or the few with the means to pay for their own protection.

Crime reflects an imperfect social organization, one that cannot satisfy the desires of all of its citizens, and the higher the crime rate the more imperfect the social organization. The short-term tactical answer for the social organism is the police force that attempts forcibly to restrain anyone who breaks the bounds. But tactics mean only temporary relief at best, smoldering warfare at worst.

Given this equation, the most obvious answer to the police-crime problem is the renovation of the social organization. Obviously that calls for a long-term extended effort, and agreement among the members of the society upon what the goals should be and the means to get to those goals. It is very possible that the complex modern industrial society cannot be organized without a certain residue of antisocial behavior.

It should be obvious that the police cannot be regarded as a separate entity from the rest of the social organization. Police practices in themselves contribute to how well the organism functions and to how much antisocial behavior there is. For example, the history of the New York City Department demonstrates that gambling, prostitution and traffic in narcotics depend for their prosperity on active or passive cooperation by the police. When Bill Devery ran the Department, the police were on the vice proprietors' payrolls. Fifty years later, Harry Gross figured his "ice" to police friends totaled roughly a million dollars a year. During the last half of the 1960s bookmakers became harder to find but off-track betting is still thriving business. However, the Syndicate has found new techniques for receiving bets and abandoned the wire or horse room so popular in the Devery era.

Numbers, the poor man's speculation, operates quite openly, unlike bookmaking. The police are passive in the face of the policy racket. No evidence of high-level payoffs has been shown, but like the bookmakers the policy operators have become much more sophisticated in hiding the numbers bank and the higher echelon executives of the industry.

Perhaps an answer will be off-track betting under license and state supervision. Policemen, like other New Yorkers, have grown up in an atmosphere of easy tolerance toward gambling. After all, churches use bingo games to raise money and civic associations run carnivals with gambling as the chief attraction and source of revenue. Speculation in stocks, commodity futures, and real estate are all highly respectable industries in the city. The state also runs a lottery and in its advertising boasts that it pays off better than the numbers game.

Betting is legal at the race track and the state accepts the lions' share of the profits as the price of a license.

If policemen are to be able to combat the highly sophisticated tactics of the numbers racket or bookmaking they will have to be permitted electronic snooping. The courts will have to hand down stronger punishment to anyone convicted of these crimes. Naturally, society must recognize that wiretaps infringe upon civil liberties; stiffer punishments will be out of proportion to the magnitude of the crimes. It is a question of priorities and goals.

Still another vice, prostitution, also continues to thrive in the city even in the midst of a sexual revolution that seems to make noncommercial satisfaction within reach of almost anyone. At the turn of the century, veteran cops mourned that "the social evil will always be with us." The chief complaints about the whores who flood midtown today are their harassment of passersby and the activities of the pimps. The cry of immorality, the rallying point for Dr. Parkhurst, does not figure in discussions of what to do about contemporary prostitution. With the laws on prostitution being construed very narrowly by the courts, the sentences light and the cottage industry pattern replacing the flashy bordellos of fifty years ago, the police would be hard pressed to take effective measures even if they felt the pressure of the community. Perhaps the solution might be to remove prostitution from the list of crimes and treat it as a mental disease. Certainly incarceration for five to fifteen days in a jail seems to offer no cure. And as a mental health matter it might be easier to treat practitioners than to arrest them. So far the evidence on mental health programs designed for drug addicts offers slim encouragement for this approach. Psychiatric facilities have been unable to handle the volume of addicts, nor can authorities agree on the most efficacious therapy. A New York State law passed in 1966 made addicts subject to detention for treatment. Previously one had to be caught in possession or sale of narcotics before the courts could order either imprisonment or treatment. However, the State program failed to make any serious inroads on the narcotics problem during the first three years of operation.

There is no evidence that prostitution supplies organized crime with capital. But drug traffic, particularly in hard stuff such as heroin, has been a mob business and the profits do fatten Syndicate investments. The demand for drugs has risen to the point where individuals without ties to organized crime have gone into the business. As far as the Mafia, or whatever name is given to organized crime, is concerned, it would appear that the police of any city are without the resources or training to deal with it. The bosses of the Syndicate have managed to isolate themselves from illegal operations by a maze of contacts, legitimate businesses, and payments to politicians beyond the reach of municipal police. In addition organized crime operates on a national scale, geographically outside the jurisdiction of the city police. New York's intelligence division may be able to funnel tidbits of significant information picked up from small predators that fall victim of city laws, but apprehension of organized crime chiefs requires the efforts of federal law-enforcement experts. However, diligent work in narcotics enforcement could reduce Mafia income.

New York's crime in the streets, assault, robbery, burglary, murder, rape, and general mayhem continues to rise, as in other cities, in spite of the frantic efforts of the police. There are now more men on the streets than ever before and they answer a call faster than ever before thanks to electronic equipment. With units such as the TPF, the caliber of personnel probably is higher than ever. But unfortunately New York, like every other city, has lost the social will to curb crime. In the ghettos the people demand more protection against muggers, thieves, and addicts, but when a cop attempts an arrest he is likely to be harassed instead of helped. Black militants inveigh against white oppression and portray the policeman as the representative of that oppression. But, so far, black militants have made no attempt to unite in any coalition against the representatives of the Syndicate that sucks millions of dollars out of the black community. Nor has the ghetto put pressure on the individual freebooters who prey on blacks. High-rise housing projects, as Jane Jacobs pointed out in *The Life and Death of American Cities,* have robbed areas of the small stores and destroyed the type of housing that provided a sense of community and human watchdogs over the neighborhood weal. Anonymity now provides a cover if not a cause for antisocial behavior.

In the more affluent areas of the city the sense of isolation led thirty-eight people to ignore the cries of Kitty Genovese, a young woman trying to escape her murderer. Until New Yorkers find the collective will to protect themselves and their city, the police will continue to fight a losing battle.

Part of the same problem is in the relationship of the police to the rest of the community. As history shows, the cop has been an outsider in New York since the establishment of the Department. But never in the past have the cops held a sourer view of the public or the public a sourer view of the cops.

One recurrent suggestion is that the Lyons Residence Law be

reestablished. Until exemptions were made for police and some other city agencies, employees of New York had to live within the city limits. A city employee, particularly a policeman, who spends only his working hours in New York may be too removed from the life of the city and may not understand the needs of the people he polices. Certainly a cop who commutes from Levittown on Long Island, a middle-class white suburb, cannot be very aware of life in Harlem. When he matches New York against his garbage-free, pollution-free, educationally oriented, less violent hometown the comparison must be odious. But the exemption of the police from the Lyons Law occurred because the city simply could not recruit enough men from the resident population. And it is questionable whether a cop who, under the Lyons Law, lived in the middle-class confines of Staten Island would be any more understanding of Bedford-Stuyvesant's problems than one commuting from Levittown.

No matter where a cop lives he will always be somewhat alien to the people he polices. The cop's daily view of life is a seamy one. He's trained to look for the unlawful act. He ignores the millions of law-abiding citizens and sees only the miscreants. His work takes him into the savage parts of the city, into the savage hearts of men and women. He is always a bearer of ill tidings, news of death, injury, or robbery. Or else he must make an arrest or issue a summons. The inconsistencies of public attitudes about laws inevitably enforces a cynical view of humans.

Until recently, however, the chief issue that disturbed the public was the policeman's vices. But now the existence of the cop as it has been traditionally conceived is being questioned. Part of the argument centers around the officer's right to use force on behalf of society. Some minority group philosophers claim that disarming civilians makes the police the iron fist of the majority, leaving nonwhites virtually powerless.

With the investigations of crime and civil disorder by federal commission, Americans have been forced to recognize that the evolution of the country has been violent, scarcely as peaceful as our mythology would have us believe. Since the United States was conceived through violent rape of virgin lands and primitive peoples, then born and sustained in bloody conflict, the police have been constantly immersed in violence or responding to it. Other Western nations have suffered revolutions but their police did not confront the violence that American officers must. Other nations did not suffer quite the internecine struggles of the U.S.; colonists against Indians, English against French, colonists against English, Tories against revolutionaries, frontiersmen against Indians, North against South, whites against blacks. Then there is the land itself. It called for violent measures to subdue it. And there are the waves of immigrants, many of whom had fled because they had already raised a voice or a hand against the established order in the old country. Some had been offered the choice of emigration to the United States or prison terms at home.

The cop's use of force reflects the vast reservoir of violence in the United States. The tradition of violence in the United States is so extreme that it is absurd to talk in terms of disarming the police. Complaints by minority peoples about police abuses in New York are outweighed by the threat of violence of citizen against citizen. The emotionally disturbed, driven by the failures of the system to provide satisfaction, and the coolly calculating who see in crime profits and power have been nurtured too long in the climate of violence. Police with the right to employ physical force must be interposed between the law-abiding and the criminal.

Yet a great deal must be done to insure that police actions do not continue to escalate the level of violence. Strict discipline and exacting rules should govern the use of police force. Given the volatile nature of city populations, a patrolman can no more be permitted indiscriminate use of physical force than a soldier can be given the discretion to launch a nuclear missile. What is required is that the police tradition of force as a preventive measure or as a punishment must be discarded. It's time to bury the ancient police thesis, "There's more law in the end of a night stick than in a library of Supreme Court decisions."

A review board that is independent of the Department and that has the power to investigate complaints from civilians provides the best tool for curbing police abuses. The amount of police abuse may be debatable but it is critically important that the citizens have confidence that their complaints will be heard and impartially judged. This matter of faith is not a trivial one. People tend to act on what they believe and not necessarily on actual conditions. If ghetto residents are convinced that the local police abuse them, no statistics on the number of unfounded charges will appease them. Only if nonwhites feel that their experiences with police will be fairly reviewed, can the police or the rest of the city expect nonwhites to lessen their antagonism toward the system of law and toward law enforcement.

When Vincent Broderick, a former Commissioner of the Police, reviewed Paul Chevigny's book on police abuses, *Police Power,* Broderick objected to Chevigny's insistence that a handful of cases demonstrated a pattern of misbehavior within the Department, and insisted that hundreds of thousands of instances of proper actions should far outbalance abuses. But only when the police themselves show their ruthless determination to eliminate Department misconduct will those who are alienated from the police be converted. And, aside from Chevigny's examples, there are too many other instances where the Department failed to exert proper discipline.

It has been suggested that decentralized community control of the police would be a solution to the tension and hostility toward the cops in some sections of the city. Fragmentation of the force would, however, reduce efficiency. Some areas of New York require extra cops during the daytime, others need them at night. Criminals pay no attention to precinct borders and control and apprehension of malefactors would be seriously jeopardized by loss of central command. There is little to be said for strict community control based upon a division of the city along neighborhood lines like school districts. Graft and corruption flourished most heartily in New York when precinct commanders had the most authority. Similarly it would be far easier for well-organized pressure groups within neighborhoods to dominate the local police and provide unequal service. The best protection for community interests lies in the review board system, with members of the board responsive to the various elements of the city.

Ever since Fiorello LaGuardia became mayor in 1933 the cliché has been "keep politics out of the police department." What has been ignored is the obverse, the police role in politics, from control of elections to lobbying for higher salaries and better working conditions, through campaigns against a Civilian Review Board and laws that restrict police behavior. The cops are politically active. Certainly, promotions based upon political pull destroy morale and efficiency. However, elected city officials must face the electorate and are held responsible for the effectiveness of the Department. Unless a mayor can exert control over the force, the danger is that it becomes an independent empire, unresponsive to the people it protects. As John Lindsay moved into his second term of office, political elements—the power of the PBA, the growing cohesion of minority groups, the conservative drift of Lindsay's middle- and upper-class white support—reasserted their influence over police policies.

Perhaps some of the abrasive relationship between police and citizens could be smoothed away if cops were better educated in the problems of the people who now live in New York. Training in sociology and psychology would contribute to an understanding of behavior and arm cops with methods to prevent and control situations such as family squabbles and race hate that creeps into criminal acts. Certainly a continuing effort must be made for the cop to be as much a part of community improvement programs as possible. If New Yorkers on occasion see in the cop a resource for a better life then some of the hostility will be dissipated. But what cannot be forgotten is that the cop does not create crime, vice, addiction, or civil dissent. And no matter how understanding the policeman becomes through training and discipline he is going to be out there on the grinding edge, confronting a substantial number of people who don't find the going system works for them.

BIBLIOGRAPHY

Arm, Walter. *The Big Payoff*. New York: Appleton-Century-Crofts, 1951.

Asbury, Herbert. *All Around the Town*. New York: Alfred A. Knopf, 1934.

Asbury, Herbert. *Gangs of New York*. New York: Garden City Publishing, 1927.

Barnes, D. M. *The Draft Riots in New York*. New York: Baker and Goodwin, 1863.

Botkin, B. A. *Sidewalks of New York*. New York: The Bobbs-Merrill Co., 1954.

Bordua, David J. *The Police*. New York: John Wiley & Sons, 1967.

Browne, William. *Stop That Clubbing*. New York: Privately printed, 1887.

Byrnes, Thomas. *Professional Criminals of America*. New York: Cassell, 1886.

Callow, Alexander. *The Tweed Ring*. New York: Oxford University Press, 1965.

Chevigny, Paul. *Police Power*. New York: Pantheon Books, 1969.

Costello, A. E. *Our Police Protectors*. New York: C. F. Roper, 1885.

Crane, Milton. *Sins of New York*. New York Boni and Gaer, 1947.

Crump, Irving, and Newton, John. *Our Police*. New York: Dodd, Mead & Co., 1935.

Curran, Henry. *Pillar to Post*. New York: Charles Scribner's Sons, 1941.

Danforth, H., and Horan, James. *The D. A.'s Man*. New York: Crown Publishers, 1957.

Dunne, Philip. *Mr. Dooley Remembers*. Boston: Atlantic Monthly Press, 1965.

Ellis, Edward Robb. *The Epic of New York City*. New York: Coward-McCann, 1966.

Feder, Sid, and Turkus, Burton. *Murder, Inc.* New York: Farrar, Strauss & Cudahy, 1951.

Fiaschetti, Michael. *You Gotta Be Tough*. New York: Doubleday & Co., 1930.

Fosdick, Raymond. *Crime in America & The Police*. New York: The Century Co., 1920.

Fosdick, Raymond. *Police Systems*. New York: The Century Co., 1920.

Flagg, Jared. *Flagg's Flats*. New York: Private printing by author, 1909.

Fowler, Gene. *Beau James*. New York: Viking Press, 1949.

Garnet, Charles. *The LaGuardia Years*. New Brunswick: Rutgers University Press, 1961.

Gerard, J. W. *London & New York, Their Crime and Police*. New York: 1853.

Greene, Francis. *The Present Condition of the Police Force.* New York: Public address, 1903.

Hapgood, Hutchins. *The Spirit of the Ghetto.* New York: Schocken Books, 1966.

Harper's

Harlow, A. H. *Old Bowery Days.* New York: Appleton-Century-Crofts, 1931.

Hickey, John. *Our Police Guardians.* New York: Privately published, 1925.

Hopkins, Ernest J. *Our Lawless Police,* New York: Viking Press, 1931.

Kahn, Roger. *The Battle For Morningside Heights.* New York: William Morrow & Co., 1970.

Katcher, Leo. *The Big Bankroll.* New York: Harper & Row, Publishers, 1950.

Klein, Herb. *The New York Police: Damned if They Do, Damned if They Don't.* New York: Crown Publishers, 1968.

Lavine, Emmanuel. *The Third Degree.* New York: Vanguard Press, 1930.

Lewis, Alfred Henry. *Richard Croker.* New York: Life Publishing, 1901.

Limpus, Lowell. *Honest Cop.* New York: E. P. Dutton & Co., 1931.

Lyford, Joseph. *The Air Tight Cage.* New York: Harper & Row, Publishers, 1966.

Mann, Arthur. *LaGuardia, A Fighter Against His Time.* Philadelphia: J. B. Lippincott Co., 1959.

Matsell, George. *Vocabulum or The Rogue's Lexicon.* New York: G. W. Matsell, 1859.

Mitgang, Herbert. *The Man Who Rode The Tiger.* J. B. Lippincott Co., 1963.

Mockridge, Norton, and Prall, Robert. *The Big Fix.* New York: Holt, Rinehart & Winston, 1954.

Moody, Richard. *The Astor Place Riot.* Bloomington: Indiana University Press, 1958.

New York, City of, Report. *Mayor's Commission on Conditions in Harlem.* 1933.

New York, City of, Report. *Special Committee to Investigate the Police Department in 1913.*

New York, State of, Report. New York City Police Department Investigating Committee (Senate), *Proceedings Before the Lexow Committee.* New York: 1894.

New York, State of, Report. *Special Committee of the Assembly to Investigate The Public Officials & Departments of City of New York* (Mazet Committee). 1898.

New York American, The

New York Herald Tribune, The

New York Times, The

Niederhoffer, Arthur. *Behind the Shield.* New York: Doubleday & Co., 1967.

North American Review

O'Connor, Richard. *Courtroom Warrior, The Combative Career of William F. Jerome.* Boston: Little, Brown & Co., 1963.

Osofsky, Gilbert. *Harlem: The Making of the Ghetto.* New York: Harper & Row, Publishers, 1968.

Outlook

Parkhurst, Charles. *My Forty Years In New York.* New York: The Macmillan Co., 1923.

Parkhurst, Charles. *Our Fight With Tammany.* New York: Charles Scribner's Sons, 1895.

Police Lawlessness Against Communists in New York. New York: American Civil Liberties Union, 1930.

Radano, Gene. *Walking the Beat.* New York: World Publishing Co., 1968.

Reid, Ed. *The Shame of New York.* New York: Random House, 1953.

Reynolds, Quentin. *Headquarters.* New York: Harper & Row, Publishers, 1955.

Riis, Jacob. *How The Other Half Lives.* New York: Sagamore Press, 1957.

Riis, Jacob. *The Making of An American.* New York: The Macmillan Co., 1901.

Root, Jonathan. *One Night in July.* New York: Coward-McCann, 1961.

Rothstein, Carolyn. *Now I'll Tell.* New York: Vanguard Press, 1935.

Scribner's Magazine

Steffens, Lincoln. *Autobiography of Lincoln Steffens.* New York: Harcourt, Brace & World, 1931.

Strong, George Templeton. *Diaries of George Templeton Strong.* Edited by Allan Nevins and Milton H. Thomas. New York: The Macmillan Co., 1952.

Turner, William. *The Police Establishment.* New York: G. P. Putnam's Sons, 1968.

United States. *National Commission on Law Observance and Enforcement* (Wickersham Committee). Washington, D. C.: 1931.

United States. *President's Commission on Law Enforcement & Administration of Justice.* Washington D. C.: 1967.

United States. *Report of the National Advisory Commission on Civil Disorder.* Washington, D. C.: 1968.

Valentine, Lewis J. *Night Stick.* New York: Dial Press, 1947.

Wakefield, Dan. *Island in the City.* New York: Houghton Mifflin Co., 1957.

Walling George. *Recollections of a New York Chief of Police.* New York: Caxton Book Concern, 1887.

Werner, M. R. *It Happened in New York.* New York: Coward-McCann, 1957.

Werner, M. R. *Tammany Hall.* New York: Garden City Publishing, 1928.

Willemse, Cornelius. *A Cop Remembers.* New York: E. P. Dutton & Co., 1933.

Willemse, Cornelius. *Behind the Green Lights.* New York: Alfred A. Knopf, 1931.